NYSTCE 008

CST

Earth Science

Teacher Certification Exam

By: Sharon Wynne, M.S
Southern Connecticut State University

"And, while there's no reason yet to panic, I think it's only prudent that we make preparations to panic."

XAMonline, INC.
Boston

XAMonline, Inc.
21 Orient Ave.
Melrose, MA 02176
Toll Free 1-800-509-4128
Email: info@xamonline.com
Web www.xamonline.com
Fax: 1-781-662-9268

Library of Congress Cataloging-in-Publication Data

Wynne, Sharon A.
CST Earth Science 008: Teacher Certification / Sharon A. Wynne. -2nd ed.
ISBN 978-1-58197-632-8
1. CST Earth Science 008. 2. Study Guides. 3. NYSTCE
4. Teachers' Certification & Licensure. 5. Careers

Printed in the United States of America **œ-1**

NYSTCE: CST Earth Science 008
ISBN: 978-1-58197-632-8

Table of Contents

SUBAREA II. SPACE SYSTEMS

SUBAREA I. FOUNDATIONS OF SCIENTIFIC INQUIRY

COMPETENCY 1.0 UNDERSTAND THE GENERAL RELATIONSHIPS AND COMMON THEMES THAT CONNECT MATHEMATICS, SCIENCE, AND TECHNOLOGY.

SKILL 1.1 Analyze similarities among systems in mathematics, science, and technology (e.g., magnitude and scale, equilibrium and stability, optimization)

Math, science, and technology have common themes in how they are applied and understood. All three use models, diagrams, and graphs to simplify a concept for analysis and interpretation. Patterns observed in these systems lead to predictions. Another common theme among these three systems is equilibrium. Equilibrium is a state in which forces are balanced, resulting in stability. Static equilibrium is stability due to a lack of changes and dynamic equilibrium is stability due to a balance between opposite forces. Scale is a ratio of size. For example, a map may have a scale of true miles per every inch drawn on the map. A model drawn to scale is a representation of something that is larger or smaller than its actual size. There is also the very literal interpretation of scale. In this context the scale would be used to measure mass, and would often be called a balance.

SKILL 1.2 Apply concepts and theories from mathematics, biology, chemistry, and physics to an Earth Science system

Earth Science and Biology

Over the course of Earth's history, living things have been greatly affected by Earth processes. Volcanic eruptions, plate tectonics, and climate change have affected whether living things have survived or how they have had to adapt in order to survive. At least four of the major mass extinctions have been caused by a climatic change triggered by some Earth event interconnecting geology, meteorology, and biology. The working explanation for the Cretaceous Tertiary extinction, the extinction that killed dinosaurs, is a climate change triggered by a large asteroid hitting the Earth 65 mya (million years ago). This impact threw great amounts of dust into the atmosphere causing a cool down of the climate. It is also believed that this impact may have triggered massive volcanic eruptions contributing to the cooling effect. In this extinction, many marine families and some of the land vertebrae went extinct. There is a debate as to what caused the worst mass extinction of Earth's history, the Permian Triassic extinction, which occurred 251 mya. The working theories include a meteorite impact and massive volcanic eruptions. During this time, 95% of all species were killed. The remaining species had to adapt to the cooling climate in order to survive.

Earth processes have also affected how humans live. The most fertile land for farming is at the base of volcanoes. We have developed technologies to irrigate farmland, build "safe" buildings in earthquake prone areas, and prevented low lying areas from flooding. Currently, human impact on the environment is being widely criticized.

Earth Science and Chemistry

Earth science and chemistry are tightly woven. In geology, the chemical composition of the rocks and the temperature and pressure at which crystals form are an obvious connection between chemistry and Earth science. In addition, chemistry and oceanography are connected inherently. The salinity of Earth's oceans are affected by the temperature at which water freezes, the density of water, and the solubility of certain chemical compounds. Chemistry and meteorology are connected through the chemical makeup of the atmosphere and the effects that human released chemicals have on the atmosphere (i.e. CFC's effect on the ozone layer and carbon dioxide's role in climate change).

Earth Science and Physics

Earthquakes, plate tectonics, and meteorology are all related to physics. Fault production and earthquakes are caused by large-scale plate tectonics forming small-scale zones of weakness in the crust. The pressure builds up along fault lines due to increases in fault stress. At some point in time, the stress on the fault line will exceed the static frictional force of the fault line, and seismic waves will be released. The frictional force and the dynamics of the Earth's motion during earthquakes are all related to physics.

Meteorology and physics are closely related. Changes in atmospheric pressure cause winds, updrafts, and storms. These pressure changes are caused by changes in temperature. Warm, moist air rises because it is less dense than the air surrounding it. As air rises and cools, it condenses, thus forming cloud systems. When meteorologists predict the weather, the physics of the interactions between volume, humidity, temperature, and pressure are studied in detail.

Earth Science and Mathematics

Mathematics can be used to solve many problems in Earth science. Examples of how mathematics can be used in Earth science include finding the relative humidity, the distance to stars, the residence time of materials in the soil, and discharge of water.

SKILL 1.3 Analyze the use of Earth science, mathematics, and other sciences in the design of a technological solution to a given problem

Science and technology are interdependent as advances in technology often lead to new scientific discoveries and new scientific discoveries often lead to new technologies. Scientists use technology to enhance the study of nature and to solve problems that nature presents. Technological design is the identification of a problem and the application of scientific knowledge to solve the problem. While technology and technological design can provide solutions to problems faced by humans, technology must exist within nature and cannot contradict physical or biological principles. In addition, technological solutions are temporary and new technologies typically provide better solutions in the future. Monetary costs, available materials, time, and available tools also limit the scope of technological design and solutions. Finally, technological solutions have intended benefits and unexpected consequences. Scientists must attempt to predict the unintended consequences and minimize any negative impact on nature or society.

The problems and needs, ranging from very simple to highly complex, that technological design can solve are nearly limitless. Disposal of toxic waste, routing of rainwater, crop irrigation, and energy creation are but a few examples of real-world problems that scientists address or attempt to address with technology. The technological design process has five basic steps:

1. Identify a problem
2. Propose designs and choose between alternative solutions
3. Implement the proposed solution
4. Evaluate the solution and its consequences
5. Report results

After the identification of a problem, the scientist must propose several designs and choose between the alternatives. Scientists often utilize simulations and models in evaluating possible solutions.

Implementation of the chosen solution involves the use of various tools depending on the problem, solution, and technology. Scientists may use both physical tools and objects as well as computer software.

After implementation of the solution, scientists evaluate the success or failure of the solution against pre-determined criteria. In evaluating the solution, scientists must consider the negative consequences as well as the planned benefits.

Finally, scientists must communicate results in different ways – orally and written, and through models, diagrams, and demonstrations.

Example:

Problem – toxic waste disposal
Chosen solution – genetically engineered microorganisms to digest waste
Implementation – use genetic engineering technology to create organism capable of converting waste to environmentally safe product
Evaluate – introduce organisms to waste site and measure formation of products and decrease in waste; also evaluate any unintended effects
Report – prepare a written report of results complete with diagrams and figures

SKILL 1.4 Use a variety of software (e.g., spreadsheets, graphing utilities, statistical packages, simulations) and information technologies to model and analyze problems in mathematics, science, and technology

Scientists use a variety of tools and technologies to perform tests, collect and display data, and analyze relationships. Examples of commonly used tools include computer-linked probes, spreadsheets, and graphing calculators.

Scientists use computer-linked probes to measure various environmental factors including temperature, dissolved oxygen, pH, ionic concentration, and pressure. The advantage of computer-linked probes, as compared to more traditional observational tools, is that the probes automatically gather data and present it in an accessible format. This property of computer-linked probes eliminates the need for constant human observation and manipulation.

Scientists use spreadsheets to organize, analyze, and display data. For example, conservation ecologists use spreadsheets to model population growth and development, apply sampling techniques, and create statistical distributions to analyze relationships. Spreadsheet use simplifies data collection and manipulation and allows the presentation of data in a logical and understandable format.

Graphing calculators are another technology with many applications to science. For example, scientists use algebraic functions to analyze growth, development, and other natural processes. Graphing calculators can manipulate algebraic data and create graphs for analysis and observation. In addition, scientists use the matrix function of graphing calculators to model problems in genetics. The use of graphing calculators simplifies the creation of graphical displays including histograms, scatter plots, and line graphs. Scientists can also transfer data and displays to computers for further analysis. Finally, scientists connect computer-linked probes, used to collect data, to graphing calculators to ease the collection, transmission, and analysis of data.

COMPETENCY 2.0 UNDERSTAND THE HISTORICAL AND CONTEMPORARY CONTEXTS OF THE EARTH SCIENCES AND THEIR APPLICATION TO EVERYDAY LIFE.

SKILL 2.1 Analyze the significance of key events in the history of the Earth sciences (e.g., the development of solar system models, the discovery of a galactic universe, the development of the plate tectonics model)

History of tectonic theory

At the beginning of the 20th century, most scientists accepted the view that the Earth's materials were largely fixed in their position because rock was thought to be too hard and brittle to permit much movement. However, in 1906, Alfred Wegener became intrigued by how the shape of the continents seem to have at one time fit together. In 1910, he began a lifelong pursuit of supporting evidence for what eventually became known as his theory of Continental Drift. Over the ensuing years of his research efforts, Wegener became convinced that the landmasses had—at one point in history—been connected, forming a giant super-continent that he later dubbed Pangea. As his research progressed, he collected data and offered evidence of this theory, most of which is still included in the proofs offered for modern tectonic theory. Not surprisingly, his controversial theory of moveable continents was not readily accepted. Starting in the late 1950's and early 1960's, some scientists began to reexamine Wegener's impressive collection of data, and much to their surprise, they discovered that Wegener's old data, as well as the new data they had collected, both supported the theory of Continental Drift. Modern geology owes much to Alfred Wegener's initial postulations. The advent of new technologies has made it possible for science to verify most of his observations, and additional, new data has expanded Wegener's original concept into the widely accepted, modern theory of tectonics.

Discovery of a galactic universe

In the late 1700's early astronomers studied hazy objects in the sky that weren't stars. However, it wasn't until the 1850's that telescopes became powerful enough to discern that the hazy objects had a spiraling structure. Almost a hundred years would pass before their identity was solved. In 1924, American astronomer Edwin Hubble determined that the objects were farther away than previously thought. This meant that for us to even see them, they must have a greater luminosity than a single star. The conclusion was obvious; the objects were other galaxies, each composed of billions of stars. Our galaxy is but one of billions of galaxies in the universe.

Formation of Earth and the solar system

Most cosmologists believe that the Earth is the indirect result of a supernova. The thin cloud (planetary nebula) of gas and dust from which the Sun and its planets are formed, was struck by the shock wave and remnant matter from an exploded star(s) outside of our galaxy. In fact, the stars manufactured every chemical element heavier than hydrogen. The turbulence caused by the shock wave caused our solar system to begin forming as it absorbed some of the heavy atoms flung outward in the supernova. In fact, our solar system is composed mostly of matter assembled from a star or stars that disappeared billions of years ago. The Nebula spun faster as it condensed and material near the center contracted inward. As more materials came together, mass and gravitational attraction increased, pulling in more mass. This cycle continued until the mass reach the point that nuclear fusion occurred and the Sun was born. Concurrently, the Proto-sun's gravitational mass pulled heavier, denser elements inward from the clouds of cosmic material surrounding it. These elements eventually coalesced through the process of accretion: the clumping together of small particles into large masses. The planets of our solar system were created.

The period of accretion lasted approximately 50 to 70 million years, ceasing when the Proto-sun experienced nuclear fusion to become the Sun. The violence associated with this nuclear reaction swept through the inner planets, clearing the system of particles, ending the period of rapid accretion. The closest planets (Mercury, Venus, and Mars) received too much heat and consequently did not develop the planetary characteristics to support life as we know it. The farthest planets did not receive enough heat to sufficiently coalesce the gasses into a solid form. Earth was the only planet in the perfect position to develop the conditions necessary to maintain life.

SKILL 2.2 Recognize the impact of society on the study of the Earth sciences (e.g., increasing commercial demand for more accurate meteorological analyses; growing populations in earthquake-prone regions; expanding markets for oil, gas, and other nonrenewable resources)

Society has had a significant influence on the Earth Sciences. Public safety personnel, farmers, and business people all make decisions based on weather patterns. Civil engineers in earthquake prone areas depend on knowledge of seismic activity to properly design roadways and buildings. The use of a dwindling supply of non-renewable resources has caused increased search for new sources of oil, gas, and coal. The study of the Earth Sciences responds to the demands of the needs of society.

Commercial demand for meteorological analyses

Commercial demand for studying weather patterns and accurate forecasting has increased over the last fifty years. Insurance companies use trends in storm tracks and flooding events to analyze risk. Businesses in the tourism industry rely on accurate information about weather in order to make decisions and predictions on their potential profits. Citizens rely on accurate information in the forecast to plan their lives. The demands for accurate forecasts for business and public safety have forced a dramatic increase in the power of forecasting computers. Mathematical models have improved forecasting accuracy. Furthermore, the study of storm systems from the inside (from aircraft sensors, etc.) has improved understanding of major storms and the effects of their conditions on storm tracks.

Growing populations in earthquake prone regions

As populations grow in earthquake prone regions, the demand for earthquake analysis and improved engineering techniques increases. Although prediction of an exact time and place for earthquakes will be forever elusive, the likelihood of rupture in a general time frame can be estimated. By studying stress and strain in the bedrock, scientists can indicate the fault lines that should be monitored for potential seismic activity. Through the study of how seismic waves react in different soil types, engineers have been able to build and fortify structures based on their location and type of soil present. Active earthquake engineering is employed when a structure is built to react to seismic waves. In some active engineering buildings, a seismograph is located in the foundation. As the earthquake occurs, the seismic wave frequency and intensity are measured. A computer then sends information to a series of pistons in the building, moving the building accordingly to avoid structural collapse. As more and more information is gathered about the nature of earthquakes, more improvements in the engineering of structures can be made.

SKILL 2.3 Assess the implications for society of Earth science phenomena in a variety of regions (e.g., volcanoes, earthquakes, erosion, rising sea levels)

An important topic in science is the effect of natural disasters and events on society and the effect human activity has on inducing such events. Naturally occurring geological, weather, and environmental events can greatly affect the lives of humans. In addition, the activities of humans can induce such events that would not normally occur.

Nature-induced hazards include floods, landslides, avalanches, volcanic eruptions, wildfires, earthquakes, hurricanes, tornadoes, droughts, and disease. Such events often occur naturally, because of changing weather patterns or geological conditions. Property damage, resource destruction, and the loss of human life are the possible outcomes of natural hazards. Thus, natural hazards are often extremely costly on both an economic and personal level.

While many nature-induced hazards occur naturally, human activity can often stimulate such events. For example, destructive land use practices such as mining can induce landslides or avalanches if not properly planned and monitored. In addition, human activities can cause other hazards including global warming and waste contamination. Global warming is an increase in the Earth's average temperature resulting, at least in part, from the burning of fuels by humans. Global warming is hazardous because it disrupts the Earth's environmental balance and can negatively affect weather patterns. Ecological and weather pattern changes can promote the natural disasters listed above. Finally, improper hazardous waste disposal by humans can contaminate the environment. One important effect of hazardous waste contamination is the stimulation of disease in human populations. Thus, hazardous waste contamination negatively affects both the environment and the people that live in it.

The most fertile land for farming is at the base of volcanoes. Obviously, this is a dangerous area for people to live, although farming communities sometimes thrive there. An inactive volcano provides fertile ground and less (if any) danger to those who live nearby.

Some scientists have estimated that if global warming continues, the polar ice caps will melt. Our sea levels would rise to enormous heights, estimated at an increase of 50 to 150 feet. Much of the present day United State's coastal shorelines would be underwater. New York City would be gone. Most of Florida would be submerged. Major California cities would be inundated with water. World wide, a warmer world would result in shifts in the Rain Belts. Crop failures would occur and be associated with famine. The mid-west United States would have a climate like present day Arizona and Canada would become a major agricultural source. The warming of the oceans could cause exceptionally strong hurricanes and typhoons.

SKILL 2.4 Analyze Earth's hazards (e.g., earthquakes, volcanoes, hurricanes, tornadoes, drought) and their effects upon humans to develop plans for emergency preparedness

Earthquake: The sudden movement of Earth materials in relation to other Earth materials, caused by the rupture of the Earth's materials. The rupture originates underground in the brittle lithospheric material. The sudden breaking of the rock material causes a release of energy. The movement of the tectonic plates causes stress on the rock. Because rock has a limited ability to stretch before breaking, the interior of a plate can move while its edges do not. The energy caused by the stress placed on a bending rock is called Elastic Energy. As tectonic plates try to move past one another, rock near the plate boundary stretches and stores elastic energy (elastic deformation). When the elastic energy overcomes the frictional forces that are resisting the movement of the rock, the rock materials "jump" along the fault. As the rocks "jump" they try to spring back to their original dimensions—elastic rebound—and they release the stored elastic energy. This causes motion in the rock that sets up vibrations that travel through the Earth. These vibrations are felt as an Earthquake or Seismic Slip.

Effects of Earthquakes

Ground Movement

Shaking: The extent of the shaking is dependent on the type of material the seismic wave encounters. Soft material amplifies the shaking.

Ground Displacement: The ground literally drops away. Vertical displacements of over 20 feet occurred during the 1964 Anchorage, Alaska earthquake.

Ground Cracks: Cracks can open either several inches or several feet.

Landslides: Loose material is set into motion by the Earthquake.

Fire: Gas and electric lines break during an earthquake, sparking and feeding fires. Water mains also are often broken, limiting the means to fight the fires. Fire accounts for 95% of all earthquake damage.

Liquefaction: In an earthquake, sand and silt liquefy, developing the consistency of quicksand. Packed sand and silt have trace amounts of water between the grains. As the shaking occurs, these move apart and more water enters. If there is a low water table, the grains eventually become flooded with water in the spaces. As the material liquefies, the structures built upon them sink. However, the material doesn't have the same rate of liquefaction, and only parts of the buildings sink, causing their structural collapse.

Tsunamis (Tidal Waves): Earthquakes can trigger an underwater landslide or cause sea floor displacements that in turn generate deep, omni-directional waves. Far out to sea these waves may be hardly noticeable. However, as they near the shoreline, the shallowing of the sea floor forces the waves upward in a springing type of motion. The tidal waves formed by the upward motion can grow to be quite immense and powerful depending on the topography of the sea floor and the magnitude of the earthquake.

Structural Damage: The shaking in an earthquake often breaks the man-made structures in the area. The structures collapse, killing, injuring, or trapping the people inside.

Elevated Roadways: Straight rebar (unfinished steel) was widely used as reinforcement for concrete support columns. In an earthquake, these bars were prone to spalling (flaking off of concrete sections), causing the sudden collapse of the entire elevated structure.

Buildings: Ground motion through building foundations often sets up a swaying motion throughout the entire structure. As the sway intensifies, the building materials fail, causing collapse of the structure.

Volcanoes

Magma: the molten liquid or semi plastic Earth material located beneath the Earth's crust. Magma is produced at Hot Spots, Spreading Centers, and Subduction Zones and varies in composition according to where it is produced.

Pyroclasts or Tephra: the angular, high velocity, quickly cooling globules of ejected material that adapts aerodynamic shapes of differing sizes.

Blocks: Large chunks of lava.

Bombs: Big pieces of lava, shaped similar to a spindle or lens.

Lapilli: Walnut sized bits of lava.

Cinders: Pea sized lava, 4 to 32 mm.

Dust and Ash: Fine particles.

Accompanying the pyroclastic ejecta is a huge release of gas that forms into a glowing gas cloud that moves rapidly down the side of the volcano. This gas cloud, the **Nuée Ardente**: a glowing, highly heated mass of gas-charged lava, travels at 600 mph when first expelled and is still moving at 200 mph when it reaches the bottom of the cone. The Nuée Ardente is very deadly. Besides being scorching hot, it causes a smothering effect by displacing or burning up all oxygen in its path. The Nuée Ardente released in the 1902 eruption of Pelée in Martinique destroyed the entire town of Saint Pierre, killing an estimated 40,000 people. The Nuée Ardente also creates extremely strong winds that can affect areas as much as 20 miles away from the volcano. You also get **Lahars**: a flowing slurry of volcanic debris and water. These mudflows have the consistency of wet concrete and can cause widespread devastation.

Hurricanes are produced by temperature and pressure differentials between the tropical seas and the atmosphere. Powered by heat from the sea, they are steered by the easterly trade winds and the temperate Westerlies, as well as their own incredible energy. Hurricane development starts in June in the Atlantic, Caribbean, and Gulf of Mexico, and lasts until the end of hurricane season in late November. Hurricanes are called by different names depending on their location. In the Indian Ocean they are called **Cyclones**. In the Atlantic, and east of the international dateline in the Pacific, they are called Hurricanes. In the western Pacific they are called **Typhoons**. Regardless of their name, a hurricane can be up to 500 miles across, last for over two weeks from inception to death, and can produce devastation on an immense scale.

Hurricane Damage

The destruction and damage caused by a hurricane or tropical storm can be severe. **Storm surge** causes most of the damage as the winds push along a wall of rising water in their path, and this rising effect is amplified on low sloping shorelines such as those found on the Gulf Coast. The intense winds can also cause damage.

Tornado: an area of extreme low pressure, with rapidly rotating winds beneath a cumulonimbus cloud. Tornadoes are normally spawned from a Super Cell Thunderstorm. They can occur when very cold air and very warm air meet, usually in the Spring. Tornadoes represent the lowest pressure points on the Earth and move across the landscape at an average speed of 30 mph. The average size of a tornado is 100 yards, but they can be as large as a mile wide. A tornado's wind speed ranges from 65 to 300 mph and has an average duration of 10 to 15 minutes, but has been known to last up to 3 hours. Tornadoes usually occur in the late afternoon (3 to 7 p.m.) in conjunction with the rear of a thunderstorm. Most tornadoes spin counter-clockwise in the northern hemisphere, and clockwise in the southern hemisphere. Worldwide, the U.S. has the most tornadoes. Texas has the most tornadoes, but Florida has the largest number per square mile. Roughly 120 deaths each year are from tornadoes.

Drought

Droughts are the result of changes in climate, changes in water sources, overgrazing of land (lack of vegetation causes water to run-off and not infiltrate back down in the ground), and over irrigation (this literally pumps the sources dry). Although we cannot do anything about the climate, improved agricultural and animal husbandry techniques have greatly aided in the retention of top cover that holds moisture. Likewise, crop rotation allows a natural replenishment of soil nutrients that help hold vegetation in place. Awareness of over irrigation has also helped to ease the problems of human-produced drought factors. Water intensive crops in many areas have been replaced with hardier, less water needy substitutes. Unfortunately, not all countries practice these improved techniques. As a result, human induced droughts remain a major threat for many underdeveloped nations.

Natural disaster preparedness

To be prepared for all natural disasters, people should:

1.) Practice evacuation from the house or building.
2.) Find the safest areas outside of the building and away from possible falling debris.
3.) Have non-perishables (including water) on hand.
4.) Have an out-of-state point of contact that everyone in the family knows in the event that people are separated.
5.) Have a plan for pets in case of an emergency.
6.) Have a second exit from each room if possible.
7.) Mark utility switches for water, gas, electric, etc. in case they need to be accessed.
8.) Have account numbers, medical information, insurance policy information, birth certificates, etc. in a plastic bag (to protect from water damage) and placed in a fire proof safe.

Government preparedness

Hurricane Katrina was a civics lesson on how to proceed with emergency management plans in the case of a natural disaster. Local and state governments need to be prepared with a realistic evacuation plan, shelters, non-perishables, and means of rescue.

Earthquake preparedness

1.) Secure heavy objects such as bookshelves to the wall.
2.) Practice an exit plan.
3.) In the event of an earthquake, crawl under a sturdy table or desk.
4.) If a table or desk is not available, cover your face and stand in a doorway or inside corner.

Hurricane preparedness

1.) Board up windows and doors.
2.) Stay away from windows.
3.) Evacuate if you are told to do so.
4.) Get to higher ground if you live in a low lying area, flood prone area, or manufactured housing.
5.) Make sure that you have plenty of non-perishables and a NOAA weather radio on hand.

Tornado preparedness

1.) Get below ground if there is a tornado warning for your area.
2.) If you are unable to get below ground, get away from windows on the interior of the house (preferably remain in a bathroom).
3.) If you don't have time to go underground, get into the bathtub and then cover yourself with a mattress.

SKILL 2.5 Recognize the applications of Earth science related technology to everyday life (e.g., GPS, weather satellites, cellular communication)

One relatively recent technology that can be used to locate points on the Earth is the **global positioning system (GPS)**. Over 20 GPS satellites broadcast signals that allow GPS receivers to obtain exact longitude, latitude, and altitude data. In the past 2 decades, GPS technology has become invaluable for navigation, military use, surveyors, and outdoor enthusiasts. Though GPS will not replace maps, these tools are incredibly powerful when used together.

Satellites: The National Weather Service heavily depends on its network of weather satellites (i.e. GOES Satellite), to provide a wide-area coverage of the Earth. These satellites primary provide infrared, water vapor, and photographic data and are used to track the formation, development and motion of major meteorological events such as hurricanes and tropical storms. In terms of orbit, there are two types of satellites: Geostationary and Polar Orbiting. Geostationary satellites move with the Earth's rotation. Since they always look at the same point, this allows for a view that shows changes over periods of time. Polar Orbiting satellites follow an orbit from pole to pole. The Earth rotates underneath the satellite and gives a view of different areas. In effect, it produces slices of the Earth. The GOES Satellite is a key source of weather information. GOES is a geostationary satellite that primarily scans the Atlantic Ocean & U.S. East Coast. There are 4 detection bands on the GOES satellite.

Cellular communication has been advanced by studies in astronomy. Bursts of energy from the Sun can disrupt wireless cell communications several times each year, usually in correlation with the solar maximum, the most active portion of the Sun's 11year cycle. The first solar radio bursts were detected inadvertently by radars deployed during World War II. After the war, solar radio studies became a recognized field of astronomical research, and the Air Force was active in collecting data. Continued research will help in the design of future wireless platforms.

COMPETENCY 3.0 Understand the process of scientific inquiry and the role of observation and experimentation in explaining natural phenomena.

SKILL 3.1 Analyze processes by which scientific knowledge develops

The process of scientific inquiry is an understanding of science through questioning, experimentation, and drawing conclusions. The steps involved in this important process are:

Observing
Identifying problem
Gathering information/research
Hypothesizing
Experimental design, which includes identifying a control, constants, independent and dependent variables
Conducting experiment and repeating the experiment for validity
Interpreting, analyzing, and evaluating data
Drawing conclusions
Communicating conclusions

Scientific inquiry begins with observation. Observation is a very important skill by itself, since it leads to experimentation and finally communicating the experimental findings to the society/public. After observing, a question is formed that starts with "why" or "how." To answer these questions, experimentation is necessary. Between observation and experimentation, there are three more important steps. These are gathering information (or researching about the problem), hypothesis, and designing the experiment.

Designing an experiment involves identifying a control, constants, independent variables, and dependent variables. A control/standard is something we compare our results with at the end of the experiment. It is a reference. Constants are the factors we keep constant in an experiment to obtain reliable results. Independent variables are factors we change in an experiment. It is important to bear in mind that there should be a constant and 3-4 independent variables present to obtain reproducible results in an experiment. The dependent variable is responsive to the independent variables. It is also the factor that will be measured in an experiment. After the experiment is concluded, it is repeated and results are graphically presented. The results are then analyzed and conclusions are drawn.

After the conclusion is drawn, the final step is communication. It is the responsibility of the scientist to share the knowledge obtained through the research. Much emphasis is put on the method of communication. The conclusions must be communicated by clearly describing the information using accurate data, visual presentation (such as bar/line/pie graphs), tables/charts, diagrams, artwork, and other appropriate media, including power point presentation. Modern technology must be used whenever it is necessary. The method of communication must be suitable to the audience. Written communication is as important as oral communication. This is essential for submitting research papers to scientific journals, newspapers, other magazines, etc.

SKILL 3.2 Assess the appropriateness of a specified experimental design to test a given hypothesis

Only certain types of questions can truly be answered by science because the scientific method relies on observable phenomenon. That is, only hypotheses that can be tested are valid. Often this means that we can control the variables in a system to an extent that allows us to truly determine their effects. If we don't have full control over the variables, for instance, in environmental biology, we can study several different naturally occurring systems in which the desired variable is different.

The scientific method is particularly useful for determining 'cause and effect' type relationships. Thus, appropriate hypotheses are often of this nature. The hypothesis is simply a prediction about a certain behavior that occurs in a system. Variables are changed to determine whether or not the hypothesis is correct. For instance, let's consider several identical potted African violets and suppose we have lights of different color, fertilizer, water, and a variety of common household items. Below are some possible questions, phrased as hypotheses, and a bit about why they are or are not valid.

1. African violets will grow taller in blue light than they will in red light. This hypothesis is valid because it could easily be tested by growing one violet under blue light and another under red. The results are easily observed by measuring the height of the violets.

2. Invisible microbes cause the leaves of African violets to turn yellow. This hypothesis is not valid because we cannot know whether a given violet is infected with the microbe. This hypothesis could be tested if we had appropriate technology to detect the presence of the microbe.

3. Lack of water will stop the growth of African violets. This hypothesis is also valid because it could be tested by denying water to one violet while continuing to water another. The hypothesis may need to be refined to more specifically define how growth will be measured, but presumably this could be easily done.

4. African violets will not grow well in swamps.
This hypothesis is not valid in our specific situation because we have only potted plants. It could be tested by actually attempting to grow African violets in a swamp, but that is not within this scenario.

SKILL 3.3 Assess the role of communication among scientists in promoting scientific progress

Scientific theory and experimentation must be repeatable. It is also possible to be disproved and is capable of change. Science depends on communication, agreement, and disagreement among scientists. It is composed of theories, laws, and hypotheses.

hypothesis - an unproved theory or educated guess followed by research to best explain a phenomena. A theory is a proven hypothesis.

theory - the formation of principles or relationships which have been verified and accepted.

law - an explanation of events that occur with uniformity under the same conditions (laws of nature, law of gravitation).

Observations, however general they may seem, lead scientists to create a viable question and an educated guess (hypothesis) about what to expect. While scientists often have laboratories set up to study a specific thing, it is likely that along the way they will find an unexpected result. It is important to be open-minded and to look at all of the information. An open-minded approach to science provides room for more questioning, and, hence, more learning. A central concept in science is that all evidence is empirical. This means that all evidence must be is observed by the five senses. The phenomenon must be both observable and measurable, with reproducible results.

The question stage of scientific inquiry involves repetition. By repeating the experiment you can discover whether or not you have reproducibility. If results are reproducible, the hypothesis is valid. If the results are not reproducible, one has more questions to ask. It is also important to recognize that one experiment is often a stepping stone for another. It is possible that data will be re-tested by the same scientist or by another, and that a different conclusion may be found. In this way, scientific competition acts as a system of checks and balances.

COMPETENCY 4.0 UNDERSTAND THE PROCESSES OF GATHERING, ORGANIZING, REPORTING, AND INTERPRETING SCIENTIFIC DATA; AND APPLY THIS UNDERSTANDING IN THE CONTEXT OF EARTH SCIENCE INVESTIGATIONS.

SKILL 4.1 Evaluate the appropriateness of a given method or procedure for collecting data for a specified purpose

Measurements may be taken in different ways. There is an appropriate measuring device for each aspect of science. A graduated cylinder is used to measure volume. A balance is used to measure mass. A microscope is used to view microscopic objects. A centrifuge is used to separate two or more parts in a liquid sample. The list goes on, but you get the point. For each variable, there is an appropriate way to measure it. The internet and teaching guides are virtually unlimited resources for laboratory ideas. You should be imparting on the students the importance of the method with which they conduct the study, the resource they use to do so, the concept of double checking their work, and the use of appropriate units.

SKILL 4.2 Select an appropriate and effective graphic representation (e.g., graph, table, diagram) for organizing, analyzing, and reporting given data

The type of graphic representation used to display observations depends on the data that is collected. Line graphs are used to compare different sets of related data or to predict data that has not yet be measured. An example of a line graph would be comparing the rate of activity of different enzymes at varying temperatures. A bar graph or histogram is used to compare different items and make comparisons based on this data. An example of a bar graph would be comparing the ages of children in a classroom. A pie chart is useful when organizing data as part of a whole. A good use for a pie chart would be displaying the percent of time students spend on various after school activities.

SKILL 4.3 Apply procedures and criteria for reporting investigative procedures and data

The knowledge and use of basic mathematical concepts and skills is a necessary aspect of scientific study. Science depends on data and the manipulation of data requires knowledge of mathematics. Scientists often use basic algebra to solve scientific problems and design experiments. For example, the substitution of variables is a common strategy in experiment design. Also, the ability to determine the equation of a curve is valuable in data manipulation, prediction and experimentation.

Understanding basic statistics, graphs, charts, and algebra are of particular importance in science. In addition, scientists must be able to represent data graphically and interpret graphs and tables. Scientists must be able to understand and apply the statistical concepts of mean, median, mode and range to sets of scientific data. Modern science uses a number of disciplines for improved understanding.

Mean: Mean is the mathematical average of all the items. To calculate the mean, all the items must be added and the result divided by the number of items. This is also called the arithmetic mean or more commonly known as the "average."

Median: The median depends on whether the number of items is odd or even. If the number is odd, then the median is the value of the item in the middle. This is the value that denotes the number of items having higher or equal value, and is equal to the number of items having equal or lesser value. If the number of the items is even, the median is the average of the two items in the middle, such that the number of items having values higher or equal to it is same as the number of items having values equal to or less than that.

Mode: Mode is the value of the item that occurs the most often when there are not many items. Bimodal is a situation where there are two items with equal frequency.

Range: Range is the difference between the maximum and minimum values. The range is the difference between two extreme points on the distribution curve.

SKILL 4.4 Analyze relationships between factors (e.g., cyclic, inverse, direct, linear) as indicated by data

When relating factors in experimental data, graphical representations often indicate that two variables vary predictably and in direct relation to each other. Two such relationships common to science systems are linear and exponential. The individual data points on the graph of a linear relationship cluster around a line of best fit. In other words, a relationship is linear if we can sketch a straight line that roughly fits the data points. The individual data points on the graph of an exponential relationship cluster around a curve of best fit. Thus, in linear relationships the y variable varies by a fixed, absolute amount for each change in x (e.g. 3 units each time). In exponential relationships, on the other hand, the y variable varies by a fixed, relative amount for each change in x (e.g. 3% each time). Consider the following examples of linear and exponential relationships.

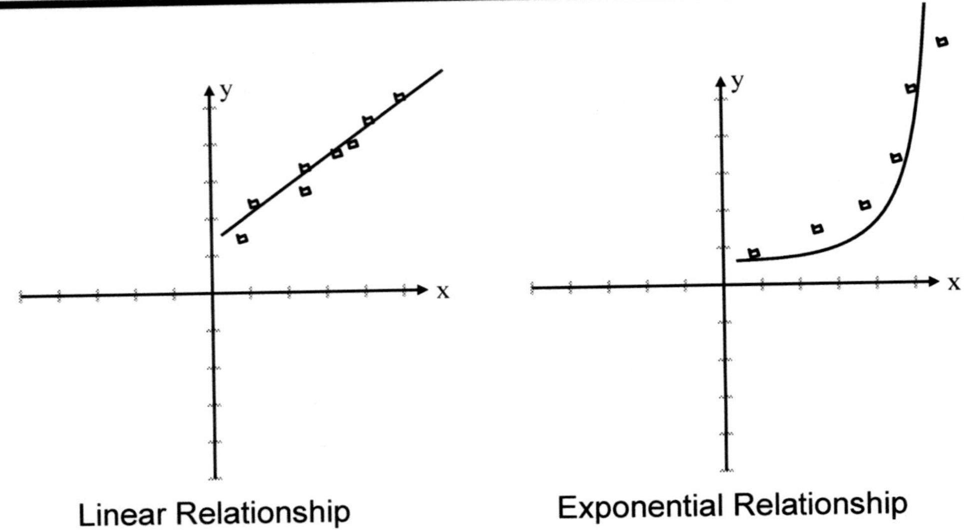

Linear Relationship Exponential Relationship

Note that the exponential relationship appears linear in parts of the curve. In addition, contrast the preceding graphs to the graph of a data set that shows no relationship between variables.

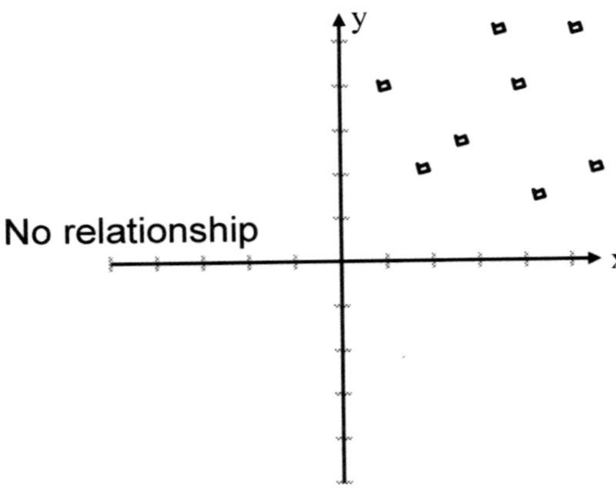

In mathematics, a direct (positive) relationship is one in which the two variables both increase or decrease in conjunction. For a direct relationship where the y-intercept is zero (0), if the value of the control variable is doubled, the dependent variable doubles also. If the size of the control is reduced to a third, the dependent is also reduced to a third. An inverse (negative) relationship is one where an increase in the value of one number results in a decrease in the value of the other number.

Extrapolation is the process of estimating data points outside a known set of data points. When extrapolating the data of a linear relationship, we extend the line of best fit beyond the known values. The extension of the line represents the estimated data points. Extrapolating data is only appropriate if we are relatively certain that the relationship is indeed linear. For example, the death rate of an emerging disease may increase rapidly at first and level off as time goes on. Thus, extrapolating the death rate as if it were linear would yield inappropriately high values at later times. Similarly, extrapolating certain data in a strictly linear fashion, with no restrictions, may yield obviously inappropriate results. For instance, if the number of plant species in a forest were decreasing with time in a linear fashion, extrapolating the data set to infinity would eventually yield a negative number of species, which is clearly unreasonable.

COMPETENCY 5.0 UNDERSTAND TYPES AND USES OF NATURAL RESOURCES, THE EFFECTS OF HUMAN ACTIVITIES ON THE ENVIRONMENT, AND THE NEED FOR STEWARDSHIP TO PRESERVE THE ENVIRONMENTAL INTEGRITY OF EARTH SYSTEMS.

SKILL 5.1 Demonstrate an understanding of the uses and importance of natural resources

There are two categories of natural resources: renewable and nonrenewable. Renewable resources are unlimited because they can be replaced as they are used. Examples of renewable resources are oxygen, wood, fresh water, and biomass. Nonrenewable resources are present in finite amounts or are used faster than they can be replaced in nature. Examples of nonrenewable resources are petroleum, coal, and natural gas.

Strategies for the management of renewable resources focus on balancing the immediate demand for resources with long-term sustainability. In addition, renewable resource management attempts to optimize the quality of the resources. For example, scientists may attempt to manage the amount of timber harvested from a forest, balancing the human need for wood with the future viability of the forest as a source of wood. Scientists attempt to increase timber production by fertilizing, manipulating trees genetically, and managing pests and density. Similar strategies exist for the management and optimization of water sources, air quality, and other plants and animals.

The main concerns in nonrenewable resource management are conservation, allocation, and environmental mitigation. Policy makers, corporations, and governments must determine how to use and distribute scarce resources. Decision makers must balance the immediate demand for resources with the need for resources in the future. This determination is often the cause of conflict and disagreement. Finally, scientists attempt to minimize and mitigate the environmental damage caused by resource extraction. Scientists devise methods of harvesting and using resources that do not unnecessarily impact the environment. After the extraction of resources from a location, scientists devise plans and methods to restore the environment to as close to its original state as possible.

SKILL 5.2 Recognize methods of locating and obtaining natural resources

Natural Resources: naturally created commodities critically important or necessary to human life and civilization. The term natural resource can also include the total quantity of a given resource commodity on Earth, both discovered and undiscovered.

A major source of contention in our modern society centers on the proper use and conservation of our natural resources. Although most people automatically think of coal, oil, iron and other minerals when they think of natural resources, the definition also includes other often overlooked resources such as forest, soil, water, air, and land.

Mineral resources are abundant. Unlike fossil fuels, there is not a major concern of "running out" of mineral resources. Pegmatite is a resource for the following minerals: feldspar, mica, and quartz. Hydrothermal sources, whether it is through contact metamorphism or the mineral solutions solidifying in cavities, are sources for gold, silver, copper, mercury, and lead. Kimberlites are pipes that grow diamond crystals. Regional metamorphism can create ore deposits of asbestos, graphite, and talc. However, the cost of maintaining a reserve and mining the mineral is of concern. In many instances, the concentration of the element being mined is not high enough to warrant further extraction. The resources are being consumed rapidly. Mineral consumption is expected to increase as developed countries become more technologically advanced. Concentrations of the minerals will become less profitable to mine. Recycling of scrap metals and other used mineral materials will become key to maintaining mineral supplies without astronomical cost.

Ninety percent of all of humans' energy needs are satisfied by fossil fuels. Just ten percent of energy needs are satisfied by renewable resources. Fossil fuels are created by natural processes underground. These resources are thousands of years old and are used heavily today. Coal mining is occurs mostly in mine shafts underground. However, strip mines have become more popular as a method of mining coal. Strip mines lead to acid mine drainage. About 40% of the materials from the mining process is waste or talus. The extraction, transportation, and burning of coal cause significant environmental problems. Fifteen percent of the Earth's oil supply is found in the Middle East. Eighty five percent of the total oil production comes from only five percent of the well fields. The current consumption of oil is of concern as oil supplies are dwindling. Although many new sources for oil and natural gas are being explored and discovered, the production of this oil and natural gas is coming at a high price. Extraction from oil shale and tar sands may increase the oil supply for a short time.

SKILL 5.3 Assess the positive and negative effects of human activities (e.g., mining, waste disposal) on Earth's environment

All forms of pollution have both local and global economic, aesthetic, and medical consequences. Air, land, and water pollution directly and indirectly affect human health. Pollution negatively influences the local and global economy by increasing medical costs, increasing pollution treatment costs (e.g. water and soil clean up), and decreasing agricultural yields. Finally, all types of pollution decrease natural beauty and diminish enjoyment of nature and the outdoors.

Air pollution, possibly the most damaging form of pollution, has both local and global consequences. Air pollution results largely from the burning of fuels. Major sources of air pollution include transportation, industrial processes, heat and power generation, and the burning of solid waste. At the local level, air pollution negatively affects quality of life by increasing medical problems and decreasing comfort and enjoyment of outdoor activities. Air pollution can cause medical problems ranging from simple throat or eye irritations to asthma and lung cancer. Globally, air pollution threatens the Earth's ozone layer and may cause global warming. Ozone depletion and global warming increase the risk of sun related health problems (e.g. skin cancer) and threaten the Earth's ecological balance and biodiversity. Possible solutions to air pollution are government controls on fuel types, industry combustion standards, and the development and use of alternative, cleaner sources of energy.

Land pollution is the destruction of the Earth's surface resulting from improper industrial and urban waste disposal, damaging agricultural practices, and mining and mineral exploitation. Land pollution greatly effects aesthetic appeal and human health. At the local level, improper waste disposal threatens the health of people living in the effected areas. Waste accumulation attracts pests and creates unsightly, dirty living conditions. Globally, damage and depletion of the soil by improper agricultural practices has great economic consequences. Overuse of pesticides and herbicides and depletion of soil nutrients causes long-term damage to the soil, leading to decreased crop yield in the future. Close regulation of waste disposal and agricultural practices is the most effective strategy for the prevention of land pollution.

Water pollution, perhaps the most prevalent form of pollution, greatly effects human health and the economy. The agricultural industry is the leading contributor to water pollution. Rain runoff carrying pesticides, herbicides, and fertilizer readily pollutes oceans, lakes, and rivers. Also contributing to water pollution are industrial effluents, sewage, and domestic waste. Water pollution negatively affects the economy because clean up and treatment of polluted water is very costly. In addition, consumption of polluted water causes health problems and increases associated medical costs. Finally, polluted water disrupts aquatic ecosystems, decreasing the availability of fish and other aquatic resources. Like air and land pollution, limiting water pollution requires strict governmental control. Proper oversight requires the implementation and enforcement of environmental standards regulating agricultural and industrial discharge into bodies of water.

On a positive note, there is a movement to reclaim old strip mines. Mining is the process by which minerals are extracted from the Earth. These minerals may often include coal, limestone, gold, silver, and many other metals. Mining causes serious disturbance of land and ecosystems. Mine reclamation is the process by which mined land is restored to a useful state, such as a productive ecosystem or industrial or municipal land. Mine reclamation has become a regular part of modern mining industry, and improves water and air quality in abandoned mine areas. Reclaimed sites may function as pasture areas, hayland, recreational areas, wild life habitat, and/or wetlands.

Mine reclamation techniques stabilize land surfaces against water and wind erosion using material placement and capping. The final step in mine reclamation is often the replacement of topsoil and its revegetation with suitable plant species. Revegetation techniques include hydroseeding, a process commonly used for large-scale or hillside properties in which grass seed is sown in a stream of water aimed at the ground, as well as native seed drilling techniques, through which seeds can be sown in well-spaced rows at specific depths. Tree planting is another important part of mine reclamation. Trees are generally planted in low densities to allow for natural propagation. Tree seeds can be pelletalized to prevent excessive movement by the wind. This method proves particularly effective on rocky, barren slopes.

Tailing basins are a common characteristic of mined areas. These depressed areas contain a finely ground concentrate that is the byproduct of smelting operations conducted at mine sites. As the content levels of these basins increase, wind erosion leads to contamination of electrometallurgical refining processes, problems for residents of nearby towns, and machinery wear. To revegetate such areas and decrease erosion, seeding is established on portions of the basin closest to prevailing winds in order to minimize damage of young plants by eroding soil. Agricultural limestone can be applied to soil approximately six weeks before seeding to raise pH, and nitrogenous fertilizers are often used to encourage growth of young plants. When planting grasses, companion crops can be employed to create shading and reduce the dry effect of wind. To deal with drainage problems found in tailing basins, wetlands are often constructed downstream of the basins. These wetlands are capable of filtering and removing contaminants through biological and chemical processes.

SKILL 5.4 Evaluate strategies for dealing with environmental concerns (e.g., buying and selling carbon credits)

Carbon Credits

The concept behind buying and selling carbon credits is simple. Governments put a cap on how much carbon dioxide individuals and industries can put into the air. If individuals and industries stay below the allowed amount of carbon dioxide, they can sell off their excess "carbon credits" to those companies or individuals that are going above the amount allowed. This gives individuals and companies a financial incentive to produce less carbon dioxide. The less carbon dioxide these companies or individuals make, the more money they can make selling their carbon credits. In order for this plan to work, however, the cap for allowed carbon dioxide emissions needs to be low enough for the incentive. If the cap is too high, many individuals and companies will have excess carbon credits, and the price of carbon credits will be too low to be an incentive to change behavior.

Funding for fuel cell development

Fuel cells are two to three times more efficient than the burning of fossil fuels. A fuel cell works by using hydrogen and oxygen to create water and heat as byproducts. Therefore, fuel cells are a very efficient and clean source of energy. Over a billion dollars has been spent in research and development of fuel cells. Fuel cells appear to be a solution for the pollution problem, economic security (in that oil will no longer be needed), and homeland security. However, as of right now, fuel cells are not feasible. Building the components, which require platinum, can be a very expensive proposition. Until the high cost of fuel cells can be addressed, the use of fuel cells does not seem feasible.

Land Use Management

One of the big issues of late has been land use management. Natural disasters and pollution issues have made it necessary to create better plans for managing land. Planning for land use can include the following:

1.) Safety of humans and property
2.) Water quality protection
3.) Protection of ecosystems
4.) Increasing recreation and access to an area
5.) Delineation of landslide prone areas and floodplains
6.) Identification of water pollution and soil pollution problems

By addressing these and other issues, environmental problems, loss of life, and loss of property can be averted.

COMPETENCY 6.0 UNDERSTAND HOW TO CREATE, USE, AND INTERPRET PHYSICAL AND MATHEMATICAL MODELS (E.G., MAPS, CHARTS, GRAPHS, DIAGRAMS, EQUATIONS) COMMONLY USED IN EARTH SCIENCE.

SKILL 6.1 Evaluate the appropriateness of alternative models for conveying given information from Earth science

Earth science lends itself to many different teaching methods. These teaching methods increase understanding of the material and develop higher level thinking skills.

Seminars

Seminars are great ways for students to make higher connections in Earth science. A seminar is a classroom conversation where the teacher acts as a moderator. In a seminar, students make connections about how Earth science relates to daily life. Topics such as environmental issues, the importance of the space program, land use issues, and emergency management issues are good seminar discussions. The opening question should be a question that students should recall from previous learning. The core questions that follow should require further research so that students can make their points. Each student should be required to participate in the seminar.

Concept Mapping

Concept mapping is a good way for students that are visual learners to organize information. The rock cycle, seasons, and weather patterns lend themselves well to concept mapping.

Science Journal

Students keeping a science journal of current events in Earth science will realize that Earth science is relevant to their lives.

Simulations

Earth science lends itself well to simulations. Simulations of rock cross sections, earthquakes, and stream formation are very easy to implement in the classroom. By performing simulations in the classroom, students are able to witness the process by which Earth processes occur.

Experimentation

Experiments such as soil testing, water testing, testing for relative humidity, and testing for the dew point will give students hands on lessons in the scientific method.

SKILL 6.2 Demonstrate an understanding of the methods by which given physical and graphic models are created

The model is a basic element of the scientific method. Many concepts in science are studied with models. A model is any simplification or substitute for what we are actually studying, understanding, or predicting. A model is a substitute, but it is similar to what it represents. We encounter models at every step of our daily living. The Periodic Table of elements is a model chemists use for predicting the properties of elements. Physicists use Newton's laws to predict how objects will interact, such as planets and spaceships. In geology, the continental drift model predicts the past positions of continents. Samples, ideas, and methods are all examples of models. At every step of scientific study models are extensively used. The primary activity of the hundreds of thousands of scientists is to produce new models, resulting in tens of thousands of scientific papers published each year.

Types of models

- Scale models: some models are basically downsized or enlarged copies of their target systems, such as models of protein, DNA, etc.
- Idealized models: An idealization is a deliberate simplification of something complicated with the objective of making it easier to understand. Some examples are frictionless planes, point masses, isolated systems, etc.
- Analogical models: standard examples of analogical models are the billiard model of a gas, the computer model of the mind, or the liquid drop model of the nucleus.
- Phenomenological models: These are usually defined as models that are independent of theories.
- Data models: These are corrected, rectified, regimented, and in many instances, idealized versions of the data we gain from immediate observation (raw data).
- Theory models: Any structure is a model if it represents an idea (theory). An example of this is a flow chart, which summarizes a set of ideas.

Uses of models

Models are crucial for understanding the structure and function of processes in science. Models help us to visualize the organs/systems they represent, much like putting a face to person. Models are useful to predict and foresee future events like hurricanes, etc.

Limitations

Though models are very useful to us, they can never replace the real thing. Models are not exactly like the true item they represent. Caution must be exercised before presenting models to the class, as they may not be accurate. It is the responsibility of the educator to analyze the model critically for the proportions, content value, and other important data. One must be careful about the representation style. This style differs from person to person.

SKILL 6.3 Classify different types of maps (e.g., topographic, star charts, weather) used in Earth science and analyzing the information conveyed by each type of map

Topographic maps use fine lines drawn in ordered patterns to show the topography and elevation of the land.

Topographic Map Symbols

A series of special symbols and lines are used to display information about the shape and elevation of the landscape. There is a set of rules that determine how these symbols and lines are drawn on the map.

Contour Interval: Shows the amount of elevation between contour lines.

Bench Mark: Shows exact elevation. Often marked with a solid triangle.

Contour Line: Connects points that have the same elevation. Contour lines are closed loops, although all of the loop may not be visible on the map.

Index Contours: The heaviest contour lines, each marked with an elevation.

Elevation: A numerical indication of the contour line's elevation.

Hachure Marks: Short lines drawn inside a closed loop that indicate a depression. The marks point down slope.

Gradient: The relative spacing of the contouring lines indicates the gradient of the slope. The closer the lines, the steeper the gradient.

Sea Level: Elevation is measured as either above or below sea level.

The Five General Rules of Contouring

1. All contour lines either close or extend to the edge of the map.
2. Contour lines are closed around hills, basins, or depressions.
3. Contour lines never cross, although they are sometimes very close. The closer they are, the steeper the slope.
4. Contour lines appear on both sides of an area where the slope reverses direction.
5. Contour lines form V's that point upstream when they cross a stream, river, or valley.

The topographic map **legend** provides a great deal of information about the map, including the scale of the map, the agency that created the map, and the year it was created.

In the upper right hand corner of the map, another legend provides the geographic name of the area covered, latitude and longitude information, and the **minute series**- the relative coverage of the map. The larger the minute series number, the larger the area covered by the map. If a topographic map shows open bodies of water, the elevation markings in the water are given as depth soundings.

Geologic Maps

A **geologic map** is a special purpose map made to show subsurface geological features. In the United States, geologic maps are usually superimposed over a topographic map (and at times over other base maps) with the addition of a color mask and letter symbols to represent the kind of geologic unit, stratigraphic contour lines, fault lines, strike and dip symbols, and various additional symbols as indicated by the map key.

The most striking feature of a geologic map is its colors. Each color represents a different geologic unit. A geologic unit is a volume of a certain kind of rock of a given age range. Sandstone of one age might be colored bright orange, while sandstone of a different age might be colored pale brown. The capital letter represents the age of the geologic unit. Geologists have divided the history of the Earth into Eons, Eras, Periods, and Epochs. The most common division of time used in letter symbols on geologic maps is the Period. Most letter symbols begin with a capital letter representing one of the four Periods: J (Jurassic), K (Cretaceous), T (Tertiary), or Q (Quaternary). Sometimes the age of a rock unit will span more than one period. In that case, both capital letters are used. For example, QT would indicate that the rock unit began to form in Tertiary time and was completed in Quaternary time. The small letters indicate either the name of the unit, if it has one, or the type of rock, if the unit has no name.

The place where two different geologic units are found next to each other is called a contact, and that is represented by different kinds of lines on the geologic map. The two main types of contacts shown on most geologic maps are depositional contacts and faults. All geologic units are formed over, under, or beside other geologic units. When different geologic units have been moved next to one another after they were formed the contact is a fault contact, which is shown on the map by a thick line. Another kind of line shown on most geologic maps is a fold axis. In addition to being moved by faults, geologic units can also be bent and warped by the same forces into rounded wavelike shapes called folds. A line that follows the crest or trough of the fold is called the fold axis. This is marked on a geologic map with a line a little thicker than a depositional contact, but thinner than a fault.

All thicknesses of lines are also modified by being solid, dashed, or dotted. Often contacts are obscured by soil, vegetation or human construction. Those places where the line is precisely located are shown as solid, but where it is uncertain it is dashed. The shorter the dash, the more uncertain the location. The lines on the map may also be modified by other symbols on the line (triangles, small tic marks, arrows, etc.) which give more information about the line. For example, faults with triangles on them show that the side with the triangles has been thrust up and over the side without the triangles. All the different symbols on the lines are explained in the map key.

A geologic map shows the distribution of rocks at the Earth's surface. However, bedrock is usually obscured so that only a small amount of outcrop is available for observation, study, or sampling. The geologist must then extrapolate the general distribution of rock types. Not only will the rock he can see help him, but so will changes in soil, vegetation and landscape, as well as various patterns detected from aerial photographs.

A geologic cross section map tells how the rocks are arranged underground. Each type of rock has its own symbol for shading and various structures have defined symbols. The geologic map and its cross section are used together to give a more complete picture.

Weather Maps

Meteorology utilizes an extensively defined set of alphanumeric notations and iconology to graphically display the collected data elements. Depending on the extent of detail desired in the presented map, the symbology conveys information about cloud types, coverage and base heights, visibility, precipitation, wind speed, air pressure tendency, temperature, and isobaric fronts.

Once you can read a station plot you can begin to perform map analyses. Meteorologists use the station plots to draw lines of constant pressure (isobars), temperature (isotherms), and dewpoint (isodrosotherms) to achieve an understanding of the current state of the atmosphere. This knowledge ultimately leads to better weather forecasts and warnings. Decoding these plots is easier than it may seem. The values are located in a form similar to a tic-tac-toe pattern.

In the upper left, the temperature is plotted in Fahrenheit. In this example, the temperature is 77°F.

Along the center, the cloud types are indicated. The top symbol is the high-level cloud type followed by the mid-level cloud type. The lowest symbol represents low-level cloud over a number that tells the height of the base of that cloud (in hundreds of feet). In this example, the high level cloud is Cirrus, the mid-level cloud is Altocumulus and the low-level cloud is a cumulonimbus with a base height of 2000 feet.

At the upper right is the atmospheric pressure reduced to mean sea level in millibars (mb) to the nearest tenth with the leading 9 or 10 omitted. In this case the pressure would be 999.8 mb. If the pressure was plotted as 024 it would be 1002.4 mb. When trying to determine whether to add a 9 or 10 use the number that will give you a value closest to 1000 mb.

On the second row, the far left-hand number is the visibility in miles. In this example, the visibility is 5 miles.

Next to the visibility is the present weather symbol. There are 95 symbols that represent the weather that is either presently occurring or has ended within the previous hour. In this example, a light rain shower was occurring at the time of the observation.

The circle symbol in the center represents the amount of total cloud cover reported in eighths. This cloud cover includes all low, middle, and high level clouds. In this example, 7/8th of the sky is covered with clouds.

This number and symbol tell how much the pressure has changed (in tenths of millibars) in the past three hours and the trend in the change of the pressure during that same period. In this example, the pressure was steady and then fell becoming 0.3 millibars LOWER than it was three hours ago.

These lines indicate wind direction and speed rounded to the nearest 5 knots. The longest line, extending from the sky cover plot, points in the direction that the wind is blowing **from**. Thus, in this case, the wind is blowing **from** the southwest. The shorter lines, called barbs, indicate the wind speed in knots (kt). The speed of the wind is calculated by the barbs. Each long barb represents 10 kt with short barbs representing 5 kt. In this example, the station plot contains two long barbs so the wind speed is 20 kt.

The 71 at the lower left is the dewpoint temperature. The dewpoint temperature is the temperature the air would have to cool to become saturated, or in other words reach a relative humidity of 100%.

The lower right area is reserved for the past weather, which is the most significant weather that has occurred within the past six hours excluding the most recent hour.

Analyze a Map on Your Own

The following are a few sources of current weather maps. Sometimes a site may be down or experiencing data losses. In such a case, try another site listed. This is not meant to be an exhaustive list. These are provided for your convenience.

- NCAR, pick your regional plot: http://www.rap.ucar.edu/weather/surface/
- UNISYS: http://weather.unisys.com/surface/sfc_map.html
- College of DuPage: http://weather.cod.edu/analysis/analysis.sfcplots.html
- NOAA http://www.nws.noaa.gov/
- Ohio State University: http://asp1.sbs.ohio-state.edu/ (Click on "Current Weather" and choose your map)

Surface Station Model

Temp (F) Weather Dewpoint (F)	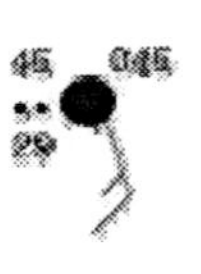	Pressure (mb) Sky Cover Wind (kts)	**Data at Surface Station** Temp 45 °F, dewpoint 29 °F, overcast, wind **from** SE at 15 knots, weather light rain, pressure 1004.5 mb

Upper Air Station Model

Temp (C) Dewpoint (C)	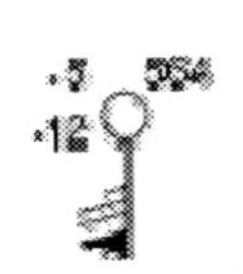	Height (m) Wind (kts)	**Data at Pressure Level - 850 mb** Temp -5 °C, dewpoint -12 °C, wind **from** S at 75 knots, height of level 1564 m

Forecast Station Model

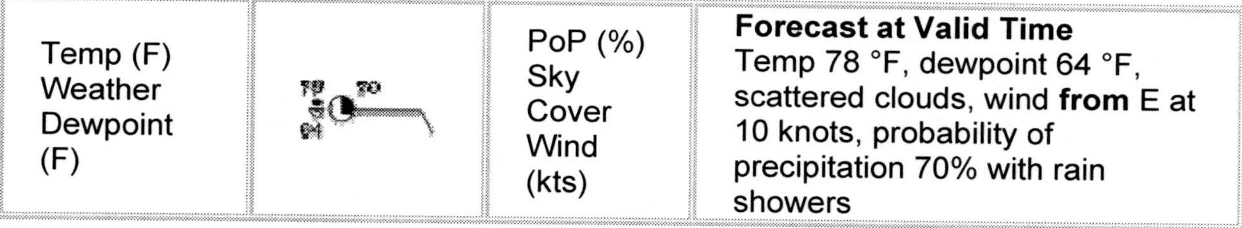

Temp (F) Weather Dewpoint (F)		PoP (%) Sky Cover Wind (kts)	**Forecast at Valid Time** Temp 78 °F, dewpoint 64 °F, scattered clouds, wind **from** E at 10 knots, probability of precipitation 70% with rain showers

Using symbols, the following map portrays the location of weather stations, as well as the temperature, dew point, and pressure found near a particular weather station. Cloud coverage, precipitation type, wind speed, wind direction, and weather fronts are also depicted on this map. Weather stations are represented by circular symbols.

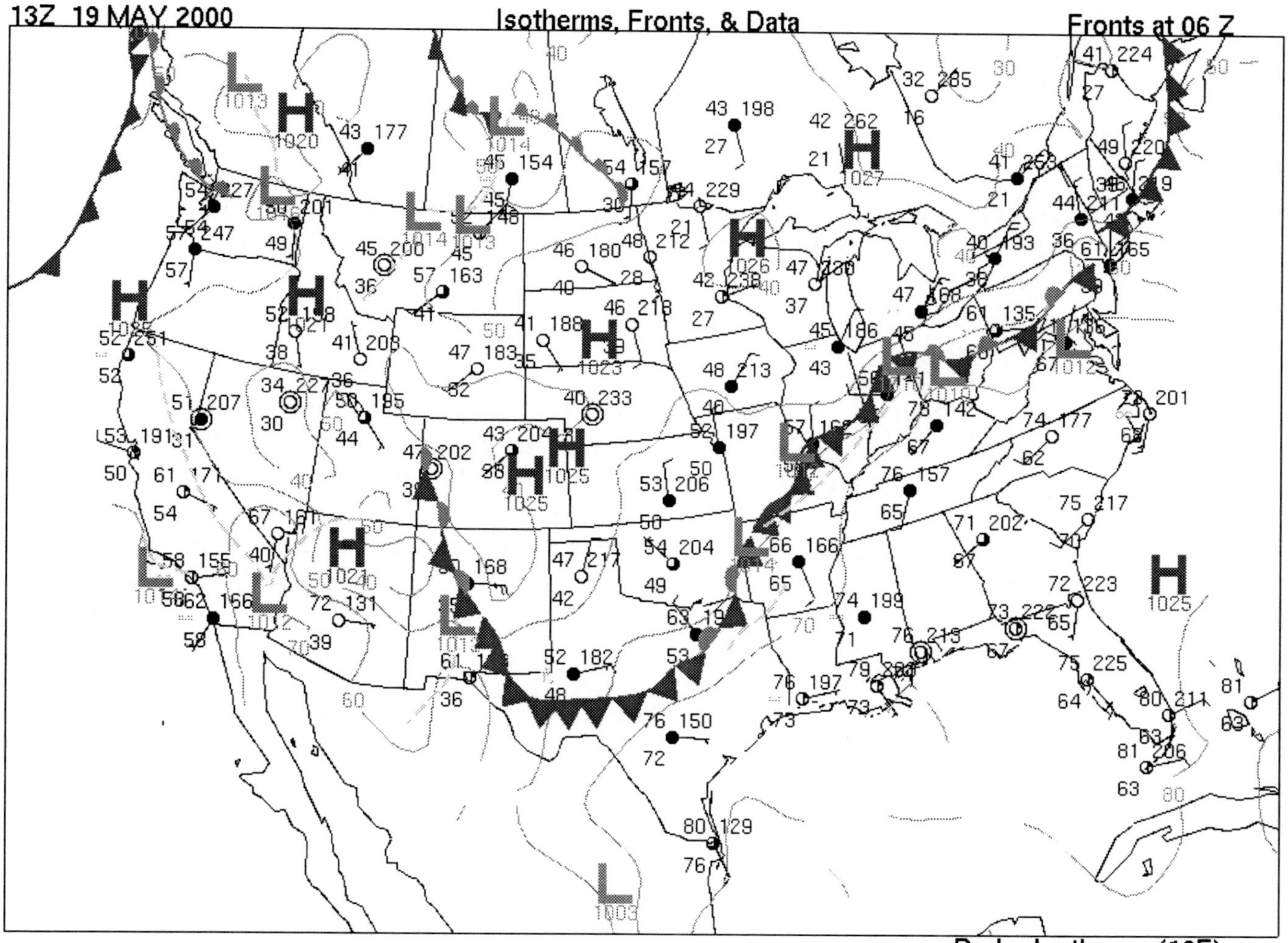

13Z 19 MAY 2000 Isotherms, Fronts, & Data Fronts at 06 Z

Red – Isotherms (10F)

Map courtesy of:
http://www.dnr.sc.gov/climate/sercc/education/saer/aer_summer_00.html

Temperature, Dew Point, and Pressure

The value for temperature is located to the upper left side of the circular weather station symbol, dew point to the lower left, and pressure to the upper right of the station symbol. According to this map, the weather station in Western Texas is recording a temperature of 52 degrees F and a dew point of 48 degrees F. The number to the upper right of the weather station symbol represents the last three digits of the pressure recorded in this area. If this recorded value is greater than 500, the initial 9 is missing. If the recorded value is less than 500, the initial 10 is missing. The pressure is determined by placing the 9 or 10 in front of the reported value and dividing by 10. Therefore, the pressure number of 182 for Western Texas indicates a pressure of 1018.2.

Front

The blue, flag-like symbols in this map indicate a cold front moving southward away from the weather station.

Cloud Coverage

Cloud coverage in Western Texas is portrayed by the degree to which the weather station circle is filled in. According to this map, skies over this weather station are overcast.

Wind Speed and Direction

Wind speed is shown on a weather map by various symbols. Calm conditions are depicted by two open circles, one inside the other. Winds 1-2 mph are depicted by a straight line, and wind speeds above 1-2 are depicted by one or more barbs and/or triangles attached to a straight line. The direction from which the long, flat wind line enters the weather station symbol is the direction from which the wind blows. Therefore, this station is reporting winds of 15-20 mph, blowing from the East–Northeast.

SKILL 6.4 Interpret diagrams relating to Earth science (e.g., cross-sections, seismic wave graphs)

Cross section

Geologists interpret the order of physical events or the geologic history of an area by observing and creating standardized diagrams of rocks. Because, in most areas, rock formations are covered by vegetation or development, or are underground, geologists must look in certain places to find rock formations that are uncovered and show deeper rocks. These include roadcuts and areas where rock faces have been exposed through weathering. An alternative is drilling into the rock and bringing a core to the surface to be examined. From these sources of information, a **stratigraphic column** is created.

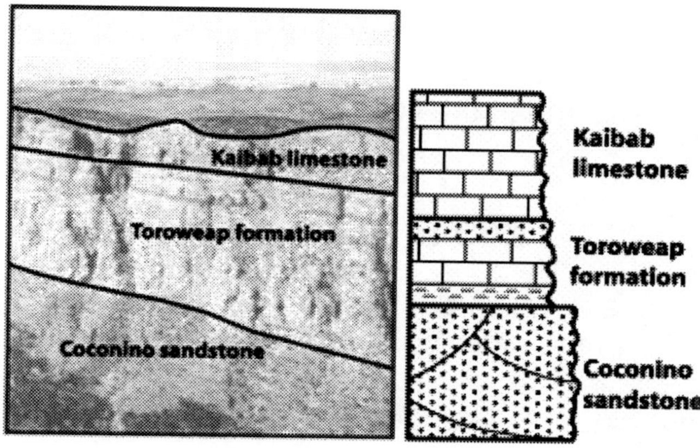

In the diagram above, rocks exposed in the Grand Canyon are translated into a stratigraphic column. This is a fairly simple column, as the most recent rocks are at the top, with the older rocks on the bottom. Because there are a lot of rocks exposed in this area of the western United States, these rock formations have been well-described and are easily recognized by geologists in the field.

The stratigraphic column contains various types of information. In this case, the rock formations are actually named. This allows this rock face to be compared to other exposed rocks distant from this site, which provides a large-scale understanding of the geology of the region. In some cases, such as a stratigraphic column for a core sample in a new area, the rocks would simply be described rather than named. In that case, they would be given names based on the type of rock, such as sandstone, shale, slate, limestone, granite, clay, etc.

Certain universal symbols are used to draw different kinds of rock layers, based on structural characteristics. For example, sandstones are drawn using dots, and limestones are drawn as bricks. From the diagram above, you can see that the Coconino sandstone has also been drawn with additional lines through it, to indicate fracturing. This can be important to geologists looking for water, oil, or natural gas deposits. A thin layer of shale is shown between the Coconino and Toroweap formations as a series of dashed lines.

In other formations, a silty shale or interbedded silts and shales might be shown as dashed lines mixed with dots. Salts may be shown using crosses, and basalts may be shown as black areas, sometimes with vertical lines if they are columnar basalts. Metamorphic rocks may be shown with wavy lines indicating folds; granite rocks as various solid colors with crosses or dots in them. Although there are certain conventions that are typically followed, each area will have its own specific formations and details that will be noted in the legend of a stratigraphic column. Colors are frequently used to indicate the actual color of the rock. Some examples of stratigraphic columns can be found in the links below:

http://www.igwa.org/iowacol.asp
http://www.deq.state.mi.us/documents/deq-gsd-info-geology-Stratigraphic.pdf

These columns also show the geologic era in which each layer was formed and the thickness of the layer, as well as shorthand letter notations for the layers.

Not all rocks appear from bottom to top, oldest to youngest. Originally they may be deposited this way, but then they can be subjected to a variety of geologic processes, including tilting, folding, uplifting, weathering, fracturing, and upwelling of magma within existing formations. These features can often be seen in roadcuts or other exposed surfaces and can confuse the interpretation of geologic events.

Tectonic Diagram

Mountains are formed due to processes related to plate tectonics. When two plates collide, the continental crust is compressed and stressed, and is crumpled and pushed both upward and downward. The result is mountain ranges extending above the surface of the continent, as well as thicker continental crust below the mountains, known as mountain roots. Volcanic activity can also produce individual mountains or chains of mountains. Various types of mountains and causes of their formation are shown and described below.

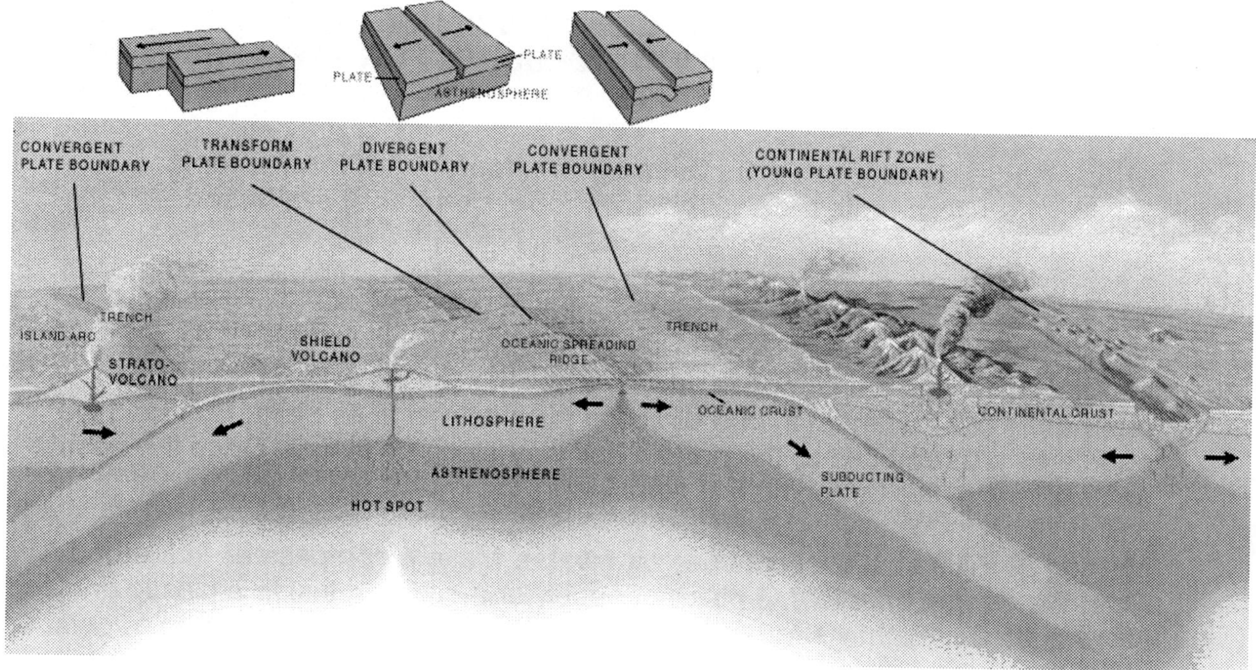

Seismic Wave Graph

Waves originating from an earthquake will appear as increased fluctuations when interpreting a seismic wave graph. Upon observing the following graph, the P and S waves are visible and are defined.

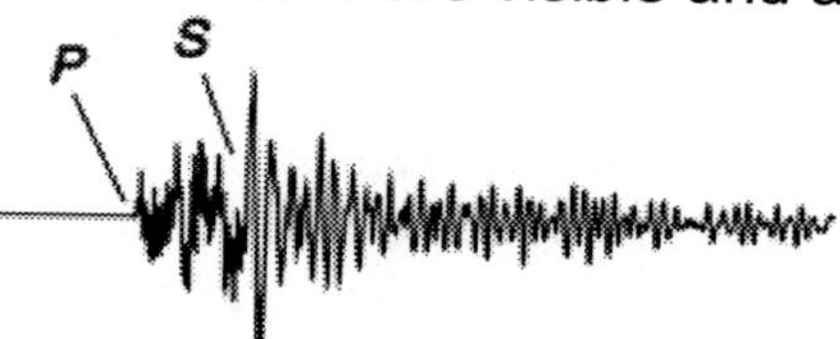

P-Wave (Primary Wave): Also sometimes called a "Push-Pull Wave or Compression Wave," the P-Wave moves through both solids and liquids. The P-Wave has a pulsating, "push-pull" type motion. It compresses material as it moves through it. The fastest moving of the seismic waves (4-7 Km/sec), the P-Wave is the first wave to reach the seismometers.

S-Wave (Secondary Wave, also called a Shake Wave): Moves only through solid material. Always shorter than a P-Wave, the S-Wave (2-5 Km/sec) is the second wave that reaches the seismometer. Motion is a sinuous "side to side" movement.

L-Wave (Surface Wave): The L-Wave is much slower than either the P- or S-Waves, but creates lots of ground movement. Because it is slower, the L-Wave takes longer to pass a location and consequently, the intense, undulating ground motion creates the greatest amount of damage in an earthquake. The L-Wave undulates with a rolling motion of the Earth, similar to ocean waves.

COMPETENCY 7.0 UNDERSTAND EQUIPMENT AND MATERIALS USED IN EARTH SCIENCE INVESTIGATIONS, AND APPLY PROCEDURES FOR THEIR PROPER AND SAFE USE.

SKILL 7.1 Identify the principles upon which given instruments (e.g., telescope, spectroscope, compass) are based

A **compass** is a tool that measures the Earth's magnetic field and determines true North. A simple compass can be made in the following ways:

Method A: To make a compass, stroke a sewing needle with a magnet repeatedly (20-25 times) in one direction from its eye to its point. Suspend the needle by a thread tied to the needle half way along its length. Once the needle quits spinning, the tip (point) will point North.

Method B: Fill a shallow container with water. Make a compass as in Method A. Float the needle on a leaf, a piece of paper, or a cork; or, inside a plastic drinking straw cut to be slightly shorter than the needle. Do not let the leaf, paper, cork, or straw break the surface of the water. The North end of the needle magnet will repel the North end of a bar magnet.

A small sticker can be placed on the North end of the needle magnet. The North pole of your compass will always point towards the direction North on the Earth. The opposite direction is South. When facing North, East is to the students' right and West is to the students' left.

Types of **telescopes** used in the study of the space sciences include optical, radio, infrared, ultraviolet, x-ray, and gamma-ray. Optical telescopes work by collecting and magnifying visible light that is given off by stars or reflected from the surfaces of the planets. However, stars also give off other types of electromagnetic radiation, including radio waves, microwaves, infrared light, ultraviolet light, X rays, and gamma rays. Therefore, specific types of non-optical instruments have been developed to collect information about the universe through these other types of electromagnetic waves.

Many of the telescopes used by astronomers are Earth-based, located in observatories around the world. However, only radio waves, visible light, and some infrared radiation can penetrate our atmosphere to reach the Earth's surface. Therefore, scientists have launched telescopes into space, where the instruments can collect other types of electromagnetic waves. Space probes are also able to gather information from distant parts of the solar system.

In addition to telescopes, scientists construct **mathematical models** and **computer simulations** to form a scientific account of events in the universe. These models and simulations are built using evidence from many sources, including the information gathered through telescopes and space probes.

The **spectroscope** is a device or an attachment for telescopes that is used to separate white light into a series of different colors according to wavelengths. This series of colors of light is called a **spectrum**. A **spectrograph** can photograph a spectrum. Wavelengths of light have distinctive colors. The color red has the longest wavelength and violet has the shortest wavelength. Wavelengths are arranged to form an electromagnetic spectrum. They range from very long radio waves to very short gamma rays. Visible light covers a small portion of the electromagnetic spectrum. Spectroscopes observe the spectra, temperatures, pressures, and also the movement of stars. The movements of stars indicate if they are moving toward or away from Earth.

SKILL 7.2 Demonstrate knowledge and applications of basic safety procedures in laboratory and field situations

All science labs should contain the following items of safety equipment. Those marked with an asterisk are required by state law.

- Fire blanket which is visible and accessible*
- Ground Fault Circuit Interrupters (GCFI) within two feet of water supplies*
- Signs designating room exits*
- Emergency shower providing a continuous flow of water*
- Emergency eye wash station which can be activated by the foot or forearm*
- Eye protection for every student and a means of sanitizing equipment*
- Emergency exhaust fans providing ventilation to the outside of the building*
- Master cut-off switches for gas, electricity, and compressed air. Switches must have permanently attached handles. Cut-off switches must be clearly labeled.*
- An ABC fire extinguisher*
- Storage cabinets for flammable materials*
- Chemical spill control kit
- Fume hood with a motor which is spark proof
- Protective laboratory aprons made of flame retardant material
- Signs which will alert potential hazardous conditions
- Containers (labeled) for broken glassware, flammables, corrosives, and waste.

Students should wear safety goggles when performing dissections, heating materials, or while using acids and bases. Hair should always be tied back and objects should never be placed in the mouth. Food should not be consumed while in the laboratory. Hands should always be washed before and after laboratory experiments. In case of an accident, eye washes and showers should be used for eye contamination or a chemical spill that covers the student's body. Small chemical spills should only be contained and cleaned by the teacher. Kitty litter or a chemical spill kit should be used to clean a spill. For large spills, the school administration and the local fire department should be notified. Biological spills should only be handled by the teacher. Contamination with biological waste can be cleaned using bleach when appropriate. Accidents and injuries should always be reported to the school administration and local health facilities. The severity of the accident or injury will determine the course of action to pursue.

It is the responsibility of the teacher to provide a safe environment for their students. Proper supervision greatly reduces the risk of injury and a teacher should never leave a class for any reason without providing alternate supervision. After an accident, two factors are considered. These are foreseeability and negligence. Foreseeability is the anticipation that an event may occur under certain circumstances. Negligence is the failure to exercise ordinary or reasonable care. Safety procedures should be a part of the science curriculum and a well-managed classroom is important to avoid danger and/or potential lawsuits.

SUBAREA II. SPACE SYSTEMS

COMPETENCY 8.0 UNDERSTAND THE STRUCTURE, COMPOSITION, AND FEATURES OF EARTH, THE MOON, AND THE SUN.

SKILL 8.1 Demonstrate an understanding of the physical characteristics of Earth (e.g., diameter, tilt of axis, distance from the Sun) and how they can be determined

EARTH	
Average Distance from the Sun	1.00 AU (1.495 x 10^8 km)
Density	5.497 g/cm^3
Diameter (equatorial)	12,756 km
Mass	5.976 x 10^{24} kg
Atmosphere	78% Nitrogen, 21% Oxygen
Solar Revolution Period	365.26 days
Axial Rotation Period	24.00 hours
Axial Tilt	23.5°
Surface Temp	-50°C to 50°C
Moons	1 The Moon

The density of planets correlates with their distance from the Sun. The inner planets (Mercury-Mars) are known as the terrestrial planets because they are rocky, and the outer planets (Jupiter and outward) are known as the icy or Jovian (gaslike) planets.

The Earth's inner core is mathematically hypothesized to be a solid iron and nickel core. The outer core, surrounding the inner core, is so hot that it is believed to be molten iron (liquid state). Combined, they are responsible for Earth's magnetism.

SKILL 8.2 Identify characteristics of the Sun (e.g., nucleogenesis)

Located at an average distance of 1.00 AU (1.495979 x 10^8 km) from the Earth, the Sun's diameter of 1.4 million kilometers is over 54 times the diameter of Earth, and at 1.989 x 10^{30} kg, its mass is roughly 330,000 times greater than Earth's. In fact, scientists estimate that the Sun contains approximately 99.8% of all the mass in our solar system. Its not surprising that the Sun's gravitational effect is so strong as to capture and hold the planets of our solar system in orbit around it. The Sun is intensely hot. At the center, it has a 140,000-kilometer diameter Core composed of hydrogen (92%) and helium (7.8%) that provide the fuel for the Sun's nuclear reactions (fusion). At approximately 15 million °C, the core gives off a tremendous amount of energy. However, the density of the Sun precludes the direct release of all this energy into space. Instead, it is slowly absorbed and re-emitted by the various layers of the Sun.

The first layer above the core is the very thick Radiative Layer. The energy produced in the core warms this layer to an average temperature of 3 million °C. On top of the radiative layer is the Convective Layer, where, as the name implies, energy is transferred via convection. This layer has an average temperature of 8,000 °C.

The Sun's atmosphere comprises its visible layers. The atmosphere is made up of three layers. The first layer is the Photosphere: the inner layer of the Sun's atmosphere that forms the Sun's visible surface. The photosphere is a very thin layer, only 400 kilometers deep, and its average temperature is around 5,500 °C. The photosphere's many small (1,000 kilometer in diameter), bright areas are referred to as Granules: the tops of rising columns of hot gas. The dark granules represent sinking columns of cooler gasses. The second layer of the atmosphere is the Chromosphere: a 2,500-kilometer thick layer of turbulent gases. The temperature in the chromosphere increases to 100,000 degrees Celsius. Spicules: jets of heated gasses shoot upward from the chromosphere, reaching average proportions of 7,000 kilometers wide by 7,000 kilometers tall. The third and final layer of the Sun's atmosphere is called the Corona: a very thin layer of gas that merges with outer space. The Corona's temperature is approximately 2 million degrees Celsius, and is heated by twisted magnetic fields that carry energy up to it. These energy particles move very fast, generating high temperatures. Prominences: red, flaming jets of gas that rise from the corona, can travel as far as 1 million kilometers outward into space. Electrons are stripped off of atoms and the reduced nuclei fly off into space, creating the Solar Wind. This wind surrounds the Earth and even reaches to the farthest regions of the solar system.

SKILL 8.3 Relate surface features of Earth's moon (e.g., maria, craters, mountains) to events in the history of the Moon

Earth's Moon is covered with mountain ranges, craters, and plains. In the early days of astronomy, the Lunar Plains: vast lava flow plains, were thought to be oceans, and were called maria or mare (Latin derivative for seas) by Galileo in the 1600's. This name is still used although we know that the plains are actually vast, dry, flat expanses of barren volcanic rock. Because the presence of igneous volcanic rock implies tectonism, we know that at one point in its development the Moon was tectonically active, producing the Lunar Highlands: lunar mountains and the lava plains. However, such activity has long ceased and for all practical purposes, the moon is tectonically dormant.

SKILL 8.4 Recognize the importance of density in the formation of the internal structure of Earth, the Moon, and the Sun

The dominant theory of our planet's history holds that a giant object (probably a meteor) smashed into the Earth very shortly after the Earth's solidification (approximately 4.5 billion years ago). The fragments- some scientists estimate as much as 1/3 of Earth's original size- of this collision were sent outward into space where much of the ejected mass continued on, but some were held in close proximity by the Earth's gravitational attraction. These fragments began orbiting the Earth and through the process of accretion, eventually coalesced into the Moon. However, unlike the Earth, the Moon did not originally have a molten core. This has led to the theory that its volcanic heat was initially caused by the collisions among gases, dust, and large fragments as gravity pulled them together. Intensive meteorite bombardment further fueled the tectonics.

The Moon has had a rough time since its inception. Meteorite bombardment melted its outermost layer down to 100 kilometers in depth. This initial swarm of meteorite activity ceased long enough for the highlands to form around 4.4 billion years ago, but the calm was not to last. Between 4.2 and 3.9 billion years ago, billions of meteorites pummeled the Moon's surface, creating huge craters and by 3.8 billion years ago, this continuous assault raised the temperature to the point that the Moon's interior turned molten. This impact-induced melting caused the denser materials to sink downward and the lighter materials to rise to the surface. Volcanic activity continued for 700 million years, lasting until approximately 3.1 billon years ago when the Moon finally cooled. Core samples taken during the six manned Apollo lunar landings in the 1970's show that the composition of the Moon mimics that of Earth in many aspects. The Moon has a molten, metallic core surrounded by silicate rocks, but the crust and mantle are too rigid and thick for any significant tectonic or seismic activity. Although seismic detectors left behind by the Apollo Astronauts have detected Moonquakes, the seismic activities have only one-billionth of the energy associated with Earthquakes.

COMPETENCY 9.0 UNDERSTAND THE INTERACTIONS AMONG THE COMPONENTS OF THE EARTH, MOON, AND SUN SYSTEM (INCLUDING ENERGY TRANSMISSION AND ABSORPTION).

SKILL 9.1 Demonstrate an understanding of the consequences of Earth's relative position and motion with respect to the Sun (e.g., length of day, change of seasons, length of year)

The change of seasons on Earth are caused by the orbit and axial tilt of the planet in relation to the Sun's Ecliptic: the rotational path of the Sun. These factors combine to vary the degree of insolation (distribution of solar energy) at a particular location and thereby change the seasons. There are four key points on the Ecliptic. These are called the Equinoxes and the Solstices.

Winter Solstice (December 21) = Shortest day of the year in the northern hemisphere.

Summer Solstice (June 21) = Longest day of the year in the northern hemisphere.

Vernal Equinox (March 21) = Marks beginning of spring.

Autumnal Equinox (Sept 21) = Marks beginning of Autumn (Fall).

These dates will vary slightly during leap years. During the summer solstice, insolation is at a maximum in the northern hemisphere, and at a minimum in the southern hemisphere. Because of the tilt and curvature of the Earth, in order to get the sun directly overhead, you must be between 23.5°N Latitude and 23.5°S Latitude (between the Tropic of Cancer and the Tropic of Capricorn). Another result is that during the summer months in the northern hemisphere, the far northern latitudes receive 24 hours of daylight. This situation is reversed during the winter months, when they experience have 24 hours of darkness.

SKILL 9.2 Relate Earth's coordinate system (e.g., latitude and longitude) to astronomical observations

The Arctic Circle

The Arctic Circle is located at 66.5° North latitude. It is the southern most point (in the Northern Hemisphere) which will experience 24 hours of sunlight once per year. It is also the southern most point in the Northern Hemisphere that there will be 24 hours of darkness once per year.

The Antarctic Circle

The Antarctic Circle is located at 66.5° South latitude. It is the northern most point (in the Southern Hemisphere) that will experience 24 hours of sunlight once a year. It is also the northern most point in the Southern Hemisphere that will experience 24 hours of darkness once a year.

The Equator

The equator is the coordinate on the globe where the Sun rises and sets on the day of the equinox. In other words, the Sun will rise due east at the equator on the equinox and the Sun will set due west at the equator on the equinox. The Sun with be at the zenith at noon on the day of the equinox. Daylight will encompass 12 hours and darkness will be 12 hours on the day of the equinox.

Tropic of Cancer

The Tropic of Cancer is located 23.5° North of the equator. It is the northern most point in the Northern Hemisphere and marks where the sun will be at the zenith at noon on the summer solstice.

Tropic of Capricorn

The Tropic of Capricorn is located at 23.5° South of the equator. It is the southern most point in the Southern Hemisphere and marks where the sun will be at the zenith at noon on the winter solstice.

Azimuth

The azimuth is the compass direction in degrees. North is 0° or 360°. If you follow clockwise from north, east is 90°, south is 180°, and west is 270°.

Ecliptic

The ecliptic is the apparent path that the Sun follows in the sky in relation to the stars.

SKILL 9.3 Analyze the consequences of the relative positions and motions of Earth, the Moon, and the Sun (e.g., phases of the Moon, tides, eclipses)

Phases of the Moon

Just as the Earth follows an orbit around the Sun, the Moon follows an eastward moving orbit around the Earth. Because the Moon's rotational period matches the Earth's and its period of revolution is 27.3 days (called the sidereal period), this keeps one side of the Moon always facing Earth. The side always facing us is called the Near Side, and the darkened side we never see is called the Far Side.

Phases of the Moon: the apparent change in shape of the Moon caused by the absence or presence of reflected sunlight as the Moon orbits around the Earth.

The orbital pattern of the Moon in relation to the Sun and Earth determines the extent of lunar illumination and, consequently, what illuminated shape is presented to the Earth. When the moon is between the Sun and the Earth, the side facing us is darkened, and we refer to this as a New Moon. The opposite pattern occurs in the second half of the complete Lunar Cycle, when the Moon is fully illuminated and bright in the night sky. This is called a Full Moon. The other phases between these extremes reflect the orbital point of the Moon as it completes its journey around the Earth.

Tides

The periodic rise and fall of the liquid bodies on Earth are the direct result of the gravitational influence of the Moon and, to a much lesser extent, the Sun. Tides are produced by the differences between gravitational forces acting on parts of an object. The side of the Earth that faces the Moon is roughly 4,000 miles (6,400 km) closer to the moon than is the Earth's center. The Moon's gravitational effect causes a bulge to form on both sides of the Earth. This double-bulge effect causes the tides to fall and rise twice each day, and the time of the high and low tides is dependent on the phase of the moon. Not all locations are uniformly affected. The tidal cycle at a particular location is actually a very complicated interaction of the location's latitude, shape of the shore, etc. Because of its distance from the Earth, the Sun's gravitational effect on tides is only half that of the Moon's. However, when the gravitational effects of both the Sun and Moon join together during a new moon and a full moon phase, the tidal effects can be extreme. During a new moon and a full moon, tidal effects are much more pronounced as the tidal bulges join together to produce very high and very low tides. This pronounced type of tide is known as a Spring Tide. During the first and third quarters of the moon phases, the Sun's effect is negligible and consequently, the tides are lower. These are called Neap Tides.

Eclipses

Eclipse: a phenomenon that occurs when a stellar body is shadowed by another and, as a result, is rendered invisible. The Earth, Moon, and Sun must be in perfect alignment with each other to form an eclipse. There are two types of eclipses: Lunar and Solar.

Lunar Eclipse: The shadow of the Earth darkens the Moon. The Moon is in the Earth's shadow.

Solar Eclipse: The Moon is between the Sun and the Earth. The Earth is in the Moon's shadow.

Both types of eclipses have two forms: partial (annular) and full (total). A total eclipse can only be seen in the equatorial regions. Most total eclipses are spaced 6 months apart. They normally are 2 to 10 minutes in duration. A partial eclipse occurs when the moon does not completely enter the Earth's shadow. The Sun never moves in between the Earth and the Moon. The orbits of the Earth and Moon cause them to move in and out of the shadow areas.

Annular eclipse: a type of solar eclipse in which the darkest part of the shadow (the Umbra), doesn't touch the Earth.

Total eclipse: a type of solar eclipse in which the darkest part of the shadow (the Umbra) does touch the Earth.

Umbra: the central region of the shadow caused by an eclipse. No light hits this region. This is typically associated with total eclipses.

Penumbra: the lighter, outer edges of the shadow created during an eclipse. Some light hits these regions. This is typically associated with annular (partial) eclipses.

The appearance of the Sun changes during a total and annular eclipse.

Annular: The moon appears as a small, dark spot in the center of the Sun.

Total: The moon covers most of the Sun, usually only showing a flaming Corona around the edges.

SKILL 9.4 Demonstrate an understanding that the Sun is the major source of energy for Earth's surface

The vast majority of energy on the Earth's surface is derived from sunlight. However, sunlight is attenuated by the Earth's atmosphere, so that not all this solar energy reaches the planet's surface. Specifically, about 1300 watts are delivered per square meter of Earth, but only about 1000 watts actually reach the surface.

It is easy for us to understand how sunlight warms the land and water on the surface of the Earth. We are similarly familiar with the capture of sunlight by solar cells, which then can be used for heating or electricity. However, it is important to understand that sunlight is the basis for many of our other sources of power. This is because sunlight is used to drive photosynthesis, which is the major method by which carbon is fixed by living things. The energy harnessed by plants is used to fuel all heterotrophs further up the food chain. When these life forms (plant or animal) die, they may ultimately be converted to fossil fuels. Thus the petroleum, oil, and other fossil fuels we use as a major power source all originally derived their energy from sunlight.

SKILL 9.5 Analyze the Sun's activity (e.g., sunspots, solar flares) and its possible effects on Earth

Large dark spots called Sunspots appear regularly on the Sun's surface. These spots vary in size from small to 150,000 kilometers in diameter and may last from hours to months. The sunspots also cause solar flares that can accelerate to velocities of 900 km/hr, sending shock waves through the solar atmosphere. The particles emitted by these flares can disrupt radio communications on Earth and cause the northern lights as the highly charged particles strike the Earth's magnetosphere.

COMPETENCY 10.0 UNDERSTAND THE SCALE AND ORGANIZATION OF THE SOLAR SYSTEM, THE ROLE OF GRAVITY IN THE SOLAR SYSTEM, AND CHARACTERISTICS OF THE BODIES WITHIN THE SOLAR SYSTEM.

SKILL 10.1 Analyze characteristics of the planets (e.g., size, density, inferred interior structure, surface temperature)

The solar system is divided into two sections: the inner and outer planets. The inner planets' composition reflects the attraction of the heavier elements by the Sun. The outer planets' composition reflects the lighter, less dense elements not attracted as much by the Sun's gravitational mass. Heavy elements sink inward to form the core. Lighter elements form the atmosphere. Our solar system consists of the Sun, planets, comets, meteors, and asteroids. The planets are ordered in the following way: Mercury, Venus, Earth, Mars (with Asteroid Belt), Jupiter, Saturn, Uranus, and Neptune. Pluto has historically been considered the ninth planet. Recently, scientists have created new requirements for the definition of a planet, and it is possible that Pluto will be considered as a celestial body. A common memory aid for remembering the order of the planets is <u>M</u>y <u>V</u>ery <u>E</u>ducated <u>M</u>other <u>J</u>ust <u>S</u>erved <u>U</u>s <u>N</u>ine <u>P</u>ies.

All the planets revolve around the Sun, and all the planets (with the exception of Venus) rotate on their axis in the same direction. Venus has a retrograde motion; it rotates backwards. Except for Pluto, all the planets follow roughly the same elliptical orbital planes around the Sun. Neptune and Pluto occasionally change places in their order. Pluto's orbit is very erratic compared to the other planets and sometimes it carriers Pluto inside of Neptune's orbit. The asteroid belt is located between Mars and Jupiter and may be the remnants a planet crushed by the massive gravitational force of Jupiter.

Comparison of the Basic Characteristics of the Inner and Outer Planets	
INNER PLANETS	**OUTER PLANETS**
Referred to as the Terrestrial Planets	Called the Gas Giants (Jovian Planets)
Similar to density to Earth	Except for Pluto, very large in size
Also referred to as the "Rocky Planets"	Primarily composed of gas
Relatively small in size	Less dense than Earth
Spin slowly on their axis	Rotate rapidly on their axis
Few, if any, moons	Many moons
Mercury	Jupiter
Venus	Saturn (Ringed)
Earth	Uranus
Mars	Neptune
+ Asteroid Belt	Pluto (Rocky)

The Inner Planets

MERCURY	
Average Distance from the Sun	0.387 AU (5.79 x 10^7 km)
Density	5.44 g/cm^3
Diameter (equatorial)	4878 km (0.38 of Earth)
Mass	3.31 x 10^{23} kg (0.055 of Earth)
Atmosphere	Only trace gasses only of H, He, Na, K
Axial Rotation Period	58.6 days
Solar Revolution Period	87.9 days
Axial Tilt	0°
Surface Temp	-173°C to 330°C
Moons	None
Composition	Silicate & Iron rocks

VENUS	
Average Distance from the Sun	0.723 AU (1.082 x 10^8 km)
Density	5.3 g/cm^3
Diameter (equatorial)	12,104 km (0.95 of Earth)
Mass	4.87 x 10^{24} kg (0.82 of Earth)
Atmosphere	Runaway Greenhouse effect 96.5% CO_2, 3.5% N.
Axial Rotation Period	243.01 days
Solar Revolution Period	224.68 days
Axial Tilt	177° (Makes the planet appear as if it was rotating clockwise)
Surface Temp	472°C
Moons	None
Composition	Unknown, crustal materials believed to be similar to Earth

EARTH	
Average Distance from the Sun	1.00 AU (1.495 x 10^8 km)
Density	5.497 g/cm^3
Diameter (equatorial)	12,756 km
Mass	5.976 x 10^{24} kg
Atmosphere	78% Nitrogen, 21% Oxygen
Axial Rotation Period	24.00 hours
Solar Revolution Period	365.26 days
Axial Tilt	23.5°
Surface Temp	-50°C to 50°C
Moons	Just one, the Moon

MARS	
Average Distance from the Sun	1.523 AU (2.279 x 10^8 km)
Density	3.94 g/cm^3
Diameter (equatorial)	6796 km (0.53 of Earth)
Mass	0.6424 x 10^{24} kg (0.1075 of Earth)
Atmosphere	95% CO_2
Axial Rotation Period	24.61 hours
Solar Revolution Period	686.9 days
Axial Tilt	23° 59'
Surface Temp	-140°C to 20°C
Moons	Deimos and Phobos. They may actually be captured asteroids because of their irregular shape.
Composition	Identical to Earth's

The Outer Planets

JUPITER	
Average Distance from the Sun	5.202 AU (7.783 x 10^8 km)
Density	1.34 g/cm^3
Diameter (equatorial)	142,900 km (11.20 of Earth)
Mass	1.899 x 10^{27} kg (317.83 of Earth)
Atmosphere	Hydrogen, Helium, and Ammonia
Axial Rotation Period	9.83 hours
Solar Revolution Period	11.867 years
Axial Tilt	3.5°
Surface Temp	29,727 °C at surface -120°C in atmosphere
Moons	47, of which only 4 are significant. These are the **Galilean Moons:** Io, Europa, Ganymede, and Callisto.
Composition	No surface, gaseous atmosphere

SATURN	
Average Distance from the Sun	9.538 AU (14.27 x 10^8 km)
Density	0.69 g/cm^3
Diameter (equatorial)	120,660 km (9.42 of Earth)
Mass	5.69 x 10^{26} kg (95.17 of Earth)
Atmosphere	Hydrogen and Helium
Axial Rotation Period	10.65 hours
Solar Revolution Period	29.461 years
Axial Tilt	26° 24'
Surface Temp	Unknown at surface and -180° in atmosphere
Moons	17 total, of which Titan is the largest and most significant.
Composition	No surface, gaseous atmosphere

URANUS	
Average Distance from the Sun	9.538 AU (14.27 x 10^8 km)
Density	1.29 g/cm^3
Diameter (equatorial)	51,118 km (4.01 of Earth)
Mass	8.69 x 10^{25} kg (14.54 of Earth)
Atmosphere	Hydrogen, Helium, and Methane
Axial Rotation Period	17.23 hours
Solar Revolution Period	84.013 years
Axial Tilt	97° 55'
Surface Temp	Unknown at surface -220° in atmosphere
Moons	15 total, of which Oberon is the largest at 1,500 km diameter.
Composition	Unknown, frozen gasses

NEPTUNE	
Average Distance from the Sun	30.061 AU (44.971 x 10^8 km)
Density	1.66 g/cm^3
Diameter (equatorial)	49,500 km (3.88 of Earth)
Mass	10.30 x 10^{26} kg (17.23 of Earth)
Atmosphere	Hydrogen, Helium, and Methane
Axial Rotation Period	16.05 hours
Solar Revolution Period	164.793 years
Axial Tilt	28° 48'
Surface Temp	Unknown at surface -216°C in atmosphere
Moons	8 total, 2 of significance, Triton and Nereid.
Composition	Unknown, mostly ice

PLUTO	
Average Distance from the Sun	39.44 AU (59.00 x 10^8 km)
Density	2.0 g/cm^3
Diameter (equatorial)	2,300 km (0.19 of Earth)
Mass	1.2 x 10^{22} kg (0.002 of Earth)
Atmosphere	Nitrogen and Methane
Axial Rotation Period	9.3 days
Solar Revolution Period	247.7 years
Axial Tilt	122°
Surface Temp	-230°C
Moons	One, Charon
Composition	Frozen nitrogen and rock

SKILL 10.2 Analyze the apparent motion of celestial objects to infer solar system models (i.e., geocentric and heliocentric)

Galileo Galilei (1633 A.D.): One of the truly brilliant minds of his time, Galileo Galilei was an Italian astronomer and inventor who built his first telescope in 1609. Contrary to popular myth, Galileo didn't invent the telescope but by using existing plans, he gradually improved upon their design. Acknowledged today as the "Father of Experimental Science," Galileo developed a careful, methodical approach to observation and collection of data on planetary motion. His conclusions eventually changed the entire direction of astronomical thought and theory.

Galileo's observed that the Moon is not flat and it has holes on its surface. The significance of Earth-like features meant that the Moon wasn't perfect. The Greek philosophy accepted at that time was that all things in the heavens were perfect. Galileo saw stars where there were none (stars not visible to the naked eye). This observation gave rise to the question of why God would put a star so far out that we have to use a device to see it? In observing Venus, he saw the phases of the planet. This meant that the geocentric theory couldn't be valid. In a true geocentric system, no gibbous (dark) phase of Venus would be possible. When observing Jupiter, Galileo saw four moons rotating around the planet. This means that an object in the perfect heavens have rotating objects around them. Galileo saw sunspots on the Sun. This meant that the Sun was not perfect.

Galileo's observations proved the heliocentric model was correct and supported Kelper's theory of planetary motion. The major significance of Galileo's observations is that they totally disproved the geocentric model of the universe, and thereby destroyed the 2,000 year old heliocentric (helio=sun, centric=center) vision of the Universe, as proposed by Aristotle.

SKILL 10.3 Recognizing physical and mathematical models (e.g., Newton's and Kepler's laws) that describe objects in the solar system and their real and apparent motions

Kepler's Law of Planetary Motion

Kepler's First Law of Planetary Motion: A planet can't travel in a circle. A planet travels an elliptical path, with the Sun at one foci point.

Kepler's Second Law of Planetary Motion: Planets must sweep out equal areas, at equal amounts of time, on these elliptical paths. When a planet is nearer to the Sun on the planet's elliptical path, it must move faster to sweep over the same area.

Kepler's Third Law of Planetary Motion: A planet's orbital period squared is proportional to its average distance from the sun cubed ($a^3 = p^2$). Therefore, the orbital period of Jupiter must be the square root of 140.6, which equals a period of about 11.8 light-years. The significance of Kepler's Law is that it overthrew the ancient concept of uniform circular motion, which supported the geocentric theory. Kepler suggested that the eccentricity of the planetary motion could be mathematically summarized as $e=c/a$.

The two major points on the elliptical orbit are the Perihelion and Aphelion.

- Perihelion: the closest point of approach to the Sun on the elliptical path. This is the point at which the planet travels the fastest in keeping with Kepler's 2nd Law.
- Aphelion: the farthest point away from the Sun on the elliptical path. This is the point at which the planet travels the slowest in keeping with Kepler's 2nd Law.

Newton's Law of Universal Gravitation

Sir Isaac Newton (1687 A.D.): Today considered the "Father of Modern Physics," Newton is justifiably famous for the development of Calculus and his work with the Laws of Motion. However, he also turned his brilliant intellect to the phenomena of gravity, postulating what has become known as Newton's Law of Universal Gravitation.

Newton's Law of Universal Gravitation states that every object attracts another object with a force that for any two objects is directly proportional to the mass of each object. In simpler terms, objects with mass attract one another.

COMPETENCY 11.0 UNDERSTAND THE PROPERTIES, MOTIONS, AND LIFE CYCLES OF STARS AND THE METHODS AND TECHNOLOGY USED TO STUDY THEM.

SKILL 11.1 Compare and contrast types of telescopes (e.g., optical, radio, infrared, ultraviolet) and the ways in which they are used to acquire information on star characteristics

Telescopes and Light

There are two main styles of optical telescopes: refractor and reflector.

Refractor Telescopes

Refraction: the bending of light. Example: Put a straw in a clear glass of water. Now look at the straw through the side of the glass. It will appear to bend at the point where the straw enters the water.

Refractor Telescope: an optical device that makes use of lenses to magnify and display received images. Professional astronomers do not use Refractor telescopes because of two main problems: first, the telescopes are affected by chromatic aberrations which make it difficult to focus on the stars, and second, because they rely solely on lenses, the telescopes have inherent weight and size restrictions. Chromatic Aberrations are a problem because as the lenses split the light into its chromatic components; each color has a different focal point based on its wavelength. This causes details on the image to blur. To compensate for this problem lenses with different refractive indexes (the degree of bending) are sandwiched together in order to compensate for the aberrations and properly focus on the image. However, this compensation method increases the size and weight of the telescope.

Reflector Telescopes

Reflection: the re-emission of light off of an object struck by the light. Example: Look at yourself in the mirror. What your eyes see is the re-emission of light waves that have struck you and the mirror.

Reflector Telescope: an optical device that makes use of a mirror or mirrors, to reflect light waves to an eyepiece (an ocular), thereby eliminating chromatic aberrations. There are different types of reflector telescopes; some use mirrors only, and others make use of both lenses and mirrors. The <u>objective</u> is the primary focus mirror in a reflector telescope and is usually curved. Any other mirrors in the telescope are referred to as secondary, tertiary, etc. depending on the number of mirrors present. On both refractor and reflector telescopes, the eyepiece is called the ocular.

The most common style of reflector telescope used is the Schmidt-Cassegrain. The two major advantages of a reflector telescope over a refractor style telescope are:

- No chromatic aberrations, which results in a much clearer and detailed image than in a refractor telescope.

- Their smaller size makes them easier to use, and they weigh less because they don't rely on the heavy, thick glass lenses required in a refractor type.

However, there are still limits to the size of a reflecting telescope. They are very expensive and it is an extremely difficult and slow process to grind the mirror to the proper specifications. The larger the mirror or mirrors required to view distant objects, the more likely it is that there will be **imperfections** in the mirror. Weight also becomes an issue depending on the size of the mirror required. The heavier and thicker the mirror required, the greater the chance that the mirror will sag, slightly distorting the image. Also, the mirror will heat and cool unevenly, causing further distortion.

Active Optics

Active Optics: a type of optical device that is composed of hexagonal pieces of mirror whose positions are controlled by a computer. Also referred to as **Active Telescopes**.

Collectively, smaller pieces of mirror weigh less than a single large mirror and, more importantly, they generally do not suffer from sagging problems. Small hexagonal shaped pieces of mirror are arranged next to each other to form a larger reflection surface. Computer-controlled thrusters mounted underneath the pieces control the mirror position and focus. Employing the smaller pieces which work in conjunction eliminates sagging and the uneven heating and cooling problems found in extremely large, single mirror type telescopes.

Example: The Keck Telescope in Hawaii is able to have a 10-meter diameter reflective surface through the use of active optics. Similarly, the Hobby-Eberly Telescope is composed of 91 hexagons has an 11-meter diameter reflective surface, making it the largest telescope on Earth.

New Generation Telescopes

The **Hubble Space Telescope** is named in honor of the American astronomer Edwin Hubble who proved the theory of an expanding universe. The Hubble Space Telescope, although only possessing a 2.4-meter diameter reflective surface, isn't affected by atmospheric constraints, and as a result, it provides a much clearer, higher resolution image of stellar objects than is possible through the use of an Earth-based telescope. Two companies competed in the design phase of manufacturing the telescope, and working models of each design were constructed. However, shortly after being positioned in space, the mirror on the winning design was discovered to have imperfections that produced a great deal of distortion in the received images. Initially, the fix for this problem seemed simple; put the losing contractor's design up in space in place of the flawed telescope. But a problem quickly arose. When NASA scientists contacted the second company, they were told that the losing model no longer was available. In any event, NASA eventually figured out a means to correct the imperfections and space shuttle astronauts successfully affected the repairs.

CCD-Charged Coupled Devices

A **CCD** is a camera plate made up of thousands of tiny pixels. The pixels carry a slight electrical charge and when photons strike a pixel, electrons are released. The release of electrons causes a flow of current through an attached wire, and this current is detected by a computer chip and used to construct images based on the number of strikes. The number of strikes also shows the intensity of the received image.

CCD cameras have a wide range of applications besides astronomy. This type of technology is being successfully employed in many of the newest, high-resolution cameras available to the general public.

Radio Telescopes

Variances in radio waves received from space can be translated into usable astronomical data. The advantages offered by use of radio telescopes are many: it's cheaper to build a radio telescope than optical telescopes, they can operate 24 hours a day and be built just about anywhere on Earth, and they open up an entirely new window of space investigation. But they initially had one major disadvantage: the useable radio waves received from space were not overly abundant and generally very weak, and you needed a huge receiving dish to detect the signals. To overcome these problems, scientists developed a technique called Radio Interferometry.

Radio Interferometry: a method of amplifying weak radio waves by lying out, in a Y-shaped pattern, a series of small radio telescopes all pointed at the same point in the sky. The telescopes add their received signals together to form an overlay of signals. Computers control the angle of incidence and correlate the incoming signals. This improves resolution and limits the size of the radio telescope dish needed for a single unit.

Black Body Radiation

When objects are heated, they give off properties of light, and you observe different colors at different temperatures. Example: Heat a needle. The color of the needle will go from red to white. The hotter you make it, the more the color will vary.

We measure the intensity of the light by the ratio of the apparent presence or absence of colors. **Intensity**: the amount of light contained in a space. Intensity varies by distance. The further away you are, you will see a drop in intensity equal to 1 over the distance squared ($1/d^2$). Intensity gives off a continuous amount of color, but the intensity of the colors seen varies in accordance with the temperature of the object.

Stars follow the same principles of emission. We observe the intensity of the stars by using a red and blue filter on a photon counter mounted to a telescope. The red and blue ratio determines the color index. From the color index, we can determine the temperature, size, properties, and material composition of the star. However, appearances can be deceiving. The hotter the object the bluer it will appear. This is because there is an inverse relationship between temperature and wavelength. Wavelength decreases as temperature increases.

SKILL 11.2 Compare and contrast types of stars (e.g., pulsars, Cepheid variables) and their characteristics

A star is a ball of hot, glowing gas that is hot enough and dense enough to trigger nuclear reactions, which fuel the star. In comparing the mass, light production, and size of the Sun to other stars, astronomers find that the Sun is a perfectly ordinary star. It behaves exactly the way they would expect a star of its size to behave. The main difference between the Sun and other stars is that the Sun is much closer to Earth.

Most stars have masses similar to that of the Sun. The majority of stars' masses are between 0.3 and 3.0 times the mass of the Sun. Theoretical calculations indicate that in order to trigger nuclear reactions and to create its own energy—that is, to become a star—a body must have a mass greater than 7 percent of the mass of the Sun. Astronomical bodies that are less massive than this become planets or objects called brown dwarfs. The largest accurately determined stellar mass is of a star called V382 Cygni and it is 27 times that of the Sun.

The range of brightness among stars is much larger than the range of mass. Astronomers measure the brightness of a star by measuring its magnitude and luminosity. Magnitude allows astronomers to rank how bright different stars appear to humans. Because of the way our eyes detect light, a lamp ten times more luminous than a second lamp will appear less than ten times brighter to human eyes. This discrepancy affects the magnitude scale, as does the tradition of giving brighter stars lower magnitudes. The lower a star's magnitude, the brighter it is. Stars with negative magnitudes are the brightest of all.

Magnitude is given in terms of absolute and apparent values. Absolute magnitude is a measurement of how bright a star would appear if viewed from a set distance away. Astronomers also measure a star's brightness in terms of its luminosity. A star's absolute luminosity or intrinsic brightness is the total amount of energy radiated by the star per second. Luminosity is often expressed in units of watts.

Cepheid stars are the stars with the most variability. They oscillate between two states. The star is compact with large temperature and pressure differences. These gradients build and cause the star to expand. In its expanded state, there is a weaker pressure gradient. Without the higher pressure gradient to support the star against gravity, the star contracts and returns to its compact state. The expending and contracting are seen as changes in its luminosity. Because of this, scientists have defined a Cepheid variable as a standard measurement with which one can determine the distance of a star to its host cluster/galaxy.

A **pulsar** is defined as a variable radio source that emits signals in very short, regular bursts. It is believed to be a rotating neutron star.

A **quasar** is defined as an object that photographs like a star but has an extremely large red shift and a variable energy output. These are believed to be the active core of a very distant galaxy.

Black holes are defined as an object that has collapsed to such a degree that light can not escape from its surface (light is trapped by the intense gravitational field).

SKILL 11.3 Use the Hertzsprung-Russell (H-R) diagram to analyze the life cycle of stars

The Characteristics of Stars

Stars are not all alike. Their energy outputs vary from 111,000th of the energy to 100,000 times the energy of Earth's Sun. The laws of physics tell us that the more energy an object has, the hotter it is. They also relate color to temperature. Therefore, by observing the color of a star, we get information about its temperature.

The Hertzsprung-Russell Diagram

In 1913, American astronomer Henry Norris Russell and Danish astronomer Ejnar Hertzsprung theorized that the energy emitted by a star is directly related to the star's color. Their supporting graph is now known as the **Hertzsprung-Russell Diagram (H-R Diagram):** a graph that shows the relationship between a star's color, temperature, and mass.

On a H-R Diagram the majority (90%) of the stars plotted form a diagonal line called the **Main Sequence**: the region of the H-R Diagram running from top left to bottom right. Hot, blue stars are at the top left while cooler, red stars are at the bottom right. The middle of the main sequence contains yellow stars, like the Sun.

Star mass is also shown on the H-R diagram, increasing from the bottom to the top of the main sequence. The stars at the bottom right have masses about one-tenth of that of Earth's Sun, and the masses increase until you reach the top left where there are stars with masses ten times greater than that of the Sun.

The truly large stars are called **Supergiant Stars**: exceptionally massive and luminous stars 10 to 1,000 times brighter than the Sun, and the smallest stars are called **Dwarf Stars**: dying stars that have collapsed in size. Although small in size, dwarf stars are extremely dense. In contrast, Supergiants are extremely large, but they may be less dense than the Earth's outer atmosphere.

SKILL 11.4 Analyze stellar life cycles to understand the formation and initial development of the solar system

A star starts as gas and dust, and then becomes a nebula, then a main sequence star, then a red giant, then a nova, then a white dwarf (the dying core of a giant star), and finally a neutron star or a black hole.

Stars are produced by the forces of gravity acting on particles of gas and dust in a cloud in an area of space. This cloud is called a nebula. Particles in this cloud attract each other and as it grows its temperature increases. With the increased temperature the star begins to glow. Fusion occurs in the core of the star releasing radiant energy at the star's surface.

The hydrogen that becomes exhausted in a small, or even an average star, causes its core to collapse and its temperature to rise. This released heat attracts nearby gases to heat, contract, carry out fusion, and produce helium. Stars at this stage are nearing the end of their life. These stars are called red giants (also called supergiants). A white dwarf is the dying core of a giant star. A nova is an ordinary star that experiences a sudden increase in brightness and then fades back to its original brightness. A supernova radiates even greater light energy. A neutron star is the result of mass left behind from the supernova. A black hole is a star with condensed matter and gravity so intense that light can not escape.

COMPETENCY 12.0 UNDERSTAND EVIDENCE REGARDING THE ORIGIN, AGE, SIZE, STRUCTURE, SCALE, AND MOTIONS OF THE UNIVERSE, THE MILKY WAY GALAXY, AND THE SOLAR SYSTEM.

SKILL 12.1 Analyze evidence for the location of the solar system within the Milky Way Galaxy

Galaxy: a large group (billions) of stars held together by the attraction of mutual gravitation. If you look into the night sky you may see a ribbon of stars packed so densely together that it appears to be a star lit cloud. You are looking at the **Milky Way Galaxy**, the galaxy in which our solar system is located. This ribbon of brilliance in the night is actually a collection of over 180 billion stars and a huge volume of interstellar dust and gasses.

You may also notice that there are groups of stars that appear closer together. These are **Globular Clusters**: a tightly grouped, high concentration of stars. These spherically arranged masses of stars are believed to be the oldest stars in the galaxy, approximately 10-20 billion years old. Each of the clusters contains between 10,000 to 1,000,000 individual stars and virtually no interstellar dust.

Although not the prevalent form, a spherical arrangement of stars is not uncommon. The Milky Way Galaxy is a **Spiral Galaxy**: a grouping of stars arranged in a thin disk. It is arranged in a spiraling geometric pattern, which has a central pivot point (nucleus) and arms radiating outward on which stars rotate around the nucleus, somewhat suggestive of the shape of a pinwheel. It is approximately 100,000 light-years in diameter and 2,000 light-years thick at the center, decreasing to 1,000 light-years thick at the edges.

Our Sun is located on one of the arms of the galaxy, roughly 30,000 light-years from the center of the galaxy, midway between the upper and lower edges. The Sun rotates around the center of the galaxy at a speed of 250 km/s, and makes one full rotation every 200 million years. This rotational pattern means that in the estimated 4.6 billion years of Earth's existence, our Sun has completed 23 rotations.

In the late 1700's early astronomers studied hazy objects in the sky that weren't stars. However, it wasn't until the 1850's that telescopes became powerful enough to discern that the hazy objects had a spiraling structure. Almost a hundred years would pass before their identity was solved. In 1924, American astronomer Edwin Hubble determined that the objects were farther away than previously thought. This meant that for us to see them they must have a greater luminosity than a single star. The conclusion was obvious- the objects were other galaxies, each composed of billions of stars. Our galaxy is but one of billions of galaxies in the universe.

SKILL 12.2 Analyze historical methods of inferring the size, structure, and motions of the galaxy and the solar system (e.g., star observations and counts)

Constellation: a region of the night sky in which a group of stellar objects form a discernible pattern; usually named after mythological gods, animals, objects, or people.

The stars visible in the night sky have always fascinated humans. Ancient humans were very dependent on stars, assigning a mystic aspect to them that influenced political and social decisions of the period. Names were assigned to the stellar patterns to produce a sense of order and purpose to the cosmos. The majority of the constellation names are based on Greek Mythology. Examples include Orion, Taurus and Pegasus. However, because the patterns appear slightly different depending on the viewer's geographical location, different names are assigned to the constellations by different cultures. For example, in the Chinese culture Taurus the Bull is the Snake and Aquarius is the Tiger.

The ancient observers believed that the Sun changed places with the stars to create nighttime. These visible stars formed the basis of the **Zodiac Constellations**: the first constellations to be named by early astronomers. The scholars who studied the Zodiac Constellations were **Astrologers**: people who studied the stellar objects in the Zodiac Constellations in order to predict the future. Besides the original twelve constellations comprising the Zodiac Constellation, modern astronomy has found and named an additional 76 others for a total of 88 constellations. Consequently, this divides the sky into 88 sections.

Locating the Stars

The positions of the stars are referenced in relation to the Earth and are described in terms of the celestial coordinates of Right Ascension and Declination.

The declination and right ascension is described in reference to the **Celestial Sphere/Globe Model.** You can picture this model as having the Earth centered in the middle of a sphere. The outer framework of the sphere rotates clockwise (east to west) in relation to the Earth. The north and south poles of the Earth correspond to the north and south celestial poles. The Earth's equator corresponds to the celestial equator. **Right Ascension** is roughly analogous to lines of Longitude and is measured eastward from the vernal equinox. **Declination** is roughly analogous to lines of Latitude and is measured in relation to the celestial equator: positive to the north, and negative to the south.

Right Ascension and Declination are measured in units of degrees and time. 1 sec = 1/3600 of a degree. Example: 15° 12' 5" Right Ascension. The sky shifts 15° every hour. That's why photo-telescopes must move with the stars.

Celestial Brightness

Over 2,000 years ago the Greek astronomer Hipparchus devised a system to classify the brightness of the stars. He ranked the brightest stars as first-class stars, the next brightest as second-class, etc., down to the faintest stars, the sixth-class. Although this system worked well for millennia, with the advent of more powerful telescopes, astronomers discovered stars that were both brighter and fainter than the brightest and faintest stars in the star catalog. To solve this problem modern astronomers extended the magnitude system into negative numbers to account for the brighter stars. Example: Sirius, the brightest star in the sky, has a magnitude of -1.42.

These numbers represent a star's **Apparent Visual Magnitude (m_v):** a star's brightness as seen from Earth. On the magnitude scale, the larger the number, the fainter the star.

The relative brightness of the stars in a particular constellation is denoted by the use of lower case Greek letters; the brightest appearing star in the constellation being Alpha (α) and the faintest appearing star being Omega (ω). The Greek alphabet symbols are used as a prefix appended to the constellation's name. The possessive form of the name is used, and this is created by appending the suffix 'is' to the name of the constellation. Example: The brightest star in the constellation Orion is noted as Alpha Orionis.

However, stellar brightness requires a more precise measurement system beyond the original model because variances in the human eye and weather conditions can dramatically affect the apparent magnitude of a star.

For the purposes of mathematical measurement, astronomers use a star's **Intensity:** a measure of the light energy from a star that hits 1 square meter in 1 second.

We can use this modern system in conjunction with the Hipparchus devised brightness classifications of first-class, etc., because a difference of 5 magnitudes corresponds to an intensity ratio of 100. This allows us to compare the intensity of one star to another based on the mathematical progression of the difference in magnitude. This progression is expressed in the formula $I_A/I_B= (2.512)\ (m_B - m_A)$.

SKILL 12.3 Analyze the evidence for current theories of the origin and evolution of Earth, the solar system, and the universe (e.g., Big Bang, inflation)

Big Bang Theory: the theory that proposes that all the mass and energy of the universe was originally concentrated at a single geometric point. For unknown reasons this mass experienced an explosion that scattered the matter throughout the universe. The concept of a massive explosion is supported by the distribution of background radiation and the measurable fact that the galaxies are moving away from each other at great speed. The Universe originated around 15 billion years ago with the "Big Bang" and continued to expand for the first 10 billion years. The universe was originally unimaginably hot, but around 1 million years after the Big Bang it cooled enough to allow the formation of atoms from the energy and particles. Most of these atoms were hydrogen and they comprise the most abundant form of matter in the universe. Around a billion years after the Big Bang, the matter had cooled enough to begin congealing into the first of the stars and galaxies.

Formation of Earth and the Solar System

Most cosmologists believe that the Earth is the indirect result of a supernova. The thin cloud (planetary nebula) of gas and dust from which the Sun and its planets are formed, was struck by the shock wave and remnant matter from an exploded star(s) outside of our galaxy. The stars manufactured every chemical element heavier than hydrogen. Turbulence caused by the shock wave caused our solar system to begin forming as it absorbed some of the heavy atoms flung outward in the supernova. In fact, our solar system is composed mostly of matter assembled from a star or stars that disappeared billions of years ago. The nebula spun faster as it condensed and material near the center contracted inward. As more materials came together, mass and gravitational attraction increased, pulling in more mass. This cycle continued until the mass reach the point that nuclear fusion occurred and the Sun was born.

Concurrently, the Proto-sun's gravitational mass pulled heavier, denser elements inward from the clouds of cosmic material surrounding it. These elements eventually coalesced through the process of Accretion: the clumping together of small particles into large masses which would eventually be the planets of our solar system. The period of accretion lasted approximately 50 to 70 million years, ceasing when the proto-sun experienced nuclear fusion to become the Sun. The violence associated with this nuclear reaction swept through the inner planets, clearing the system of particles and ending the period of rapid accretion. The closest planets (Mercury, Venus and Mars) received too much heat and did not develop the planetary characteristics to support life. The farthest planets did not receive enough heat to sufficiently coalesce the gasses into solid form. Earth was the only planet in the perfect position to develop the conditions necessary to maintain life.

SKILL 12.4 Analyze types of evidence used to infer scales of the solar system, the Milky Way galaxy, and the universe (e.g., in relation to relative size and distance)

Measurement Units in Astronomy

Astronomical distances represent mind-boggling amounts of space. Because our standard units of distance measurement (i.e. kilometers) would result in so large of a number that it would become almost incomprehensible, physicists use different units of measurement to reference the vast distances involved in astronomy. The standard distance measurement is the **AU (Astronomical Unit).** The **AU** is the mean distance between the Sun and the Earth. 1 AU = 1.495979×10^{11}m. Outside of our solar system, the standard unit of distance measurement is the **Parsec.** 1 Parsec = 206,265 AU or 3.26 Light Years (LY). Parallax is the apparent change in the position of an object due to a change in the location of the observer. In astronomy, a parallax is measured in seconds of arc. 1 second of arc = 1/3600 of a degree. The concept of measuring distances by parallax is based on the mathematical discipline of trigonometry. Photos of distant stars are taken at different times, usually 6 months apart. The apparent shift in position of the star in comparison to the previous photo is the parallax. By measuring angles, we can use the trigonometric functions of sine, cosine, and tangent to determine a distance to the object. The smaller the parallax is, the greater the distance to the star. Light-year (LY is the distance light travels in one year. Because the speed of light is 3.00×10^8 m/sec, one light year represents a distance of 9.5×10^{12} km or 63,000 AU.

Radio Interferometry

Radio Interferometery is a method of amplifying weak radio waves by laying a series of small radio telescopes in a Y-shaped pattern where they are all pointed at the same point in the sky. The telescopes add their received signals together to form an overlay of signals. Computers control the angle of incidence and correlate the incoming signals. This improves resolution and limits the size of the radio telescope dish needed for a single unit. We measure the intensity of the light by the ratios of the apparent presence or absence of colors. Intensity: the amount of light contained in a space. Intensity varies by distance. The further away you are, you will see a drop in intensity equal to 1 over the distance squared ($1/d^2$). Intensity gives off a continuous amount of colors, but the intensity of the colors seen varies in accordance with the temperature of the object. Stars follow the same principles of emission. We observe the intensity of the stars by using a red and a blue filter on a photon counter mounted on a telescope. The red and blue ratio determines the color index. From the color index, we can determine the temperature, size, properties, and material composition of the star.

SKILL 12.5 Recognize the historical, present, and future role of technology and exploration in obtaining knowledge about the universe

Detecting Motion of Stars

Doppler Effect: the apparent change in frequency of light or sound that occurs when the source of the wave is moving relative to the observer. The Doppler Effect can be used to measure the motion of an object both on Earth and in space. The motion of the stars can be determined by observing the Doppler Effect associated with their movements. As a star moves awav from us it has a red shift and its emitted light wavelength is longer. As a star moves toward us, it has a blue shift and its emitted light wavelength is shorter. Red and Blue shift doesn't refer to the color of the star. Doppler technology can also detect rotation.

Examining the Visible Light Spectrum

We use a Spectrograph or Spectroscope to examine the visible light spectra of an object. A basic spectroscope is composed of a barrier (with an aperture), a prism, and a screen. The aperture in the barrier focuses the light onto the prism, which splits the received light into its spectrum components and displays it on the screen. There are three different types of spectra: Continuous, Absorption, and Emission. The received spectra are unique to each element and act as the fingerprint of the element. By observing the spectra, we can determine a star's temperature and elemental composition. Plus, if the lines are shifted, we can also determine how far and at what speed the star is moving.

The Hertzsprung-Russell Diagram

In 1913 American astronomer Henry Norris Russell and Danish astronomer Ejnar Hertzsprung theorized that the energy emitted by a star is directly related to the star's color. Their supporting graph is now known as the Hertzsprung-Russell Diagram (H-R Diagram): a graph that shows the relationship between a star's color, temperature, and mass. The hottest stars look bluer than cooler stars. The elements comprising the star are absorbing the red color wavelengths and re-emitting the blue color wavelengths. We compare received data to known data and apply Kirchhoff's Laws to determine the type of gas and materials of which the star is composed. On a H-R Diagram the majority (90%) of the stars plotted form a diagonal line called the Main Sequence: the region of the H-R Diagram running from top left to bottom right. Hot, blue stars are at the top left and cooler, red stars are at the bottom right. The middle of main sequence contains yellow stars. The star mass is also shown on the H-R diagram, increasing from the bottom to the top of the main sequence. The stars at the bottom right have masses about one-tenth of that of Earth's sun, and the masses increase until you reach the top left where there are stars with masses ten times greater than that of the Sun. We can also use the H-R Diagram to illustrate the life cycle of stars.

Planetary Exploration

One of the primary means of learning more about the planetary bodies of the solar system is through space exploration. Beginning in the 1960's when the first probes journeyed toward Earth's Moon, a planned sequence of spacecraft has visited some of the planetary objects in our solar system.

SUBAREA III. ATMOSPHERIC SYSTEMS

COMPETENCY 13.0 UNDERSTAND THE COMPOSITION, STRUCTURE, AND PROPERTIES OF EARTH'S ATMOSPHERE AND THE MECHANISMS AND EFFECTS OF ENERGY TRANSFER INVOLVING THE EARTH-ATMOSPHERE SYSTEM.

SKILL 13.1 Compare and contrast properties of the atmosphere (e.g., density, composition, temperature) from Earth's surface through the thermosphere and understand the significance of changes in these properties

The Earth's physical environment is divided into three major parts called the atmosphere, the hydrosphere, and the lithoshpere. The atmosphere is the layer of air that surrounds the Earth. The hydrosphere is the water portion of the planet (70% of the Earth is covered by water). The lithosphere is the solid portion of the Earth. The Earth's lithosphere includes the crust, mantle, outer core, and inner core.

Dry air is composed of three basic components: dry gas, water vapor, and solid particles (dust from soil, etc.). The most abundant dry gases in the atmosphere are:

(N_2)	Nitrogen	78.09 %	makes up about 4/5 of gases in atmosphere
(O_2)	Oxygen	20.95 %	
(Ar)	Argon	0.93 %	
(CO_2)	Carbon Dioxide	0.03 %	

The atmosphere is divided into four main layers based on their temperature. These layers are labeled troposphere, stratosphere, mesosphere, and thermosphere.

Troposphere - this layer is the closest to the Earth's surface. All weather phenomena occurs here because it is the layer with the most water vapor and dust. Air temperature decreases with increasing altitude. The average thickness of the troposphere is 7 miles (11 km).

Stratosphere - this layer contains very little water and subsequently clouds within this layer are extremely rare. The Ozone layer is located in the upper portion of the stratosphere. Air temperature is fairly constant but does increase somewhat with height due to the absorption of solar energy and ultra violet rays from the ozone layer.

Mesosphere - air temperature again decreases with height in this layer. It is the coldest layer with temperatures in the range of -100° C at the top.

Thermosphere - extends upward into space. Oxygen molecules in this layer absorb energy from the Sun, causing temperatures to increase with height. The lower part of the thermosphere is called the Ionosphere. Charged particles or ions and free electrons can be found here. When gases in the Ionosphere are excited by solar radiation, the gases give off light and glow in the sky. These glowing lights are called the Aurora Borealis in the Northern Hemisphere and Aurora Australis in the Southern Hemisphere. The upper portion of the thermosphere is called the Exosphere. Gas molecules are very far apart in this layer. Layers of Exosphere are also known as the Van Allen Belts and are held together by the Earth's magnetic field.

The interior of the Earth is divided in to three chemically distinct layers. Starting from the middle and moving towards the surface these are the core, the mantle, and the crust. Much of what we know about the inner structure of the Earth has been inferred from various data. Subsequently, there is still some uncertainty about the composition and conditions in the Earth's interior.

The crust is the thinnest layer. It is not clear how long the Earth has actually had a solid crust; most of the rocks are less than 100 million years, though some are 4.4 billion years old. The crust of the Earth is the outermost layer and continues down for between 5 and 70 km beneath the surface. Thin areas generally exist under ocean basins (oceanic crust) and thicker crust underlies the continents (continental crust). Oceanic crust is composed largely of iron magnesium silicate rocks, while continental crust is less dense and consists mainly of sodium potassium aluminum silicate rocks. The crust is the least dense layer of the Earth and is rich in those materials that "floated" during Earth's formation. Additionally, some heavier elements that bound to lighter materials are present in the crust.

Rocks are made up of minerals consisting of chemical elements or chemical compounds. A chemical element is the simplest kind of substance. A chemical element can not be broken down into simpler substances by ordinary means. Gold, silver, oxygen, and carbon are examples of chemical elements. A chemical compound consists of two or more elements combined in fixed proportions by weight. Salt, water, table salt, and natural gas are examples of chemical compounds. Elements in the Earth's crust are combinations of 88 different elements. Three common groups of minerals in the Earth's crust are silicates, carbonates, and oxides. The two most common and abundant elements in the Earth's crust are oxygen and silicon.

ELEMENT	SYMBOL	APPROX. % BY WEIGHT
Oxygen	O_2	47
Silicon	Si	28
Aluminum	Al	8
Iron	Fe	5
Calcium	Ca	4
Sodium	Na	3
Potassium	K	3
Magnesium	Mg	2

The boundary separating the crust from the mantle is known as the Mohorovic Discountinity, named after its discovering scientist. It is commonly called the Moho. The mantle is located directly beneath the crust. The Earth's mantle begins about 35 km beneath the surface and stretches all the way to 3000 km beneath the surface, where the outer core begins. Since the mantle stretches so far into the Earth's center, its temperature varies widely; near the boundary with the crust it is approximately 1000°C, while near the outer core it may reach nearly 4000°C. Mantle rocks are dense and contain more iron than rocks contained in the crust. Within the mantle one can find silicate rocks which are rich in iron and magnesium. The silicate rocks exists as solids, but the high heat means they are ductile enough to "flow" over long time scales. In general, the mantle is semi-solid/plastic and the viscosity varies as pressures and temperatures change at varying depths. The outer core of the Earth begins about 3000 km beneath the surface. Geologists think the outer core is a hot molten liquid, though far more viscous than that of the mantle. The outer core is composed of iron and nickel. Even deeper, approximately 5000 km beneath the surface, is the solid inner core. The inner core has a radius of about 1200 km. Temperatures in the core exceed 4000°C. Scientists agree that the core is extremely dense, most likely made of solid iron nickel because of the intense pressure exerted by the surrounding zones. This conclusion is based on the fact that the Earth is known to have an average density of 5515 kg/m^3 even though the material close to the surface has an average density of only 3000 kg/m^3. Therefore, a denser core must exist. Additionally, it is hypothesized that when the Earth was forming, the densest material sank into the middle of the planet. Thus, it is not surprising that the core is about 80% iron. In fact, there is some speculation that the entire inner core is a single iron crystal, while the outer core is a mix of liquid iron and nickel.

Interactions between the Layers

It is not the case that these layers exist as separate entities, with little interaction between them. For instance, it is generally believed that swirling of the iron-rich liquid in the outer core results in the Earth's magnetic field, which is readily apparent on the surface. Heat also moves out from the core to the mantle and crust. The core still retains heat from the formation of the Earth and additional heat is generated by the decay of radioactive isotopes. While most of the heat in our atmosphere comes from the Sun, radiant heat from the core does warm oceans and other large bodies of water. There is also a great deal of interaction between the mantle and the crust. The slow convection of rocks in the mantle is responsible for the shifting of tectonic plates on the crust. Matter can also move between the layers as occurs during the rock cycle. Within the rock cycle, igneous rocks are formed when magma escapes from the mantle as lava during volcanic eruption. Rocks may also be forced back into the mantle, where the high heat and pressure recreate them as metamorphic rocks.

SKILL 13.2 Analyze how various wavelengths of solar radiation (e.g., ultraviolet, visible light, infrared) are affected as the radiation enters and passes through the atmosphere and is absorbed and re-radiated from Earth's surface

The Sun emits light at different wavelengths in the electromagnetic spectrum. UV light is electromagnetic radiation with a wavelength shorter than that of visible light. The three types of UV light (near UV, far UV, and deep UV) fall within the wavelength range of 200 to 1 nm.

Visible light is the portion of the electromagnetic spectrum that can be detected by the human eye. This type of electromagnetic radiation typically falls within the wavelength range of 400 to 700 nm, and is also known as short wave radiation.

Infrared (IR) radiation is electromagnetic radiation of a wavelength longer than that of visible light. Infrared radiation falls within the wavelength range of 750 nm to 1 mm, and is also known as long wave radiation.

The Earth's atmosphere selectively controls the passage of solar radiation towards the Earth's surface. Thus, not all solar radiation received at the periphery of the atmosphere reaches the Earth's surface. Upon entering the Earth's atmosphere, large amounts of solar radiation can be absorbed or scattered in all directions by atmospheric gases, vapors, and dust particles.

The scattering of solar radiation is the process by which small particles and gas molecules diffuse part of the incoming solar radiation in random directions without altering the wavelength of the electromagnetic energy. There are two types of atmospheric scattering: selective scattering and non-selective scattering.

These two processes are determined by the different sizes of particles in the atmosphere.

Selective Scattering

Selective scattering occurs when atmospheric gases or particles are smaller in dimension than the wavelength of a particular type of solar radiation. During the process of selective scattering, radiation with shorter wavelengths are scattered more extensively than those with longer wavelengths. Thus, selective atmospheric scattering is inversely proportional to the wavelength of solar radiation and has an increasingly large effect on distinct types of light in the following order: Infrared Light < Visible Light < UV Light. The scattering effect on UV light is approximately ten times as great as on the red rays of sunlight.

Non-Selective Scattering

This type of scattering occurs in the lower atmosphere due to the presence of dust, fog, and clouds with particle sizes more than ten times the wavelength of the components of solar radiation. The amount of non-selective scattering is equal for all wavelengths.

Absorption

Atmospheric absorption is the process in which solar radiation is retained by a substance, such as an atmospheric particle or gas, transferred into heat energy and then converted into long wave radiation emissions. The degree to which a certain type of solar radiation is absorbed is wavelength-dependant. Most entering ultraviolet radiation measuring less than 200 nm in wavelength, is absorbed by oxygen and nitrogen in the ozone layer of the upper atmosphere. Infrared solar radiation, with its wavelengths greater than 700 nm, is absorbed to a smaller extent by vaporous or condensed atmospheric carbon dioxide, ozone, and water.

Due to the absorption and scattering effects of the atmosphere, little UV radiation and only 50% of short wave radiation actually interacts with the Earth's surface. When short wave radiation reaches the surface, it is absorbed, transformed into heat, and re-emitted in the form of long wave radiation (infrared radiation).

SKILL 13.3 Analyze the processes by which energy is transferred to and within the atmosphere (e.g., radiation, convection, conduction)

Energy is transferred in Earth's atmosphere in three ways. Earth gets most of its energy from the Sun in the form of waves. This transfer of energy by waves is termed **radiation**. The transfer of thermal energy through matter by actual contact of molecules is called **conduction**. For example, heated rocks and sandy beaches transfer heat to the surrounding air. The transfer of thermal energy due to air density differences is called **convection**. Convection currents circulate in a constant exchange of cold, dense air for less dense, warm air.

An example of all three methods of heat transfer occurs in the thermos bottle or Dewar flask. The bottle is constructed of double walls of Pyrex glass that have a space in between. Air is evacuated from the space between the walls and the inner wall is coated in silver. The lack of air between the walls decreases heat loss by convection and conduction. The heat inside is reflected by the silver, cutting down heat transfer by radiation. Hot liquids remain hotter and cold liquids remain colder longer.

SKILL 13.4 Analyze global wind patterns in terms of latitudinal and altitudinal variations in insolation and the Coriolis effect

Solar Radiation (Insolation)

This distribution of solar energy is called **insolation**. Solar radiation isn't distributed evenly across the Earth because of the Earth's curvature, axial tilt, and orbit. This results in uneven heating of the atmosphere, and is why the temperature is warmer at the equator and colder at the poles.

Because of Earth's curvature and tilt, the energy striking the polar areas is spread over a larger area. At the equator it is more concentrated. The same amount of energy is striking the atmosphere, but it is striking a larger or smaller area. In effect, this dilutes the energy received by a particular area.

The effect of insolation is very important to life on Earth. The absence of solar radiation would cause the creation of very cold air masses and the thermal blanket of the atmosphere would not have heat to hold and reradiate. In short order, the world would become an icy rock.

Air as an Insulator

Air in the atmosphere is a good insulator, analogous to a goose-down blanket.

Convection Cells: The ground absorbs energy during the morning hours and re-radiates the absorbed energy in a narrow band near the surface. This heats the air near the surface. The air near the surface absorbs the energy and expands. Convection is the primary means of transferring heat to the air.

As the molecules move faster (because of the heat transfer), the air expands, becomes less dense, and rises. The air continues to rise, but begins to cool, again becoming denser. Then it starts to sink back to the surface. This cycle of rising, warming air and sinking, cooling air is called a convection cell.

Parcel of Air (Air Mass): a large area of air, which assumes a characteristic temperature, pressure, and humidity from sitting over a landmass. Horizontally, the parcel has relatively uniform temperature, pressure, and humidity. Vertically, the parcel may have widely differing temperatures, pressures, and humidity. Remember: when you think of air parcels, think in the horizontal plane.

Coriolis Effect

The **Coriolis Effect** is the deflection of air or water currents caused by the rotation of the Earth. This creates global wind patterns that affect the climate. These wind patterns also represent rain patterns. The wind patterns between 30°N and 0°N are called the **Trade Winds**. The wind patterns between 30°N and 60°N are called the **Prevailing Westerlies**. All the great deserts of the world lie between the Tropics at 0° and 30°North and South latitudes. A shift in the wind patterns would also shift the deserts. The optimum growing zone is between 30° and 60° North and South latitudes.

If global warming takes place, it could cause the melting of the polar ice caps that in turn could raise sea levels. This would inundate land areas and lead to economic disaster.

The Earth's climate is in a very delicate balance. A change to the global warming or cooling patterns would affect retained heat, which would further affect the growing zones. In example, global warming would cause the expansion of the tropics, while global cooling would cause a contraction of the tropic zone.

Global Wind Patterns

The rise and fall of heat at the 0°, 30°, 60° and 90° latitudes drive convection cells by causing the pressure gradients to speed up or slow down. The **Jet Streams** are zones of very strong, moving air confined to narrow columns and marks the zones where the cold Polar air and the warmer air meet. This produces the greatest pressure gradients. The Jet Streams can be either straight or dramatically dip, thus creating ridges and troughs on the 500-300mb pressure surface.

The flatter the isobars, the more evenly balanced the weather. The more pronounced the ridges and troughs, the more pronounced the swings in the weather.

The ITCZ (**Inter Tropical Convergence Zone**) controls the weather in the tropics, and it moves north and south of the equator. The ITCZ is responsible for the formation of Monsoon rains.

The **Horse Latitudes** are located between 0° and 30° north and south latitudes.

The **Doldrums**, an area of no wind, is located at 0°.

The **Trade Winds** are very strong and blow all the time in the Horse Latitudes. The Trade Winds also provide direct heating to the coastal climate in this zone.

The **Prevailing Westerlies** are found between 30° and 60° north and south latitude. These cause storms and winds to move in a west to east pattern.

Polar Winds are the product of the presence or absence of sunlight, not polar cells.

Equation of Motion (EOM)

The Equation of Motion predicts how water moves. Wind is the initial mover of water. The moving surface water couples to water below it and moves the deeper water in varying degrees according to depth.

The general equation for dealing with force is F= Ma, where Force = mass times acceleration). However, for oceanography, the terms used are somewhat different and more specialized to the field.

Pressure Gradient = gi where g=gravity and i=the slope of the pressure gradient

Coriolis Effect =fV where f=planetary vorticity, and V=velocity.

Wind Stress = A d^2V where A=area, d^2 =diameter squared, and V=velocity.

Pressure Gradient: the difference between high and low pressure areas. The difference between the areas represents a range of varying high and low pressure. Changes in temperature and density occur within this area. The pressure gradient is a major player in determining ocean circulation. Example: The Gulf Stream is one of the strongest, most consistent ocean currents.

COMPETENCY 14.0 UNDERSTAND THE PROPERTIES OF WATER, CONDITIONS IN THE ATMOSPHERE THAT RESULT IN PHASE CHANGES, AND THE ENERGY RELATIONSHIPS OF PHASE CHANGES TO CLOUD FORMATION AND PRECIPITATION.

SKILL 14.1 Relate the physical properties of water (e.g., high specific heat, surface tension) to the chemical structure and properties of water molecules

Significance of Water

Water (H_2O) is significantly different from its immediate Hydrogen compound cousins. **Compounds** are substances that contain two or more elements in a fixed proportion. Generally, the heavier molecules have higher boiling and freezing states based upon molecular weight.

A group of atoms held together by chemical bonds is called a **molecule**. The bonds form when the small, negatively charged electrons found near the outside of an atom are shared or transferred between the atoms. The bonds formed by the shared pair of electrons are known as **covalent bonds**.

Most substances tend to adopt a solid or gaseous form. Water is different. It wants to be a liquid. A water molecule forms when covalent bonds are established between two hydrogen atoms and one oxygen atom.

However, unlike the other hydrogen compounds, water has its two hydrogen molecules on one side of the atom. It's a polar molecule.

This arrangement of atoms is based on the distribution of the water molecule's oxygen electrons. The electrons cause the geometric shape of the molecule to be angular. This angular shape makes the molecule electrically asymmetrical (polar).

This polar arrangement gives water some very special properties.

- The polar molecule acts similar to a magnet. Its positive ends (the hydrogen) attract particles having a negative charge, and its negative end (the oxygen) attracts particles that have a positive charge. This arrangement is the basis for the water molecule's rightful description as the "**Universal Solvent**." When water comes into contact with compounds- for example salts- held together by the attraction of opposite charges, the water molecule separates that compound's elements from each other.

- Another unique property of water is that water likes itself; it has a natural tendency to stick to itself. Once again, this property is based upon the polar nature of the water molecule. It attracts other water molecules. When the molecules stick together, they are attached through Hydrogen Bonds, giving the molecule a property called **cohesion**. Cohesion gives water an unusually strong surface tension, and its capillary action makes the water spread. When the water spreads, **adhesion**, the tendency of water to stick to other materials, allows water to adhere to solids, making them wet.

- Water is the only known substance that readily exists in all three states of matter: liquid, solid, and gas. The hydrogen bonds holding water together are important. If they didn't exist, water would fly apart to form a gas. However, water primarily wants to be a liquid, and its liquid state range is averaged at 16°C.

Water and the States of Energy

Specific Heat: the amount of heat required to raise or lower the temperature of 1 gram of a substance by one degree Celsius.

Heat Capacity: the ability of a substance to resist a change in temperature. Water has an extremely high heat capacity. It is very resistant to changes in temperature.

It takes a great deal of energy transfer to heat up water, but it also takes a great amount of energy loss to cool it down. When we heat water we are actually transferring energy from a heat source to the water. The water molecules absorb the energy and move faster. This causes the temperature of the water to rise.

Matter can change state if enough heat (energy) is applied or removed.

SKILL 14.2 Analyze energy changes involved in the transition between phases of water (e.g., latent heat)

Matter can change state if the temperature of the substance is increased or lowered. When we apply heat from a source to a substance, we are actually transferring energy from the heat source to the substance. The molecules absorb the energy and move faster. This causes the temperature of the substance to rise.

Latent Heat: the amount of heat energy required to change matter from one state to another. Example: The amount of temperature change needed to cause evaporation or condensation of water.

Heat Capacity: The ability of a substance to resist a change in temperature. Example: Water has an extremely high heat capacity and is very resistant to changes in temperature. It takes a great deal of energy transfer to heat up water, but conversely, it also takes a great amount of energy loss to cool it down.

Specific Heat: The amount of heat required to raise or lower the temperature of 1 gram of a substance by 1 degree Celsius.

Heat of Vaporization: The amount of heat energy required to change 1 gram of water from a liquid to a vapor, or back. The heat of vaporization is equal to 540 cal/gram. Example: 1 gram of water at 99° C requires 1 cal of heat to raise the boiling point of water to a temperature of 100° C. However, the water will not turn into steam until an additional 540 cal is added. This is because of water's high heat capacity. The requirement for additional calories to force a change of state works in our favor because without the law of heat of vaporization, the oceans would vaporize. The oceans remain as a liquid and absorb heat (energy) until the extra 540 calories have been absorbed (added), causing vaporization. Fortunately, this vaporization occurs only in very small amounts in relation to the mass (volume) of the oceans. Rain represents the opposite pattern of the Heat of Vaporization. In rain, 540 calories have been removed, changing the state of water from a vapor (gas) to a liquid.

Heat of Fusion: the amount of heat energy expressed in calories required to change 1 gram of water from a solid to a liquid, or back. The heat of fusion is equal to 80 cal/gram. It takes more heat transfer to cause a change from a liquid to a vapor, or a vapor to a liquid (evaporation), than it does to change a solid to a liquid, or a liquid to a solid (fusion). Glaciers, ice caps, and the Polar Ice Packs are made possible by the heat of fusion. It takes much less energy to make ice than it does to melt it.

SKILL 14.3 Analyze atmospheric conditions under which fog and clouds with various characteristics form (e.g., adiabatic temperature changes, dew point, atmospheric stability)

Fog: a cloud that touches the ground. Fog forms when cold air moves over a warmer surface. Fog is very common along shorelines because the specific heat of water retains heat and is consequently much warmer than the overlaying air. Fog can also form inland where the same basic conditions exist.

Clouds

Clouds are classified by their physical appearance and given special Latin names corresponding to the cloud's appearance and the altitude where they occur. Classification by appearance results in three simple categories: cirrus, stratus, and cumulus clouds. Cirrus clouds appear fibrous. Stratus clouds appear layered. Cumulus clouds appear as heaps or puffs, similar to cotton balls in a pile. Classification by altitude results in four groupings: high, middle, low, and clouds that show vertical development. Other adjectives are added to the names of the clouds to show specific characteristics.

Calculating Dew Point

Calculating dew point is based upon a comparison of the difference between the dry bulb temperature versus the wet bulb temperature. Standardized tables are used to predict the dew point. This is calculated by taking the dry bulb temperature and subtracting the wet bulb temperature. The difference is then indexed against the dry bulb temperature.

Cloud Classifications

High Clouds: -13 °F (-25 °C): Composed almost exclusively of ice crystals.

Cirrus >23,000 ft (7,000 m). Nearly transparent, delicate silky strands (mare's tails) or patches.

Cirrostratus >23,000 ft (7,000 m). A thin veil or sheet that partially or totally covers the sky. Nearly transparent, the sun or moon readily shines through.

Cirrocumulus >23,000 ft (7,000 m). Small, white, rounded patches arranged in a wave or spotted mackerel pattern.

Middle Clouds: 32 to -13 °F (0 to -25 °C): Composed of super-cooled water droplets or a mixture of droplets and ice crystals.

Altostratus 6600 - 23,000 ft (2000 - 7000 m). Uniform white or bluish-gray layers that partially or totally obscure the sky layer.

Altocumulus 6600 - 23,000 ft (2000 - 7000 m). Roll-like puffs or patches that form into parallel bands or waves.

Low Clouds: > 23 °F (-5 °C): Composed mostly of water droplets.

Stratocumulus 0-6,600 ft (0-2000 m). Large irregularly shaped puffs or rolls separated by bands of clear sky.

Stratus 0-6600 ft (0-2000 m). Uniform gray layer that stretches from horizon to horizon. Drizzle may fall from the cloud.

Nimbostratus 0-13,120 ft (0-4000 m). Thick, uniform gray layer from which precipitation (significant rain or snow) is falling.

Clouds with Vertical Development: Water droplets build upward and spread laterally.

> Cumulus 0-9840 ft (0-3000 m). Resemble cotton balls dotting the sky.
> Cumulonimbus 0-9840 ft (0-3000 m). Often associated with thunderstorms, these large puffy, clouds have smooth or flattened tops, and can produce heavy rain and thunder.

Expansion, Compression, and the Adiabatic Process

One way that air cools and increases in relative humidity is by **Expansional Cooling**. As a parcel of air is heated by the Earth's surface, it will start to rise. This rising air encounters lower pressures as it increases in altitude, and will start to expand. As the air expands in volume, it begins to cool. With the expansion in volume, the molecules don't strike each other as often, and without this release of kinetic energy, the temperature goes down. Example: This same principle applies when you let air out of or put air into an automobile tire. Feel the outgoing air from a tire. It is cool. That's because as the pressure is decreased the air expands and the temperature drops.

Compressional Warming: utilizes the reverse principle. When you place air under pressure, it occupies less volume. This in turn causes the molecules to strike each other more often. Consequently, the energy released cause a rise in temperature. In the atmosphere, compressional warming causes a decrease in relative humidity.

Adiabatic Process: a process in which heat is neither absorbed nor taken away. The Expansional Cooling and Compressional Warming of unsaturated air in the atmosphere are adiabatic processes. During its ascent or descent, a parcel of air is neither heated nor cooled by radiation, conduction, phase changes of water, or mixing with its surroundings. Heating and cooling is solely accomplished by the expansion or contraction of the air in response to pressure changes.

The rate of cooling and warming is expressed as the **Dry Adiabatic Lapse Rate** (lapse refers to temperature change with altitude).

- Rising air cools: The cooling rate is 10.0 °C per 1000-meter increase in altitude (5.4 °F per 1000 feet increase in altitude).
- Sinking air warms: The warming rate is 10.0 °C per 1000-meter decrease in altitude (5.4 °F per 1000 feet decrease in altitude).

However, when air cools to the point of reaching saturation (100% humidity), the effect of expansional cooling is partially negated, and the Wet Adiabatic Lapse Rate is used to express the cooling rate. Unlike the dry lapse rate, the wet lapse rate varies with temperature. This in turn means that some latent heat is released which offsets the expansional cooling effects.

For convenience, the average value of 6°C per 1000-meter increase in altitude, 3.3°F per 1000 feet increase in altitude, is used as the **standard Moist Adiabatic Lapse Rate**.

Atmospheric Stability

Warm air rises and will continue to rise until it meets air that is as cold or colder than the rising air. When rising air cools to the dew point, clouds form due to condensation. Air can rise even if it is only a few degrees warmer than the surrounding air.

Atmospheric stability is determined by comparing the temperature change of an ascending or descending air parcel with the temperature profile of the ambient air layer in which the parcel ascends or descends. Air is considered as either **stable** or **unstable**.

Air layers become more stable when they descend, and less stable when they ascend. Unstable air will remain unstable until it encounters air of the same temperature or cooler.

In stable air, there is no vertical movement. In unstable air, there is a great deal of vertical movement.

Stable Air

Stable air exists when there is no vertical movement of the air. An ascending air parcel becomes cooler (denser) than the ambient air, and a descending air parcel becomes warmer (less dense) than the ambient air. Any upward or downward displacement of an air parcel in stable air gives rise to forces that tend to return the parcel to its original altitude.

Once stable air becomes colder than the surrounding air it sinks. It will sink to the altitude in which the temperature of the ambient air equals that of the sinking air. If a warm air mass is over a cold air mass, the air is very stable.

During the nighttime, **Radiational Cooling** of the ground tends to stabilize the overlying air. However, during the daytime, solar heating of the ground tends to destabilize the overlying air masses.

Unstable Air

Stable air can easily become unstable through **Radiational Heating**. As the ground heats up, the air also heats up and becomes unstable. The unstable air will continue to rise vertically until it encounters air as cold, or colder, than it is.

The stability of air is affected by the relative humidity of the air mass, which can cause **Conditional Stability**. The air mass is considered stable if the environment is dry, but is unstable if the air becomes saturated.

Stability is an ever-changing situation throughout the day due to heating of the Earth's surface and atmosphere. Sometimes a layer of stable air can become trapped between two layers of unstable air. This is called an **inversion** and is the result of the fact that stability can change with altitude.

Air tends to stabilize over a colder surface and destabilize over a warmer surface.

SKILL 14.4 Understand conditions under which precipitation forms and predicting the type of precipitation that will fall to Earth's surface under given conditions

All forms of precipitation start from an interaction of water vapor and other particulate matter in the atmosphere. These particulates act as a nucleus for raindrops as the water vapor particles attach themselves to the other airborne particles. Because one of water's properties is that its water particles attract other water particles, the raindrop grows as water vapor particles accrete around the nuclei.

Drizzle: any form of liquid precipitation where the drops are less than 0.02 inches in diameter.

Rain: any form of liquid precipitation where the drops are greater than 0.02 inches in diameter.

Virga: the meteorological condition where rain evaporates before touching the ground. You see rain but it never hits the ground.

Snow: water molecules that form into ice crystals through the process of freezing. The shape of a snowflake depends on the temperature at which it formed.

Needles 0°C to -10°C.
Dendrites -10°C to -20°C.
Plates -20°C to -30°C.
Columns -30°C to -40°C.

Freezing Rain: drops fall as rain but immediately depose (freeze) upon hitting an extremely cold surface such as power lines, roofs, or the ground. This is also called an **Ice Storm**.

Rime Ice: ice droplets that have tiny air bubbles trapped within the ice, producing an opaque layer of granular ice.

Sleet: officially called ice pellets, these are drops of rain 5mm or less in diameter. Sleet freezes before hitting the ground and bounces when it strikes a surface.

Hail: precipitation in the form of balls or lumps of ice. Hail forms when an ice pellet is transported through a cloud that contains varied concentrations of super cooled water droplets. The pellet may descend slowly through the entire cloud or it may be caught in a cycle of updraft and downdraft. The ice pellet grows by accreting (adding) freezing water droplets. Eventually, the weight of the hail grows too heavy to be supported by the air column and it falls to the ground as a hailstone. The size of the stone depends on the amount of time spent in the cloud.

COMPTENCY 15.0 UNDERSTAND CHARACTERISTICS OF WEATHER SYSTEMS AND LOCAL WEATHER, THE RELATIONSHIP BETWEEN THEM, AND THE METHODS AND INSTRUMENTS USED TO COLLECT AND DISPLAY WEATHER DATA.

SKILL 15.1 Interpret symbols used on weather maps and analyzing the methods used to generate weather maps (e.g., computer models)

Weather maps provide graphical or pictorial images of weather to meteorologists and everyday people. There are several different types of weather maps including satellite, radar, front, precipitation, wind speed and direction, temperature, cloud, and pressure trend.

Satellite

These weather maps are generated using data collected from satellites, such as that of NOAA (National Oceanic and Atmospheric Administration or National Weather Service). These maps display images taken in the infrared band of light and show relative warmth of objects. Satellite weather is mostly used to observe cloud formation. Colder objects are displayed as brighter patches, where warmer objects are displayed as darker patches. Lower layers of clouds are generally warmer and appear gray on weather maps. Colder, higher clouds are highlighted using a color system that portrays their relative temperatures and altitudes. This color system is defined by the weather map's legend.

Radar

Weather radar is used to locate precipitation, calculate its motion, estimate its type, and forecast its future position and intensity. A pulse of energy is sent through a cloud and the amount of echo returned will give the intensity of its precipitation. The echo is actually a reflection of the energy and a computer will generate a color code to indicate the amount of precipitation. Doppler radar, used by meteorologists, is capable of detecting the motion of rain droplets in addition to intensity of the precipitation. Radar maps are generated using data acquired by Doppler sources. These maps generally portray the location of areas of precipitation, as well as its intensity, using the color legend displayed next.

Radar Intensity Colors on a Weather Map

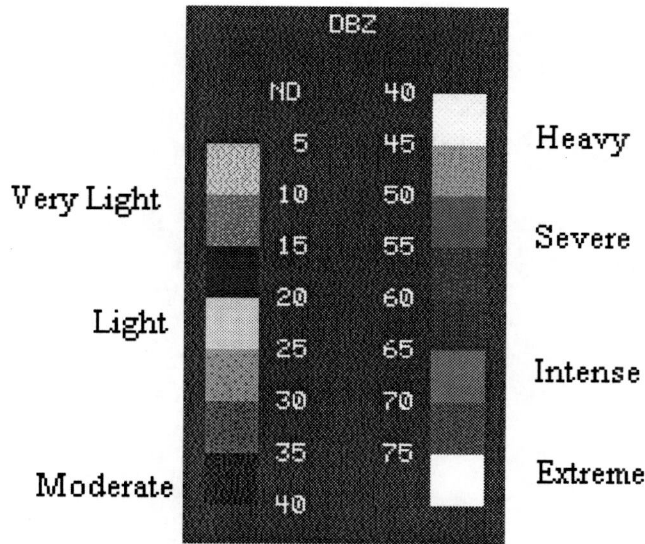

Courtesy of (http://weather.about.com/od/forecastingtechniques/ss/mapsymbols_7.htm).

To generate weather maps meteorologists collect weather data daily at multiple locations using high altitude weather balloons, weather equipment and gauges, satellites, and computers. This information is then converted into maps with weather symbols.

Fronts

Meteorologists use an extensive system of symbols to represent a large variety of weather events. Weather fronts are the boundaries between air masses with different characteristics such as temperature, humidity, and air pressure. Movement of a front depends largely on the conditions inside its air mass.

FRONTAL SYMBOLS USED ON WEATHER MAPS

SYMBOL	EXPLANATION
	Symbol for a warm front
	Symbol for a cold front
	Symbol for a stationary front
	Symbol for an occluded front

Courtesy of (http://nsidc.org/arcticmet/factors/pressure.html).

Precipitation

The following diagram provides symbols for precipitation.

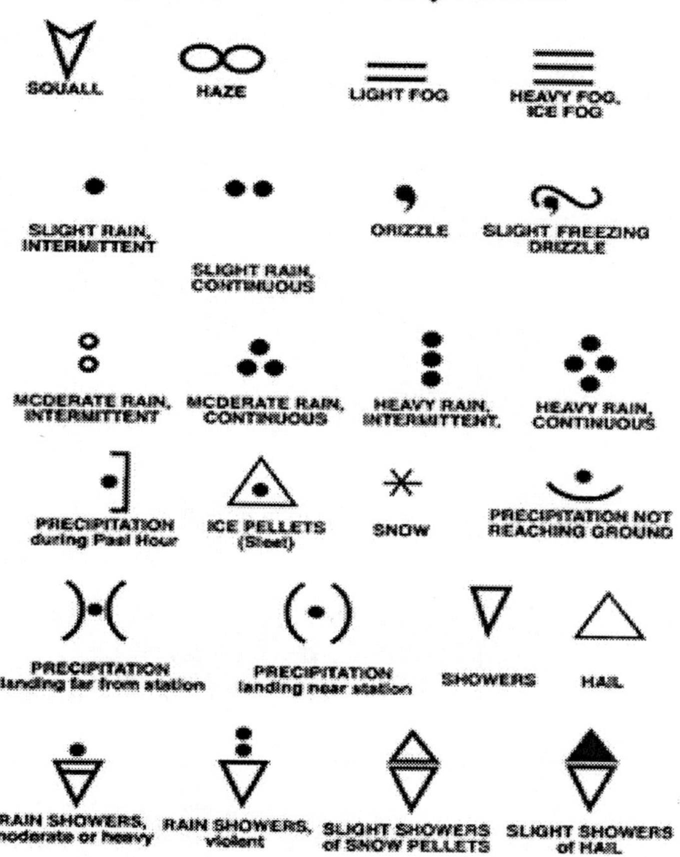

Courtesy of (http://weather.about.com/od/forecastingtechniques/ss/mapsymbols_6.htm).

Wind Speed and Direction

Wind barbs are used to show wind intensity with a series of small pennants. Wind direction is indicated by the compass direction in which the wind diagram points. Wind speed is measured in knots, where 1 knot = 1.1507788 miles per hour.

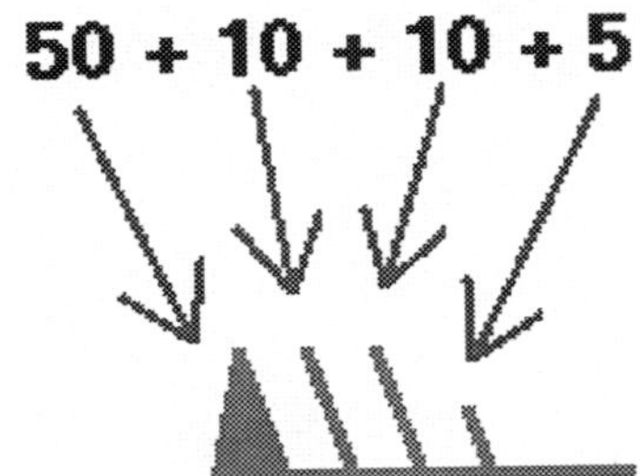

Wind blowing from the west at 75 knots

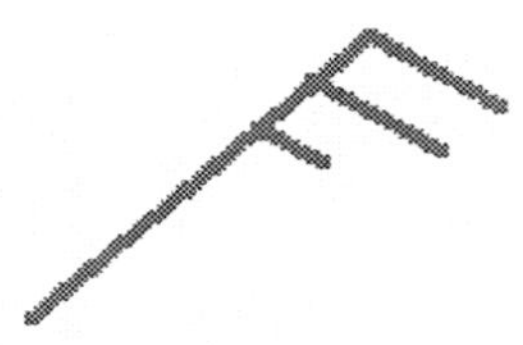

Wind blowing from the northeast at 25 knots

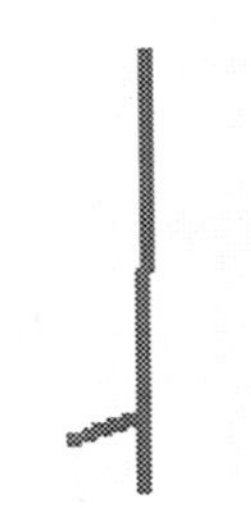

Wind blowing from the south at 5 knots

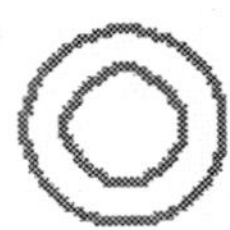

Calm winds

Courtesy of (http://www.hpc.ncep.noaa.gov/html/stationplot_buoy.shtml).

Temperature

Weather maps generally represent temperature with actual numbers instead of symbols. This method can be seen on the following map.

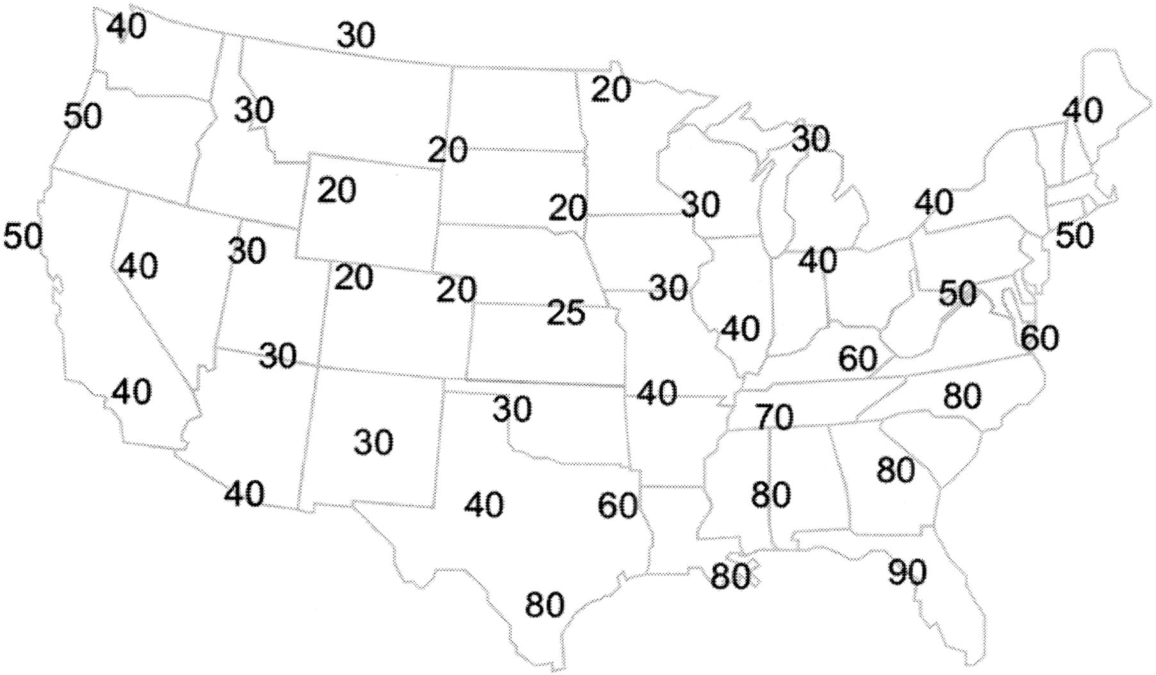

Courtesy of (http://www.srh.weather.gov/srh/jetstream/synoptic/temp.htm).

Cloud Cover

In addition to radar images of clouds, weather maps are also generated using the following cloud cover symbols. The amount that the circle is filled at the center of the station plot reflects the approximate amount of the sky that is covered by clouds.

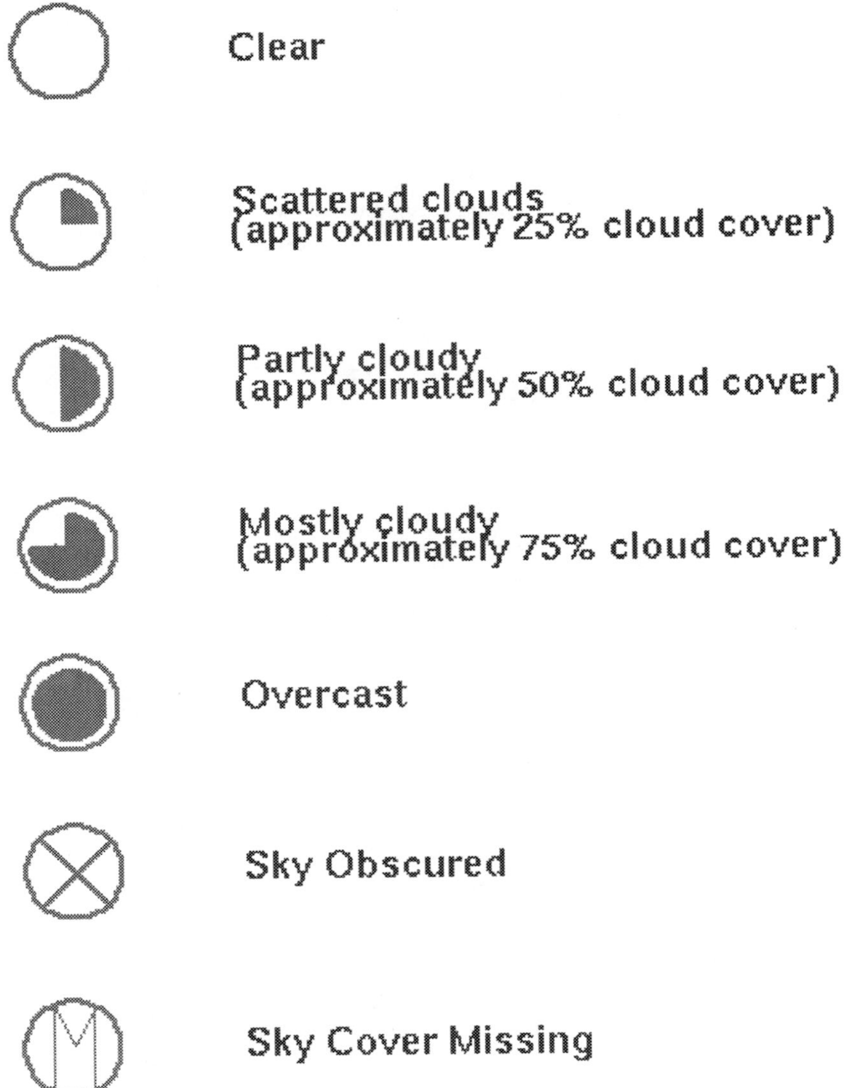

Courtesy of (http://www.hpc.ncep.noaa.gov/html/stationplot_buoy.shtml).

Pressure

A particular pressure trend is represented on a weather map with a number and a symbol. The number provides the 3-hour change in tenths of millibars, while the symbol provides a graphic illustration of how this change occurred.

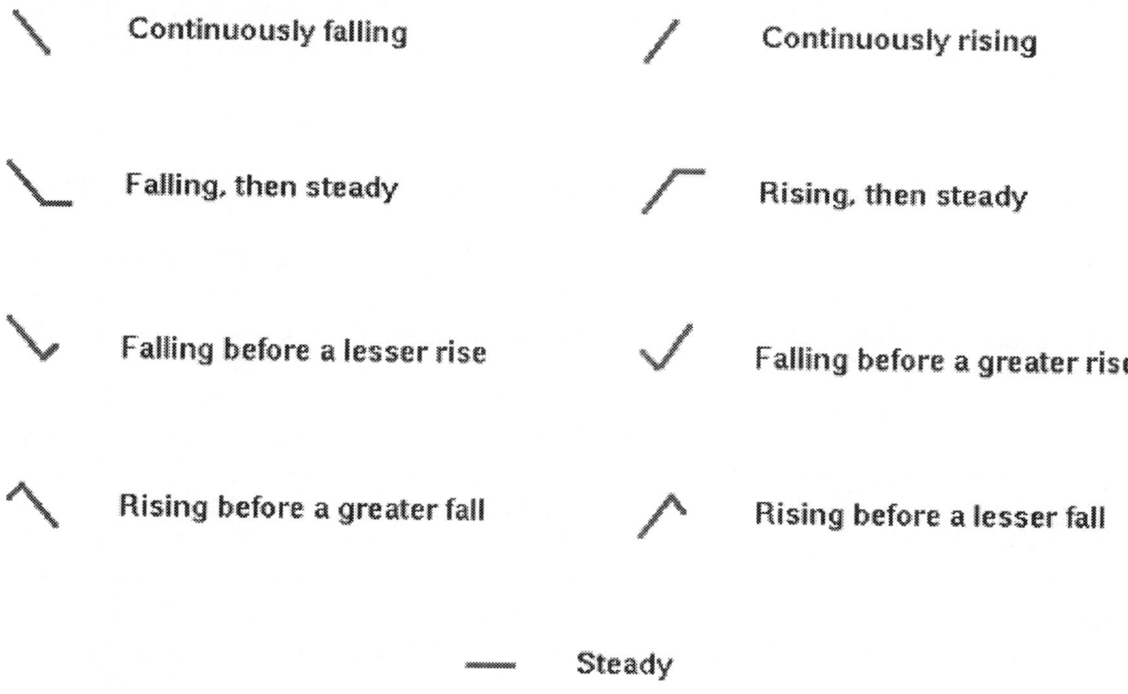

Courtesy of (http://www.hpc.ncep.noaa.gov/html/stationplot).

SKILL 15.2 Analyze types and characteristics of air masses, their movements, and the kinds of fronts that form between air masses

Parcel of Air (Air Mass): a large area of air that assumes a characteristic temperature, pressure, and humidity from sitting over a landmass. Horizontally, the parcel has relatively uniform temperature, pressure, and humidity. Vertically, the parcel may have widely differing temperatures, pressures, and humidity.

Meteorological Terms

Isobar: a line on a meteorological map that connects locations of equal pressure.

Front: a narrow zone of transition between air masses of different densities that is usually due to temperature contrasts. Because they are associated with temperature, fronts are usually referred to as either warm or cold.

Warm Front: a front whose movement causes the warm air (less dense) to advance, while the cold air (more dense) retreats. A warm front usually triggers a cloud development sequence of cirrus, cirrostratus, altostratus, nimbostratus, and stratus. It may result in an onset of light rain or snowfall immediately ahead of the front, which gives way to steady precipitation (light to moderate) as the cloud sequence forms, until the front passes, a time frame that may exceed 24 hours. The gentle rains associated with a warm front are normally welcomed by farmers. However, if it is cold enough for snow to fall, the snow may significantly accumulate. If the air is unstable, cumulonimbus clouds may develop, and brief, intense thunderstorms may punctuate the otherwise gentle rain or snowfall.

Cold Front: a front whose movement causes cold air (more dense) to displace warm air (less dense). The results of cold front situations depend on the stability of the air. If the air is stable, nimbostratus and altostratus clouds may form, and brief showers may immediately precede the front. If the air is unstable, there is greater uplift, cumulonimbus clouds may tower over nimbostratus clouds. Cirrus clouds are blown downstream from the cumulonimbus clouds by high altitude winds. Thunderstorms may occur, accompanied by gusty surface winds and hail, as well as other, more violent weather. If the cold front moves quickly (roughly 28 mph or greater), a squall line of thunderstorms may form either right ahead of the front or up to 180 miles ahead of it.

Occluded Front: a front where a cold front has caught up to a warm front and has intermingled, usually by sliding under the warmer air. Cold fronts generally move faster than warm fronts and occasionally overrun slow moving warm fronts. The weather ahead of an occluded front is similar to that of a warm front during its advance, but switches to that of a cold front as the cold front passes through.

Stationary Front: a front that shows no overall movement. The weather produced by this front can vary widely and depends on the amount of moisture present and the relative motions of the air pockets along the front. Most of the precipitation falls on the cold side of the front.

SKILL 15.3 Analyze the relationship between the jet stream and weather

The **Jet Streams** are zones of very strong, moving air confined to narrow columns and mark the zones where the cold Polar air and the warmer air meet This produces the greatest pressure gradients. The Jet Streams can be either straight or dramatically dip, creating ridges and troughs on the 500-300mb pressure surface. The flatter the isobars, the more evenly balanced the weather. The more pronounced the ridges and troughs, the more pronounced the swings in the weather. The jet stream carries warm air from the tropics northward along North America. This warm air brings humidity and often storms.

SKILL 15.4 Analyze the horizontal and vertical movements of surface air in high-pressure and low-pressure systems

Temperature differences cause the pressure differences that result in **wind**. The pressure moves the wind from high to low pressure areas. The greater the difference in pressure, the larger the gradient, and the faster the wind will move. On a weather map, closely spaced isobars indicate high winds. The winds at altitudes, with no friction present, form an undulating surface-like topography and flow easily to low-pressure areas. These winds are called **Geostrophic Winds**. Geostrophic Winds are affected by the Pressure Gradient Force (PGF) and the Coriolis Effect. This causes the winds to move in either a clockwise motion (high pressure areas), or a counter-clockwise motion (low pressure areas). The winds blow parallel to the isobars because of the Coriolis Effect, and upper level winds always follow the isobars. Geostrophic Winds are also referred to as **Gradient Winds**.

Surface Winds are found at less than 1,000 meters altitude. These winds are no longer balanced because the terrain introduces friction, which in turn, reduces the Coriolis Effect and causes a 30° deflection of the wind from the PGF (Pressure Gradient Force).

The **Buys-Ballot Law** defines the relationship between pressure and surface winds. If you stand with your back to the wind and turn 30° clockwise, the low pressure will be on your left, and the high pressure will be on your right.

Horizontal Divergence and **Horizontal Convergence** are the terms used to describe the rising or sinking (vertical deflection) of air. On a weather map these are pictured as either troughs or ridges. High pressure converges on the ridges and low pressure diverges on the trough.

SKILL 15.5 Analyze the effects of the relationship between land and water on weather (e.g., lake-effect snow, land and sea breezes)

Waves are formed as the result of wind moving across a body of water.

Sea Breezes are caused by the temperature differentials between the land and oceans. During the day, the land is hot and the water is cool. At night the situation is reversed; the land is cool while the water is warmer.

Land Breezes follow the reverse pattern of sea breezes, with daytime causing airflow from the land to the sea and from the sea toward land at night.

Monsoons are seasonal land and sea breezes that are characterized by extreme rains during the summer and dry winters. Monsoons are found almost exclusively in tropical zones because the temperature differentials are greatest in those areas.

Lake Effect Snow/Rain is caused by air moving over a large body of water. The air absorbs large amounts of moisture and then releases it as snow or rain (dependent on temperature) over urban heat islands. Example: Situated near large lakes, Chicago, Illinois and Buffalo, New York often experience unexpected precipitation or early snowfall during the Fall months because of the lake effect. This usually ceases when the lakes freeze over during the winter months.

SKILL 15.6 Demonstrate an understanding of the use of weather instruments (e.g., thermometer, barometer, psychrometer) for collecting given types of weather data

There are two kinds of weather instruments that measure air pressure, the aneroid barometer and the mercury barometer. As air exerts varying pressures on a metal diaphragm within an **aneroid barometer**, a sensitive metal pointer linked to the diaphragm moves either up or down a graduated scale that indicates units of pressure. A **mercury barometer** operates when atmospheric pressure pushes on a pool of mercury in an open dish containing an evacuated glass tube. Air pressure forces the pool of mercury up into the tube. The higher the air pressure, the higher up the tube the mercury will rise. The tube is scaled to reflect units of atmospheric pressure in inches of Hg.

There are two kinds of weather instruments used to measure relative humidity, the psychrometer and the hair hygrometer. The **psychrometer** or "sling psychrometer" consists of two identical mercury thermometers. In order to calculate the water vapor/moisture in the air, one end of one thermometer is covered with a wick that is dipped in water. Spinning the entire instrument allows evaporation of water from the wick. Measuring the difference between the two thermometer readings determines the relative humidity. The hair hygrometer is another type of sensing method that indicates the contraction or expansion when recording relative humidity. The operating principle of a hair hygrometer relies on the fact the human hair stretches whenever it becomes damp.

An **anemometer** measures wind speed and a **wind vane** measures wind direction.

Evangelista Torricelli (1608-1647), an Italian mathematician, developed the first barometer. Galileo Galilei (1564-1642), an Italian astronomer and physicist, invented the first thermometer. Christoph Buys-Ballot (1817-1890), a former director of the Netherlands Meteorological Institute, devised the "baric wind law." This is better known as the Buys-Ballot's Law. This law states that in the northern hemisphere, when a person stands with his back to the wind, the lowest pressure is always toward the left. In the southern hemisphere the opposite phenomenon occurs.

COMPETENCY 16.0 UNDERSTAND THE IMPACT OF WEATHER ON HUMANS AND THE PRINCIPLES AND TECHNOLOGY OF WEATHER FORECASTING.

SKILL 16.1 Analyze the use of weather models in forecasting

The National Weather Service runs the 500 active weather stations used for national forecasting. However, there are thousands of local weather stations that contribute observations. They collect temperature, precipitation, and humidity data and provide remarks about local conditions. The collected data is sent to the National Meteorological Center in Maryland where it is plotted and then sent on to other weather centers throughout the world. The collected data is used to develop mathematical models that are then used to predict the weather. These models have been used since the late 1950's and place differing emphasis on the various aspects of the factors involved. A typical model will consist of 6-8 different equational factors. The data elements are disseminated to the National Weather Service, which uses them to calculate model results based on 12, 24, 36, 48, and 72-hour predictions. However, the further out you extend the predictions, the less accurate the prediction is likely to be. This is because of the wide variation in the data elements that can occur between the time of prediction and the realization of the prediction time. The data is also sent to local meteorological offices and radio and television stations for local interpretation.

The local forecast often includes a great deal of **Kentucky Windage**: experience based guesses by local meteorologists, and can vary considerably from the forecasts of the National Weather Service. The accuracy of local forecasting is dependent on the experience and expertise of the local meteorologist. Forecasting is only as good as the data collected and local intuition (experience) modifications. Four main types of forecast are developed:

1. Persistence: This doesn't change much and is inaccurate.

2. Steady State (Trend): This is a guesstimate as to what the system will do based on the assumption that there will be no change in the data parameters.

3. Analog: This is the best type of forecast basis. It takes the data numbers and plugs them into equations, the equations into models, and uses the models for forecasting. This is also called Numerical Forecasting.

4. Climatological: This type of forecast is often vague and is based on long-standing trends. Example: The weather predictions in the "Old Farmer's Almanac."

SKILL 16.2 Predict weather in a given location based on one or more weather maps

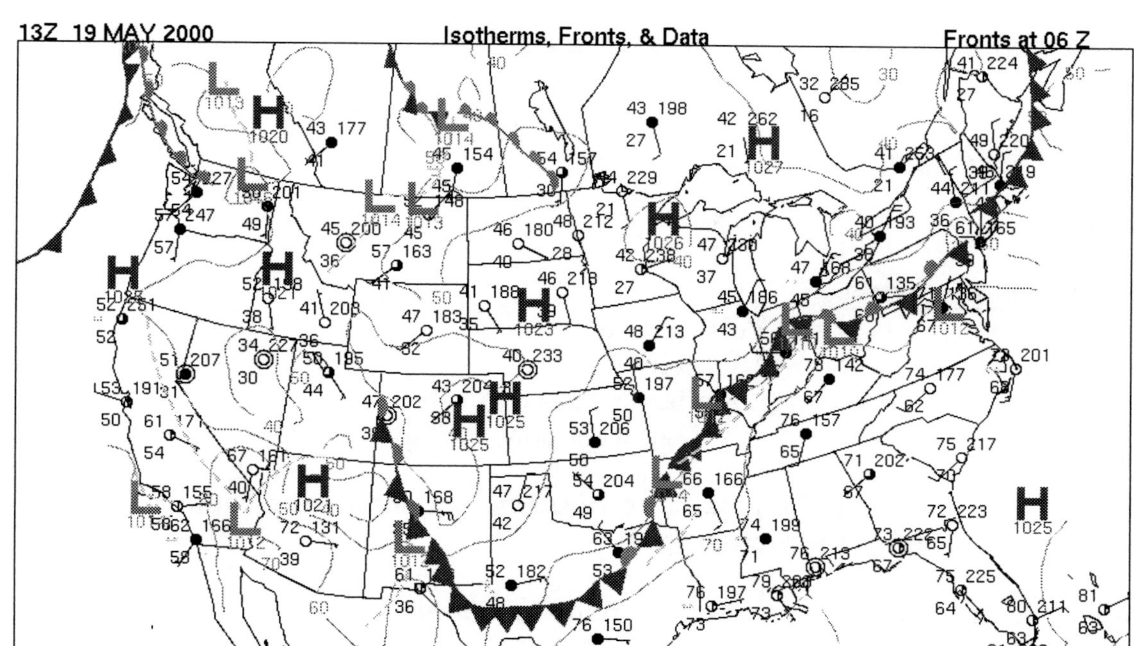

http://www.dnr.sc.gov/climate/sercc/education/saer/aer_summer_00.ht

This map can be used to predict future weather conditions at the weather station in central Arkansas represented by the circle symbol.

This map indicates that a cold front is moving toward the weather station from West to East, as do most weather conditions in the United States. Cold weather fronts occur when a cold air mass of high density pushes under a warm air mass, causing moisture in the warm air to quickly rise, cool, and condense. Heavy precipitation in the near future can be predicted for this area.

This weather map indicates that a low-pressure system is moving toward the weather station with the approaching cold front. Low-pressure systems allow air to rise and moisture to condense, and are associated with precipitation. The cloud coverage symbol of a completely dark circle indicates that skies are overcast. This state could be due to the presence of nimbostratus clouds, which form dark sheets that block sunlight and are often responsible for lengthy periods of precipitation. Therefore, all conditions for Arkansas portrayed on this weather map indicate imminent precipitation.

Forecasting Language

Cloud Forecast Forecasted	% Cloud Coverage
Fair	< 40%
Partly Cloudy/Partly Sunny	30 to 70%
Cloudy	90%

Precipitation Forecast Forecasted	%Probability
Slight Chance	10 to 20%
Chance	30 to 50%
Occasional	> 50%, but for only ½ of the time period covered

SKILL 16.3 Evaluate the role of computers, satellites, and radars in weather forecasting

Meteorologists use a combination of many resources to forecast weather. **Satellites** in space send us pictures of the atmosphere (clouds). From these images, meteorologists can learn about the amount, density, and type of clouds present. This is especially helpful when tracking storms forming over water, such as a hurricane. For **radar** maps, a beam of energy is emitted. How much of that beam is reflected back and the time needed for the beam to return are measured. Those measurements are plotted to give meteorologists an idea of what is in the sky. For example, rain, snow, and sleet will reflect the energy beam back to the radar. More return energy is mapped by bright colors. This is why a television station's broadcasting map of a storm center is often red or orange. When a small amount of the energy beam is detected by the radar, we say there is low reflectivity and this is indicated by darker colors. **Temperature** maps are also color coded. As you might expect, red indicates hot and blue indicates cold with gradients in between the two. Numerals are often superimposed over colors to add specificity. There are also maps showing wind presence/direction and storm fronts. All of these maps together help a meteorologist to predict weather.

SKILL 16.4 Analyze types and effects of hazardous weather to determine appropriate precautions and demonstrate an understanding of the role of weather services in issuing weather alerts

Tornadoes

Tornado: an area of extreme low pressure, with rapidly rotating winds beneath a cumulonimbus cloud. Tornadoes are normally spawned from a Super Cell Thunderstorm. They occur when very cold air and very warm air meet, usually in the Spring.

Tornadoes represent the lowest pressure points on the Earth and move across the landscape at an average speed of 30 mph. The average size of a tornado is 100 yards, but they can be as large as a mile wide. A tornado's wind speed ranges from 65 to 300 mph and has an average duration of 10 to 15 minutes, but has been known to last up to 3 hours. Tornadoes usually occur in the late afternoon (3 to 7 p.m.), in conjunction with the rear of a thunderstorm. Most tornadoes spin counter-clockwise in the northern hemisphere and spin clockwise in the southern hemisphere. They are not dependent on the Coriolis Effect because of the way they are formed.

Worldwide, the U.S. has the most tornadoes and most of these occur in the Spring. Texas has the most tornadoes, but Florida has the largest number per square mile. Tornadoes are without a doubt the most violent of all storms. Roughly 120 people each year are killed in the United States by tornadoes.

Formation of a Tornado

Technically, tornadoes are actually classified as mesocyclones that form within super cell thunderstorms. Temperature differentials within the thunderstorm cause an up and down draft effect that induces a horizontal spinning motion. An increase in the up and down motion tightens the spin and a strong draft may eventually tilt the **mesocyclone** into a vertical position. When this occurs, the bottom of the cloud wall drops down as a funnel cloud. If the funnel cloud touches the ground, it becomes a tornado. Approximately 50% of mesocyclones produce tornadoes.

Tornadoes are very rare in **Pop-Up** and **Squall Line Thunderstorms**. These are both isolated storm fronts of very short duration and speeds. Although there is an induced spin similar to a mesocyclone, it is on a much smaller scale. Tornadoes sometimes form **families**: multiple funnels within the same super cell thunderstorm. If all of these funnels touch the ground, a very rare tornado formation known as a **Rake** can, as the name implies, affect a much wider area in its movement path.

Detection and Tracking

Doppler Radar is the primary device used in tracking tornadoes. The radar measures the funnel's speed and movement by using false color techniques. Movement is graphically displayed with red/yellow patterns indicating a movement away from the radar, and blue/green patterns indicating movement toward the radar.

Mobile tornado tracking devices include TOTO (Totable Tornado Observatory) which was developed by researchers at the University of Oklahoma at Norman, Turtles, expendable ground sensors that measure temperature and pressure, and portable Doppler radars.

Authorities may issue a **Tornado Watch** if meteorological conditions could/ probably will cause the formation of mesocyclones. A **Tornado Warning** is issued when a funnel cloud is spotted. Tornadoes are also noted for producing unusual effects (besides total destruction) in their path.

Observers have routinely reported such phenomena as straws driven into tree trunks, people lifted into the air and then gently returned to the ground miles away, and homes left intact while homes on either side were devastated. For example, while assisting in the cleanup efforts after a tornado struck Topeka, Kansas, in 1967, the author of this book viewed a home that, although it had completely lost its roof and exterior walls, had its interior furnishings untouched by the tornado. Despite the violence visited on the home by the tornado, the furniture and the evening meal on the table had remained in their original positions.

Waterspouts and **Dust Devils** are on a smaller scale and are far less powerful versions of mesocyclones. Waterspouts occur only over water, and thermal currents not associated with super cell thunderstorms cause dust devils.

The Fujita Scale

The **Fujita Scale** is used to measure the intensity and damage associated with tornadoes. Numbered from 0 to 6, ascending numbers on the Fujita Scale indicate higher wind speeds and damage.

Intensity	Wind (mph)	Typical Damage
Weak		
F0	<72	broken branches, shallow trees uprooted, damages signs and chimneys
F1	72-112	damage to roofs, moving auto swept off road, mobile homes overturned
Strong		
F2	113-157	roofs torn off homes, mobile homes completely destroyed, large trees uprooted
F3	158-206	trains overturned, roofs and walls torn off of well constructed houses
Violent		
F4	207-260	frame houses completely destroyed, cars picked up and blown windward
F5	261-318	steel reinforced concrete structures badly damaged
F6	>319	might occur in a small part of an F4 or F5 tornado. Damage would be indistinguishable from that of the main body of the tornado.

Hurricanes

Hurricanes are produced by temperature and pressure differentials between the tropical seas and the atmosphere.

Powered by heat from the sea, they are steered by the easterly trade winds and the temperate Westerlies, as well as their own incredible energy. Hurricane development starts in June in the Atlantic, Caribbean, and Gulf of Mexico, and lasts until the end of the hurricane season in late November.

Hurricanes are called by different names depending on their location. In the Indian Ocean they are called **Cyclones**. In the Atlantic, and east of the international dateline in the Pacific, they are called Hurricanes. In the western Pacific they are called **Typhoons**. Regardless of the name, a hurricane can be up to 500 miles across, last for over two weeks from inception to death, and can produce devastation on an immense scale.

Formation of a Hurricane

Hurricanes start as an upper atmospheric disturbance at the 500mb altitude. This is a trough of low pressure called a **Tropical Wave**.

Recipe for a hurricane

Warm water of at least 200 feet in depth and 79° F in temperature.
Converging surface winds.

Diverging upper atmosphere winds, diverging at a faster rate than the surface winds are converging.

High humidity and unstable air (warm air rising).

Moderate strength winds aloft, and they must blow from the same direction to add momentum to the self-propagating effect.

Warm water feeds hurricanes. The greater the mass of water available, the greater the spin induced by the winds going in the same direction. The storm essentially rotates counter- clockwise around itself, pulling in more wind in a self-perpetuating effect.

Divergence causes the storm to grow as the condensation of the cloud mass releases heat to further feed the storm. Bands of clear air form between the spiral bands (thunderstorms) of the hurricane and a clear, low-pressure **eye** forms at the center of the storm.

The tightness of the eye indicates the relative strength of the storm. The more pronounced and tight the eye is, the stronger the storm. The highest winds are located next to the eye wall. Although as a general rule, hurricanes move east to west, a hurricane's path is determined by its interaction with areas of high and low pressure cells. These cells steer the storm with lows repelling it, and highs attracting it.

Hurricanes die when they move over land or cold water. The hurricane's energy dissipates slowly when robbed of its water or heat source. Stable air breaks the self-propagating effect.

Formation Sequence

Tropical Wave: a trough of low pressure in the trade wind easterlies, very common throughout the tropics during the Summer and Fall.

Tropical Disturbance: a moving area of thunderstorms in the tropics that maintains an identity for a period of 24 hours or more.

Tropical Depression: the first sign of a developing storm, with sustained surface winds of 38 mph or less. Tropical Depressions show some rotation and are assigned a number by the National Hurricane Center in Miami, and the storm's progression and development are tracked.

Tropical Storm: a tropical cyclone in which the maximum sustained surface winds have reached 39 mph or stronger. The storm has well defined rotation, is assigned a name, and is continuously watched for further development.

Hurricane: a tropical cyclone in which the maximum sustained surface winds reach 74 mph or greater. The Northeast (right hand) quadrant of the storm is the strongest because of addition of wind to forward momentum.

The Saffir-Simpson Scale

The **Saffir-Simpson Scale** is used to classify hurricanes into five categories, with increasing numbers corresponding to lower central pressures, greater wind speeds, and large storm surges.

Category	Pressure (mb)	Wind Speed (mph)	Storm Surge(m)	Damage
1	≥980	74-95	1-2	minimal
2	965-979	96-110	2-3	moderate
3	945-964	111-130	3-4	extensive
4	920-944	131-155	4-6	extreme
5	<920	>155	>6	catastrophic

Hurricane Damage

The destruction and damage caused by a hurricane or tropical storm can be severe. **Storm surge** causes most of the damage as the winds push along a wall of rising water in their path, and this rising effect is amplified on low sloping shorelines such as those found on the Gulf Coast. The intense winds can also cause damage. Some notable storms are listed below.

Galveston, Texas, 1900: A 20 feet storm surge killed over 6,000 people and literally destroyed the majority of this Gulf Coast city.

Florida Keys, 1935: A category 5 hurricane, the biggest of the 20th century, was recorded as having 150-200 mph winds and a barometric pressure of 892 mb.

Hurricane Camille, Florida and South Carolina, 1969:This category 5 hurricane with a barometric pressure of 990 mb, scored a direct hit on the Gulf Coast, killing 300 people and causing severe flooding as far north as Virginia.

Hurricane Andrew, Gulf Coast, 1992: Classified as a category 4/5 hurricane, this was the fastest moving storm ever recorded. Moving at 20 mph, the hurricane had maximum sustained winds of 150 mph and gusts up to 175 mph, and re-intensified just prior to making landfall. Andrew was a notable exception to the damage rule in that it was the winds, not the storm surge (16.9 feet), which caused the majority of the 26.5 billion dollars of damage. Over 80,000 houses were destroyed and an additional 50,000 houses suffered greater than 50% damage. 70,000 acres of mangrove swamp was uprooted as this storm cut a 25 mile wide path of destruction in Florida and Louisiana.

Lightning

Lightning: a brilliant flash of light produced by an electrical discharge of about 100 million volts. Lightning flashes when the attraction between positive and negative charges (ions) becomes strong enough to overcome the air's normally high resistance to electrical flow.

Normally, the surface of the Earth is negatively charged and the upper troposphere is positively charged. However, this distribution changes when a cumulonimbus cloud develops. Charges separate within the cloud so that the upper portion and a small region near the base become positively charged. Likewise, the cloud induces a positive charge on the ground directly beneath it.

As a thunderstorm matures, electrical resistance of the air breaks down and lightning can flow either between oppositely charged areas of the cloud, or between the cloud and the ground. Lightning flashes follow a predictable sequence of events.

Electrons (negatively charged) begin a zigzagging downward path in a forked pattern called a **Step Leader**. When the stepped leader is within 100 meters (328 feet) of the ground it draws a **Return Stroke**, a streamer of positive charge ions sent upward, normally through a tall object such as a tree or flagpole.

When the leader and return stroke meet, a powerful electrical current begins to flow as an intense wave of positively charged ions travel upward at 31,000 miles per second. The entire lightning sequence takes place in less than two tenths of a second.

Following the initial electrical discharge, **Dart Leaders**: additional surges of electrons, flow along the same path and are met by return strokes from the ground. A typical lightning discharge consists of two to four dart leaders plus their return strokes.

Lightning heats the air along the conducting path to temperatures that exceed 45,000° F (25,000° C), and can cause serve burns or death to people near the strike area. This heating also expands the air violently, initiating a sound wave we call **thunder**.

National Weather Service

The National Weather Service (NWS) is one of six scientific agencies that comprise the National Oceanic and Atmospheric Administration (NOAA) of the United States Government. The NWS is responsible for the collection of weather, hydrologic, and climate data at national and regional centers, and for the provision of forecasts and warnings for the United States based on this data. The NWS has developed a multi-tiered set of terms to provide observation-based weather forecasts and alerts to the United States public.

Outlook

This alert is issued daily to address potentially hazardous weather or hydrologic events that may occur in the next seven days. A hazardous weather outlook is intended to provide information to those who may need a considerable amount of time to prepare for future weather events, such severe thunderstorms, heavy rains, flooding, winter weather, extremes of heat or cold, etc. This type of alert may also be issued on an event-driven basis, such as the Flood Potential Outlook and Severe Weather Outlook.

Watch

This alert is issued when the risk of a hazardous weather or hydrologic event has increased significantly, but its occurrence, location, or timing remains uncertain. Similar to outlooks, watches are intended to provide information to those who may need time to prepare for a weather event. A weather watch suggests that hazardous weather is possible, but not certain, and that people should establish a plan of action in case the weather event occurs. Watches also recommend that people listen for later information and warnings, especially when planning travel or outdoor activities.

Warning

A warning is issued when a hazardous weather or hydrologic event is occurring, imminent, or likely. Warnings are therefore more serious than watches. This type of alert means that weather conditions pose a threat to life or property, and that people in the path of the storm need to take protective action.

Advisory

Advisories are similar to warnings in that they are issued when a hazardous weather or hydrologic event is occurring, imminent, or likely. However, advisories indicate that conditions are less serious than those of weather warnings.

SKILL 16.5 Analyze the impact of weather on humans in different climatic regions

Some of the most common natural events are hurricanes, tornadoes, floods, snow and ice, extreme heat, etc. The US government studies these natural hazards and helps people through agencies like FEMA (Federal Emergency Management Agency). FEMA coordinates all of the relief activities so that people can receive assistance as soon as possible.

Hurricanes

The term hurricane is derived from Huracan, a god of evil recognized by the Tainos, an ancient aborigines Central American tribe. Hurricanes form over tropical waters (between 8 to 20 degrees Celsius or 80 degrees Fahrenheit or greater). The hurricane season in the northern hemisphere runs from June to November. There are 5 types of hurricanes based on a classification system, which was designed in 1970 by Herbert Saffir, an engineer, and Robert Simpson, the then director of the National Hurricane Center and is called the Saffir-Simpson scale. On this scale 1 is the weakest and 5 is the strongest, referring to the damage sustained. Categories 3,4, and 5 are considered as major (intense) hurricanes capable of inflicting great damage and loss of life. At the center of the hurricane is an area mostly free of clouds, sinking air, and light winds, called the eye. The National Hurricane Center issues warnings about hurricanes and people need to follow them and take necessary precautions including stocking food, filling gas in vehicles, and leaving homes when they are advised to.

Tornadoes

A tornado is a rotating column of air extending from a thunderstorm to the ground and is capable of tremendous destruction with wind speeds of 250 mph or more. The path of the tornado can be 1 mile wide and 50 miles long. Tornadoes are the most violent storms and about 1,000 occur each year. There are nearly 80 deaths and 1500 injuries every year due to the destructive effect of tornadoes. They come in all shapes and sizes and they occur mostly in the southern states. The peak season for tornadoes is March to May. Tornadoes are assessed one of five categories depending on the wind speed. The best precaution is to stay indoors when a tornado warning is given and not venture outdoors to observe.

Flooding

Flooding kills people and destroys homes in many parts of the United States. About 125 people die of flooding in the US every year. Property damage runs into billions of dollars and of late these figures have risen consistently. Flooding is caused by a number of reasons, including flooding during hurricanes due to heavy rains, coastal flooding (sea/ocean waves), inland flooding from snow melting or swollen rivers, flooding from failure of dams, impoundments or other water regulatory systems, flash floods from sudden large downpours and also from ice jams (melting of ice due to heat). Every year the US government spends billions of dollars assisting its citizens. People need to leave their homes in the event of flooding and also insure their properties against flood and other natural disasters.

Snow and ice

Snow and ice are well known hazards to those living in mountainous areas (regions north of 35 degrees latitude). During the winter months, prolonged power outages, automobile accidents, transportation delays, damage to buildings, and dangerous walkways are often attributed to snow and ice. Although slippery surfaces are often the primary cause of such problems, reduced visibility is responsible for many accidents. Snow can be warm causing wet and slushy conditions, or cold, creating dry and powdery conditions. The latter leads to blizzards when mixed with high winds. Blizzards can reduce the visibility to zero. Drifting can block roadways, airport runways, and even bury buildings. Snow and ice are often associated with low wind chills, which are dangerous to exposed skin.

Snow and ice reduce visibility and when they accumulate on the surface, they reduce traction and put strain on power lines, roofs and other structures. The most important part of dealing with snow and ice is forecasting and issuing warnings for the purpose of community preparation. Communities can prepare for winter storms by stocking sand and salt to improve road conditions, advising people to use caution when leaving their homes and to stock plenty of food before a storm in case they are confined to their homes.

Extreme heat

Extreme heat is very dangerous to people in tropical and sub-tropical areas. Sometimes even in places which are colder in winter, summer can be very hot and heat waves can sweep through. From 1979 to 2002, excessive heat exposure caused 8,966 deaths in the US. During this period, more people in the country died from extreme heat than any other natural hazard. The elderly, children, and people with certain medical conditions (such as heart disease) are at greater risk. Even healthy individuals can become victims to heat if they exercise strenuously in extreme heat. It is often referred to as "Heat Stroke" in the tropics. This can be avoided by taking some precautions. The most important of which is to remain indoors, install air conditioning in homes, and increase the intake of water and fruit juices. It is important from a humanitarian point to check on neighbors who may be susceptible.

COMPETENCY 17.0 UNDERSTAND THE LOCATIONS AND CHARACTERISTICS OF EARTH'S MAJOR CLIMATIC REGIONS AND ANALYZE FACTORS THAT AFFECT LOCAL CLIMATE AND THE RELATIONSHIP BETWEEN WEATHER AND CLIMATE.

SKILL 17.1 Infer the climatic zone in which a given area is located based on temperature and precipitation data

The Köppen climate system explains that the origin of the climate is based on the average monthly and yearly temperatures, location of the landmass, precipitation rates, and seasonality of the precipitation. When Köppen, a climatologist, created his classification system, he determined that one of the best indicators for climate is native plant life. He created the Köppen climate system map with native vegetation in mind.

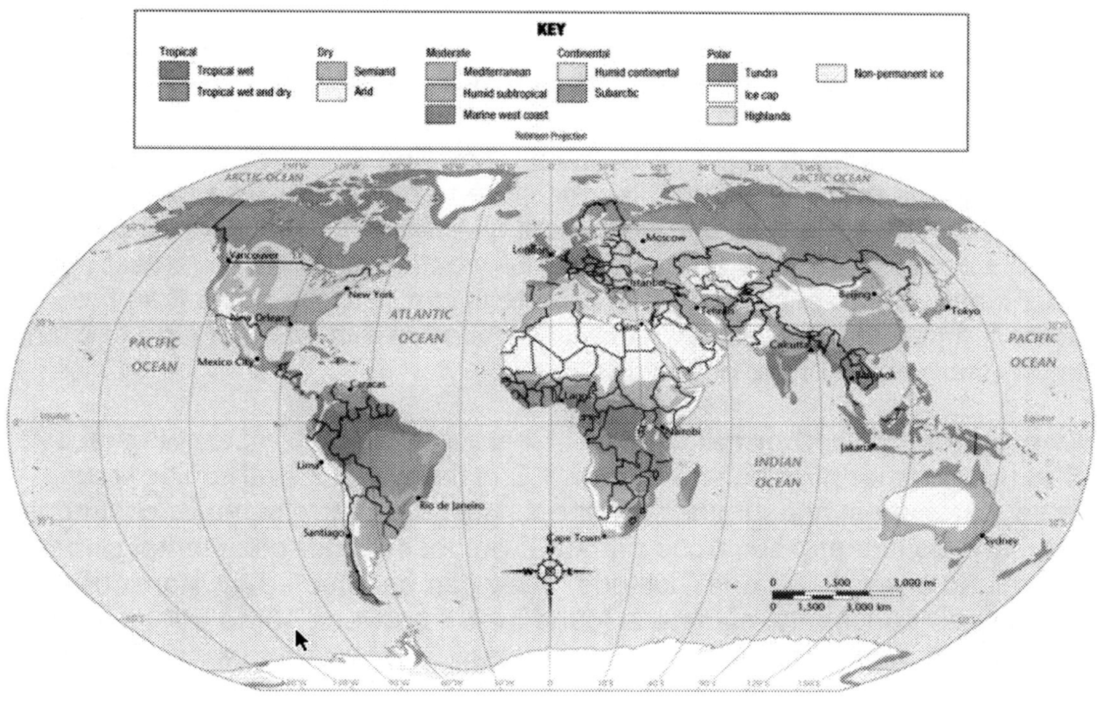

Types of Climate

1). Tropical/Megathermal Climate: Characterized by a constant high temperature over 18°C or 64.4°F. There are three subcategories: tropical rain forest, tropical monsoon, and tropical Savanna. The tropical rain forest climate has more than 60 mm of rain each month of the year. There are no season changes. The tropical monsoon climate will have more than 100 mm of rain total in the year, but may have some months that fall below 60 mm of rain due to change in wind direction as the seasons change. The tropical savanna climates have a prominent dry season and have less than 100 mm of rain each year.

2). Arid and Semiarid Climate: The precipitation of the region is less than the evapotranspiration of the region.

3). Temperate/Mesothermal Climate: The average temperature is above 10°C for the warmest months and between -3°C and 18°C in the coldest months. There are four subcategories: Mediterranean climate, humid subtropical, maritime temperate, and maritime subarctic. The Mediterranean climate is found on the western sides of continents. It has moderate temperatures and experiences a polar front in the winter and a tropical front in the summer. Summers are usually hot and dry. The humid subtropical climate is found on the interior of the continents or on the east coast of the continents. The summers are usually very humid due to the trade winds bringing moisture to the region. The maritime temperate climate experiences a polar front all year. It is usually found on the continents between 45° and 55° latitude. The weather is usually overcast year round. Finally, the maritime subarctic climate is closer to the poles than the maritime temperate climates and is usually limited to thin strips of land or islands off the western coast of the continents.

4). Continental/Microthermal Climate: Characterized by temperatures above 10°C in the summer months and below -3°C in the winter months. There are three subcategories: hot summer continental climate, warm summer continental climate, and continental subarctic climate. The hot summer continental climate occurs inland around 30° to 40° latitude. They can be affected by monsoons. The warm summer continental climate is found inland between 40° to 50° latitude in North America, and up to 60° latitude in Eastern Europe due to wind patterns. The continental subarctic climate exists inland in the 50° to 60° latitude.

5). Polar Climates: Temperatures are below 10°C all year. There are two subcategories: the tundra climate and the ice cap climate. The tundra climate is dry and has an average temperature between 0° and 10°C in the warmest months. The ice cap climate has temperature below 0°C year round.

Variation in Climate

Weather consists of hourly and daily changes in the atmosphere over a region. Climate is the average of all weather conditions in a region over a period of time. Many factors are used to determine the climate of a region including temperature and precipitation. Climate varies from one place to another because of the unequal heating of the Earth's surface. This varied heating of the surface is the result of the unequal distribution of land masses, oceans, and polar ice caps.

Climate varies over time. The diurnal cycle is how the weather has changed in the last 24 hours. Over the course of a year, regions experience seasonal changes. The climate of a region may vary due to changes in atmospheric dust, large dust storms, and volcanic eruptions. Over the course of 10 years, changes in climate may take place due to the El Niño and La Niña cycles in Earth's oceans. Climate change over the course of 100 years can be attributed to solar variability and changes within ocean temperature. Over the last 100 years, significant climate changes have been noted in some regions due to deforestation and increased carbon dioxide output. Climate variability over 1000 years can be linked to thermocline circulation in the oceans and changes in the carbon cycle. Paleoclimatology indicates that climate variation on the 100,000 year time frame can be attributed to the Milankovich cycles, solar variability, precession, and orbit eccentricity. By studying variations in climate, paleoclimatologists can determine how current changes in climate are related to long term trends. This can help scientists to further understand humanity's effect on climate change.

SKILL 17.2 Analyze factors that affect the climate in a given region (e.g., insolation, water vapor, wind patterns, topography)

A number of factors affect the climate of a given location. These factors include latitude, elevation, topography, insolation, and proximity to large bodies of water and cold or warm ocean currents.

Latitude

Latitude is the measure of how far you are north or south of the equator. Latitude has a pronounced effect on climate because it determines how much solar energy a location receives. Locations close to the equator receive more direct sun light and, thus, more radiant energy and heat. Locations distant from the equator (and nearer the Earth's poles) receive less direct sun light as the sun's rays strike the Earth at an angle. Thus, locations closer to the poles receive less radiant energy and heat.

Locations between the Tropics of Capricorn and Cancer, located approximately 23 degrees south and north of the equator respectively, experience a tropical climate, typified by hot, moist weather throughout the year. The Arctic and Antarctic Circles, located at approximately 66 degrees north and south of the equator respectively, define the Polar Regions. Locations north of the Arctic Circle and south of the Antarctic Circle experience a polar climate, typified by extremely cold temperatures and varying lengths of days. Finally, the temperate zones, defined as the areas between the tropics and the Polar Regions, experience seasonal climates, typified by cold weather in the winter and warm weather in the summer.

Elevation

In general, elevation, or distance above sea level, has a clear effect on climate. When comparing two locations at the same latitude, the one with the higher elevation will have a cooler climate. As you go up a mountain, for instance, the air pressure decreases and the air gets less dense. Less dense air does not hold heat as well as more dense air does. Thus, locations at higher elevations have consistently cooler climates.

Topography

The climate, topology, and atmospheric processes all combine to trap pollutants. **Inversion**: an atmospheric condition where the air temperature rises. Inversion is driven by temperature. Warm air rises only so far. If it encounters an atmospheric pressure cell of colder air it will stall. Colder surface air attempting to rise won't go past the higher altitude warm air. This traps pockets of pollutants in the air.

Topology also acts to trap pollutants. Mountains and valleys are the key locations. In valleys, the normal flow of air is downward during the daytime, and at nighttime, from the valley floor up the sides of the mountains. However, during winter months the airflow pattern can reverse and become a down flow all the time. The down-flowing cold air traps the warm air layer filled with pollutants in the valley.

The Radiant Heat Energy Balance (The Radiation Budget)

Radiation Budget: the balanced exchange cycle of radiation absorbed and released by the Earth's surface, water, and atmosphere. The Sun drives a radiation exchange interaction with the Earth every day as the Sun's radiated energy enters the Earth's sphere of influence. The 19% absorbed by the CO_2, dust, clouds and water vapor in the atmosphere traps the heat and holds it to moderate the temperature (especially at night). In the desert, there is little water vapor present to trap the heat. That's why it's so cold at night. The interaction between the Earth's upper atmosphere, waters, and land keeps the world at a moderate ambient temperature of approximately 55 degrees F.

Solar Radiation (Insolation)

This distribution of solar energy is called **insolation**. Solar radiation isn't distributed evenly across the Earth because of the Earth's curvature, axial tilt, and orbit. This results in uneven heating of the atmosphere, and is why the temperature is warmer at the equator and colder at the poles.

Because of the curvature and tilt, the energy striking the polar areas is spread over a larger area. At the equator it is more concentrated. The same amount of energy is striking the atmosphere, but it is striking a larger or smaller area. In effect this dilutes the energy received by a particular area.

The effect of insolation is very important to life on Earth. The absence of solar radiation would cause the creation of very cold air masses and the thermal blanket of the atmosphere would not have heat to hold and reradiate. In short order, the world would become an icy rock.

Proximity to Large Bodies of Water

Large bodies of water have a pronounced affect on the climate of surrounding landmasses, by moderating temperatures and increasing precipitation. Coastal areas generally experience cooler temperatures during the summer and warmer temperatures during the winter than their inland counterparts. This moderation of temperature results from the ability of large bodies of water to absorb a large amount of solar energy. During the summer, bodies of water trap heat, keeping temperatures cooler. Conversely, during the winter, the latent heat stored in the water escapes to warm the atmosphere slightly. Finally, coastal areas generally receive more precipitation because the bodies of water serve as a direct source of moisture.

Cold or Warm Ocean Currents

There is a direct relationship between the temperature of ocean currents and the temperature of surrounding landmasses. Coastal areas near warm ocean currents experience warmer climates than coastal areas at similar latitudes near cold ocean currents. Warm ocean currents heat the air above the ocean, while cold ocean currents cool the air above the ocean. The varying atmospheric temperatures and related wind patterns act to warm or cool the related coastal regions.

SKILL 17.3 Analyze the relationship between the climate of a region and its weather

Climate: the characteristic weather of a region over long periods of time.

Weather: the state of the atmosphere at a particular time and place.

The Hydrologic Cycle is greatly influenced by the climate. Warm air rises and holds more water than cold air. Cold air sinks and holds less water than warm air. This temperature differential balances the cycle of water. Much of Earth's water is locked in glacial ice. As the climate changes, glaciers melt or freeze, changing the volume of water available.

Climate Basics

Radiation Budget: the balanced exchange cycle of radiation absorbed and released by the Earth's surface, water, and atmosphere. The Sun drives a radiation exchange with the Earth everyday as the Sun's radiated energy enters the Earth's sphere of influence. The 19% absorbed by the $C0_2$, dust, clouds and water vapor in the atmosphere traps the heat and holds onto it to moderate the temperature (especially at night). In the desert, there is little water vapor present to trap the heat. That is why it is so cold at night. The interaction between the Earth's upper atmosphere, waters, and land keeps the world at a moderate ambient temperature of approximately 55 degrees Fahrenheit.

Climate Zones

The movement of the air forms **Convection Currents** that affect the weather and climate in three zones. The patterns created in these zones distribute the heat between the poles and the equator. The **Coriolis Effect** is the deflection of air or water currents caused by the rotation of the Earth. This creates global wind patterns that affect the climate. These wind patterns also represent rain patterns. The wind patterns between 30°N and O°N are called the **Trade Winds**. The wind patterns between 30°N and 60°N are called the **Prevailing Westerlies**. All of the great deserts of the world lie between the Tropics at 0° and 30°North and South latitudes. A shift in the wind patterns would also shift the deserts. The optimum growing zone is between 30° and 60° North and South latitudes. If global warming takes place, it could cause the melting of the polar ice caps that in turn could raise sea levels. This would inundate land areas and lead to economic disaster. The Earth's climate is a very delicate balance. A change to the global warming or cooling patterns would affect retained heat, which would further affect the growing zones. In example, global warming would cause the expansion of the tropics, while global cooling would cause a contraction of the tropic zone.

SKILL 17.4 Recognize seasonal changes in weather in various world regions and analyze factors that influence these changes (e.g., insolation, ocean current patterns)

Hurricanes are produced by temperature and pressure differentials between the tropical seas and the atmosphere. Powered by heat from the sea, they are steered by the Easterly Trade Winds and the temperate Westerlies, as well as their own incredible energy. Hurricane development starts in June in the Atlantic Ocean, Caribbean Sea, and Gulf of Mexico, and lasts until the end of hurricane season in late November.

Monsoons are seasonal land and sea breezes that are characterized by extreme rains during the summer and dry winters. Monsoons are found almost exclusively in tropical zones because temperature differentials are greatest in those areas.

Mountains and Valley Breezes are the result of thermal differences and topography. During the day the thermal currents rise up from the valley floor and move up the sides of the mountains. At night, the mountains act as a lingering heat source, retaining the heat in the valleys.

A **Chinook Breeze** occurs when the Prevailing Westerlies are squeezed between the bottom of the Stratosphere and the top of large mountain ranges. This causes a heating and expansion of the air as it moves over the mountains, drying the area and melting snow. This effect can be intensified by the presence of high and low pressure systems.

Example: The Chinook Breeze is most heavily concentrated on the Eastern edge of the Rocky Mountains. Its presence can cause an early melt of the snow, increasing the likelihood of flooding downstream.

Santa Ana Winds are a specialized form of Chinook Breeze. They are formed when air moves down the valleys to the coast when a high-pressure area is present. The wind is very warm and dry, creating dangerous fire conditions.

A **Haboob** is experienced in deserts and is a dynamic of thunderstorms that do not have enough condensation to precipitate. It is characterized by violent up and down drafts that pick up sand and carry it high into the atmosphere. This sand can 'rain' down thousands of miles away.

Urban Heat Islands are the result of concentrated masses of buildings and concrete and asphalt paving. Heat produced by activities in the urban areas and reradiated by the concrete masses will form a rising thermal zone over the urban area. This is why it is usually 10 degrees or more warmer in the city than rural areas. The concrete buildings and asphalt paving absorbs more heat than grass and fields in the countryside.

Lake Effect Snow/Rain is caused by air moving over a large body of water. The air absorbs large amounts of moisture and then releases it as snow or rain (dependent on temperature) over urban heat islands

El Nino is a reverse of the normal weather patterns in the Pacific. A low-pressure area normally sits in the Pacific Ocean west of Hawaii and a high-pressure area normally sits off of the California coast. When an El Nino forms, these pressure areas shift eastward, causing the low-pressure area to be situated below Hawaii and the high-pressure area to move inland over California. Because of the shift in pressure areas, an El Nino affects the wind patterns (especially the jet stream and trade winds), and creates a wide variety of effects, including a direct impact on commercial fishing. Normally, there is a shallow warm water layer over the colder, deeper waters along the coastlines. The temperature disparity causes an upwelling of rich nutrients from the lower layers of the cold water, creating a feeding zone that attracts a variety of marine life forms. In an El Nino situation, the warm water layer increases in both area coverage and depth. It extends downward, blocking the nutrient rich upwell from reaching the feeding zone. Although many species can migrate to more friendly waters, some have limited mobility and die. In any event, the fishery area can become permanently barren depending on the intensity, duration, and repetition of El Nino events. Other effects of El Nino are both direct and indirect.

Direct Effects

- In the west, fires and drought.
- In the east, rain, landslides, and fish migration.

Indirect Effects

- Greater chance of hurricanes in Hawaii.
- Lesser chance of hurricanes in Virginia because of weakened Trade Winds.
- Less rain during September and October.
- Coastal erosion in the western states.
- Fewer storms that deposit snow in the Cascades in Washington and Oregon.
- The Jet Streams are altered as the high pressure areas move.

A **La Nina** is the opposite of El Nino. However, it does not have as great effect. It causes the East to be wetter and the west to be drier. Many scientists believe that both of these conditions are caused by a change in the surface temperature of the water of the Pacific Ocean.

COMPETENCY 18.0 UNDERSTAND THE IMPACT OF HUMAN ACTIVITIES AND NATURAL PROCESSES ON THE ATMOSPHERE, THEORIES ABOUT THE LONG-RANGE EFFECTS OF HUMAN ACTIVITIES ON GLOBAL CLIMATE, AND METHODS OF CONTROLLING AND MINIMIZING THESE EFFECTS.

SKILL 18.1 Identify common air pollutants (e.g., sulfur dioxide, chlorofluorocarbons) and their sources and demonstrating an understanding of the effects of air pollutants and atmospheric chemical reactions involving these pollutants

Sulfur Compounds: Some sulfur compounds are naturally released. The primary natural sources are volcanoes. The man-made sources are mostly due to the combustion of coal and oil products. When released, the sulfur combines with the atmosphere and changes to an oxidizer, Sulfur Dioxide (SO_2). Further chemical modifications transform this into Sulfate, and when combined with water, it changes to Sulfuric Acid ($S0_4$). This acid precipitation is commonly known as Acid Rain. The solution to the problem is to use low sulfur content coal. Since the EPA mandated its use, there has been an 11% drop in the amount of acid rain.

Nitrogenous Compounds: 5% of all nitrogenous compounds occur naturally from bacterial decay, rice paddies, wetlands, and swamp decay. 95% of them are caused by man-made, high temperature combustion. Auto exhaust is the primary offender. The nitrogenous compounds oxidize and combine with H_20 (water) to form into SO_4 (acid rain).

Carbon Oxides: Carbon Monoxide (CO) is deadly because it replaces oxygen molecules in the blood, causing Carbon Monoxide poisoning. Carbon Monoxide is produced by combustion of oil and gas, with auto exhaust as the primary offender.

Particulates: These are Aerosols (small bits of solids suspended in water drops). Aerosols block solar radiation and make the air look dirty. The source of the particulate (dust, soot, ash) can be either man-made or natural. 40% comes from industrial processes. 17% comes from vehicle emissions. 30% comes from natural sources: salt spray, dust, and volcanoes. 13% comes from all other miscellaneous sources. The most dangerous of the particulates are <2.5 microns in size. These microscopic sized particles cause lung problems. Some sources are asbestos, cigarette smoke, and coal dust. Example: Long exposure to coal dust can cause "Black Lung" disease. The sulfur in the dust particulates literally burns acid holes in the lungs.

Metals: Metal substances are the byproducts of a variety of manufacturing processes. Some sources are sandblasting, leaded gasoline, and leaded paint. Example: Since the EPA banned the use of lead in gasoline and paint there has been a major decline in lead accumulation in the environment. The major problem with metals is that almost all of them are carcinogenic, and because the metals accumulate in the fatty tissues of the body, they also cause long-term problems with nervous system disruption.

Photochemical Oxidants: The oxidation process can change normally harmless chemicals into dangerous substances. Example: When Oxygen (0_2) is exposed to ultra-violet radiation (UV), it becomes Ozone (0_3). Although Ozone is necessary in the upper atmosphere, when the human body is exposed to it, it causes lung damage. Example: Nitrogen compounds under certain circumstances can transform into $N0_3$. This compound is a major component of smog that irritates the soft tissues and mucous membranes.

Volatile Organic Compounds (VOCs): These are organic chemical gases that occur both naturally and through man-made processes.

Natural sources: Plants, wetlands, rice paddies, and ruminant animals release Methane. Conifer trees release Terpene. Terpene forms a haze in the atmosphere. It is what forms the haze over the Great Smoky Mountains and the Azure Mountains.

Man-made Sources: Any synthetic organic chemical (such as Benzene, Toluene, and Formaldehyde) and all hydrocarbons emissions such as gasoline fumes.

SKILL 18.2 Demonstrate an understanding of factors that affect local air pollutant concentrations (e.g., population density)

Normal, daily human activity can generate emissions that produce air pollution. These activities may include transportation, electricity use, solvent use, adhesives, paints, and home heating and cooling. As population density increases at particular geographic locations, the frequency of such activities increases, affecting local air pollution. Human use of products that release CFC's into the atmosphere contributes to increased air pollution. In areas of higher population density (urban areas) the two largest sources of air pollutants are transportation and fuel combustion.

Transportation

Automobiles produce high levels of carbon monoxides and nitrogen oxides, both of which are greenhouse gases. As populations rise, vehicle use also rises. Recent studies performed for the Federal Highway Administration found that, generally, traffic volumes tend to rise at least 80% of the rate of population density increase. This rise is explained by the increasing number of people who own and use cars in a growing city. In addition to the increased number of cars used by a growing population is the problem of increased traffic. As the number of cars increases in a particular geographic location due to growing population density, the traffic slows down and becomes subject to more stop-and-go operation. This situation further increases the amount of time an automobile is in use, worsening air pollution.

Fuel Combustion

Another source of air pollution is fuel combustion by stationary sources including residential, commercial, and industrial heating and cooling and coal-burning power plants. Fuel combustion is the dominant source of sulfur dioxide air pollution. As population density increases, the number of people requiring and using energy increases. More power is needed to construct new homes and industries, to heat and cool a larger number of homes and buildings and to generate more food and commercial products. Energy used in all of these situations may be produced by the burning of fossil fuels, thus increasing the amount of greenhouse gases released into the atmosphere.

SKILL 18.3 Analyze theories of global climate change (e.g., greenhouse effect, glaciation)

One of the major environmental issues of today is the controversy over **Global Climate** change. Many scientists forcefully contend that we are experiencing a period of global warming, and that our dependence on modern technology is the major reason behind the warming. Not surprisingly, other scientists equally oppose this theory. Much of the controversy depends on the source of information as to whether humankind is at fault.

Is the Earth Warming or Cooling?

In the 1970's the scientific issue was whether there was going to be another ice age. However, as we approached the new millennium, the issue shifted to concern about warming. The controversy is based on interpretations of the historical records. Temperatures have been recorded based upon four temperature readings per day from each collection location. The collected readings are sent to the World Metrological Organization where the readings are correlated and averaged. That data indicates a rise in average temperature.

However, the temperature readings only have been collected for the past 100 years.

Problems with the Collected Data

- **How were the records constructed?**

Weather stations use an averaging method. In 1945 the World Meteorological Organization dictated the method of collection, type of shelter, height off of the ground, equipment used, etc. in order to normalize the temperature readings world wide. This make previously collected records suspect as to the means through which they were collected.

- **The locations of weather stations.**

The big problem is where to place the weather collection stations. In example, where is the ideal place to collect ambient temperature? In reality, the stations were placed at locations where they could be monitored roughly 24 hours a day. Most of the stations are placed at airports. However, because of the expanse of heat absorbing building materials (i.e. concrete and asphalt) airports are usually hotter than surrounding areas. Stations located within other **Urban Heat Islands** (i.e. the cities) are also subject to same problem.

- **How to collect and analyze correct data?**

The most accurate method to measure global temperature is to use space satellite technology. Since 1979, the GOES Satellite has collected temperature readings. Instead of sampling only the cities, the GOES samples all areas in blocks of data, including the oceans. Data taken during the period of 1979-1998 showed no net warming. However, from a scientific point of view this is not a long enough period of sampling to be fully conclusive.

Has the Climate Always Been the Same?

Paleoclimate: the climate of the past. The paleoclimate is studied by CLIMAP, an organization that is focused on past climatological situations. Both Fine and Gross methods are used to determine the past climate.

Gross Methods

The study of arboreal forests, cactus, coral, etc, gives a rough idea of the past climate based on the fossil record. It can also show the presence of species that favored warm or cold climates, providing clues as to what the climate in a location used to be.

The study of historical records also provides important information. People write about what is going on in their lives. In-depth research in old texts, letters, etc., can provide clues. 100 years ago grapes grew in England. This is not so today.

As the climate changes, people comment on the change, or popular culture reflects the fears and issues caused by the changes. Stories of trolls, ogres, and dwarfs were probably reflecting medical conditions caused by the little ice ages. The little ice ages caused a shortage of food. This led to dietary deficiencies and malnutrition. The malnutrition manifests itself as stunted growth, gnarled joints, etc, which gave rise to fairy tales of deformed creatures.

Studying what the topographical records indicate is also useful. Example: Large Rivers used to run through the Sahara Desert. The presence or absence of ancient seabeds, riverbeds, etc. may provide clues of past climate changes.

Fine Methods

Fine methods focus on improved scientific methods of taking past temperatures.

Oxygen Isotope Ratio Measurements: all living things utilizing oxygen retain a percentage of oxygen within their cellular structure. The change in the ratio of O_{18} and O_{16} provides clues as to the type of climate they lived in. Carbonate shells and coral remains on the ocean floor are key fossils. More O_{18} indicates a colder climate. More O_{16} indicates a warmer climate. The oxygen trapped within the $CaCO_3$ bones and shells gives a record of the air at the time the creature lived.

Air Bubbles trapped within Glacial Ice: Analysis of the ice sheets in Antarctica, Greenland and Siberia provide clues. As you drill down the layers of ice provide a record of changes, much like tree ring dating techniques. Analysis of the air bubbles is very accurate. It provides data on temperature, gaseous content concentrations, etc. The analytical methods used can be applied to samples as far back as 160,000 years in the past.

Climate Trends

What we know about the climate in the distant past is based entirely on Gross methods (lithology and the fossil records). There were long periods of warm, stable climate punctuated by climatic changes.

Climatic Disruptions: a period of glaciation followed by a warmer stable period that is interrupted by interglacial periods of 5 million years.

Reasons for Climate Change

The Greenhouse Effect

The Greenhouse Effect is predicated on a rise in the trapped gases in the atmosphere.

CO_2, Methane and Water Vapor all absorb reflected heat. CO_2 makes up 0.03% of the atmosphere. If the CO_2 level rises, more reflected heat is trapped, and the balance of the **Radiation Budget** is upset.

When greenhouse gases and heat build up, the Earth's surface and atmospheric temperatures rise. The theory contends that if we cut the amount of rising CO_2 in the atmosphere, temperatures will fall.

Sources of greenhouse gases

Gasoline burning engines and Aerosols (CO_2)
Vegetation & Microwave devices (CO_2)
Rice Paddies & Ruminant animals (Methane)

CO_2 levels have risen this century, with the most dramatic rise since the 1960's. However, the data is not conclusive when compared to the past. The only thing certain is that there is a one-to-one correlation between temperature and CO_2.

Are the oceans a CO_2 sink? The possibility of the oceans acting as a major source of CO_2 release cannot be discounted. Warm liquids hold less gas. As liquids cool, the gas goes into solution. Therefore, a change in the ocean temperatures either releases or holds more gases.

Global Cooling

The Ice Age began about 2-3 million years ago. This age saw the advancement and retreat of glacial ice over millions of years. Many scientists hypothesize that something in the atmosphere blocked much of the incoming solar radiation and thereby caused global cooling, giving rise to the development of the ice sheets. We have evidence of frequent volcanic eruptions in the past that may have caused this effect.

About 12,000 years ago, a vast sheet of ice covered a large part of the northern United States. This huge, frozen mass had moved southward from the northern regions of Canada as several large bodies of slow-moving ice, or glaciers. A time period in which glaciers advance over a large portion of a continent is called an ice age. A glacier is a large mass of ice that moves or flows over the land in response to gravity. Significant amongst the climatic disruptions over the past 2 million years were the several periods of widespread glaciations during the Pleistocene and Holocene Epochs. These glaciations have are collectively called the "Great Ice Age." During these periods, ice and snow - an estimated 40 million km^3 - covered approximately one-third of the Earth's surface. The glaciations also caused a 50 to 75 foot drop in sea level worldwide, which in turn caused land bridges between continents to form. Around 12,000 years ago, a warming trend began, causing extinctions of life forms that could not adapt. These included the Saber Tooth Tiger (Smilon), Wooly Mammoths and Mastodons, the North American horse, Giant Ground Sloth, and Giant Beavers.

COMPETENCY 19.0 UNDERSTAND GEOCHEMICAL SYSTEMS, THE PROCESSES OF MINERAL AND ROCK FORMATION, AND THE CHARACTERISTICS OF DIFFERENT TYPES OF MINERALS AND ROCKS AND THE METHODS USED TO IDENTIFY AND CLASSIFY THEM.

SKILL 19.1 Demonstrate the ability to utilize a classification scheme (e.g., based on physical properties, crystal structure, chemical composition) to identify common rock-forming minerals

Minerals

A mineral is a naturally occurring homogenous element or compound of homogenous elements with a definite chemical composition (within limits), and a highly ordered atomic arrangement (crystalline structure).

Some minerals are single elements. An example of this is a diamond, which is solely Carbon (C). Some minerals are simple combinations of atoms. Examples of this are Halite (NaCl) and Pyrite (FeS_2). Other minerals are complex combinations of atoms. An example of this is Tourmaline whose formula is $Na(MgFe)_3Alo(BO_3)(Si_2O_{18})(OH)_4$.

.

The $(Mg, Fe)_x$ portion of the formula indicates that the Magnesium and Iron may combine in any combination of 3 atoms as long as both elements are present in the final composition. This type of formula variance is why the definition of a mineral states that the chemical composition must be within limits. This variance in formula also causes variance in coloration of the same mineral. Variance in color is caused by small impurities.

Crystalline structure, form or shape (not chemical composition) is the key defining factor in identifying minerals. Crystalline structure is defined as the most efficient arrangement of atoms that form a crystal shape.

Minerals are arranged in specific patterns based on their elemental composition. For example, Halite (NaCl) forms into cube shapes, while a diamond's structure is a complex latticework of diamond shapes.

Crystal Habit: the shape of the mineral. Some minerals possess distinctive shapes.

Cleavage: how the mineral breaks under pressure. Most minerals have a tendency to break in a preferred direction along smooth surfaces. Where the atoms connect, it forms a weak point. In example, Mica is resistant to breaking but peels quite easily. Not all minerals have cleavage. Instead, some have fractures (they shatter like glass).

Hardness: how hard the mineral is. Hardness is based upon the arrangement of atoms within the crystalline structure. Hardness is graded from 1 to 10 using Mohs Scale of Hardness. General classification is acceptable based on the scratch test.

Mohs Scale of Hardness

1. Talc
2. Gypsum
3. Calcite
4. Fluorite
5. Apatite
6. Orthoclase (Feldspar)
7. Quartz
8. Topaz
9. Corundum
10. Diamond

Soft: Able to be scratched with a fingernail.
Hard: Able to scratch glass with the mineral.
Medium: not able to be scratched with a fingernail, nor able to scratch glass with the mineral.

Specific Gravity: the ratio of the mineral's weight to water. Because the weight of the mineral is based upon the arrangement of the atoms, minerals will vary in specific gravity (e.g., water = 1, but rock = 2.65).

Color: the color of the mineral in solid form. Although some minerals, such as Sulfur, are distinctly colored- always some shade of yellow- it's relatively common to find color variations within the same mineral. As a result, identifying minerals using color as the sole basis for identification can easily lead to misidentification.

Streak: the color of the mineral in powdered form. Some minerals leave a distinctive color streak when the mineral is scratched across a Streak Plate (a piece of unglazed porcelain).

Additional (Secondary) identifying Properties

Luster: the surface appearance of the mineral.
Examples of luster are Pearly, Waxy, Shiny, Dull, Earthy and Glassy.

Magnetism: inherent magnetic qualities.
Example: Magtletite=yes, Quartz=no.

Fluorescence: Some minerals glow under a black light.
Example: Lapis Lazuli.

Reaction to Acid: Some minerals have a distinctive reaction when exposed to acids. For example: Any mineral with calcium carbonate ($CaCO_3$) will fizz when diluted hydrochloric acid (HCl) is dropped on it.

Striations: distinctive marks on the surface of the mineral. These marks are usually parallel lines on the mineral's surface. In example, Feldspar is often heavily striated.

Taste: Some minerals have a distinctive taste.
Example: Halite (NaCl) (more commonly known as table salt).

Minerals are divided into three common types: Silicates, Orebites, and Carbonates.

Silicates

Silicates are the most common type, making up 90% of all minerals.
The Silica tetrahedron of Oxygen (O_2) and Silicon (Si_4) is the basic crystalline structure of a silicate.

The silicates are subdivided into two divisions: pure silica (Quartz) and silica combined with other elements (Ferromags and non-Ferromags). Both Ferromags and non-Ferromags are silicates. The difference is that one has iron and magnesium in it and the other doesn't.

Any silicate mineral that is a Ferromag has iron (Fe) and magnesium (Mg) in its formula. Ferromags are dark in color and dense in mass. An example of a ferromag is Hornblende.

Non-Ferromags are silicate minerals with chemicals other than iron or magnesium in their chemical composition. They are light in both color and mass density. An example of a nonferromag is Feldspar.

If examined in a thin, wafer-like section, their crystalline structure clearly shows that the silica tetrahedrons form chains in distinctive patterns that are indicative of the grouping of the silicate.

Single-Chain Structure

The corners of the tetrahedron coincide with the centers of the oxygen ions. When other elements combine with the silicate tetrahedron, they do so at the junction points of the chains. In the case of Biotite (Mica), it has iron combined in a thin sheet over the entire surface of the tetrahedron.

Silicate Structures include Double-Chain (Amphibole Group: "Hornblende") and Sheet Silicate styles (Mica Group: "Biotite").

The iron is what gives the Biotite its dark color as compared to another mineral. Muscovite, which doesn't have iron in it, has a transparent appearance similar to cellophane.

Orebites: economically important ore minerals. Minerals such as iron, copper, gold, silver, zinc, lead, and calcium are extracted from base ores through a variety of processes.

Carbonates: form the group of minerals that have calcium carbonate ($CaCO_3$) in their chemical formulas. Carbonates are a very important group of minerals. These are often found in shells and fossils. Rocks that have calcium carbonate in them are called carbonated rocks. Examples of carbonates include **Coral reefs** (composed of calcium carbonate) and **Coquina** (a biomass of shells compressed to form a carbonate mineral).

Mineral Chemistry and Analysis

Minerals are described by their chemical composition, which, within specific limits, can widely vary. These variable compositions consist of **end members** within a specific group/family/class, and the variability is reflected by the percentage of elements within a specific mineral. Albite ($NaAlSiO_3$) and anorthite ($CaAl_2Si_2O_3$) are both types of feldspar, and their chemical formulas represent the end members of their particular group. Note that they share a common composition of aluminum (Al), silica (Si), and oxygen (O). They differ in that albite also contains Sodium (Na) while anorthite also contains calcium (Ca).

The minerals themselves are divided into families and then further subdivided into groups. Mineral classifications within each of the groups reflect both chemical composition and crystalline structure.

Mineral Families: Native elements (i.e. gold), Sulfides, Oxides, Halides, Carbonates, and Silicates.

Minerals are crystalline solids. The structure reflects the repetitive, periodic array of atoms. This array- the **lattice**- forms the basis for the **unit cell**: the basic repeating unit in a crystal that possesses the symmetry and properties of the mineral. The angles present at the bonding points of the atoms determine the fundamental geometric shape of the crystal. These shapes are classified as either isometric (cubic), tetragonal, orthorhombic, hexagonal, monoclinic, triclinic, or rhobohedral.

The chemical analysis of minerals is often displayed in a variety of graphic formats that address chemical composition and mineral stability. The primary formats used are either a Chemical Composition diagram or a **Pressure-Temperature (PT) diagram**.

A chemical composition diagram is used to show the molecular percentage of elements that combine to form the multiple minerals within a particular mineral group system. The format of the diagram consists of a triangle with the native elements shown at the apex and lower corners.

Percentile marks are shown along the sides of the triangle and a series of dots and lines section off specific areas that reflect the percentage of native element present for each member of the group. The percentages present are read at the intersection point on the line.

A pressure-temperature diagram is often used to display the stability of a particular mineral or group of minerals. A PT diagram uses a basic graph format with pressure shown on the y-axis and temperature shown on the x-axis. It is read as you would read any standard graph.

SKILL 19.2 Analyze the processes by which different kinds of rocks are formed (e.g., rock cycle)

The **rock cycle** is a dynamic process of ongoing change that reflects the recycling of the Earth's materials. Although the processes involved in the rock cycle are dynamic, they follow a geological, rather than human time scale, and consequently, changes occur so slowly that they are not readily observable. To help understand the recycling processes, the rock cycle is often graphically presented in the form of a circle with one process following another until the cycle is complete. However, the formation and decomposition of the Earth's materials often do not happen in a neatly fixed pattern of events. Depending on the circumstances involved in any specific event, the recycling sequence may be interrupted, and the material may go directly from one stage to another, skipping stages in between. Example: Igneous rock material may go directly to a metamorphic stage or sedimentary materials may be carried back into a melt.

Sedimentary Rocks

Sediments are basically various sized fragments of broken or eroded rock material. As weathering processes break down the parent material, the sediments are transported, sorted and deposited in piles. These sediment piles may lithify into sedimentary rocks.

Fragmentation, Transportation and Sorting

Wind and Running Water

Wind is very effective in transporting sediments in areas of little vegetation. The haze over the Grand Canyon is actually sand from Monument Valley over 50 miles away.

Sand dunes are essentially piles of wind-blown micro-rock. Pebbles in mountain pools and streambeds are pieces of the mountain broken off and carried to another location by water movement. The pebbles are polished and rounded by the abrasive action of tumbling into each other as the water carries them downstream.

The piles of sorted and transported sediment can be quite extensive in terms of depth and area covered. Everything east of Richmond, Virginia is a sedimentary base. The sediments came from the erosion of the Appalachian Mountains.

The **velocity** achieved by most transport agents determines what and how far materials are transported, and those materials tend to be of relatively uniform size. The exception is those materials moved by glaciers. A **glacier** acts like a giant bulldozer, moving most everything in its path, big or small.

Fining: the process of sorting materials by size. Geologists describe sedimentary rocks by size. To determine the size, they use the **Wentworth Scale.**

Wentworth Scale

Name	Size	Size Analogy
Boulder	Larger than 256mm	Basketball
Cobbles	> 64mm and < 64mm	Tennis ball
Pebbles	> 2mm and < 64mm	Pea sized
Sand	1/16mm to 2mm	Coarse/ med/ fine grains
Silt	1/256mm to 1/16mm	none
Clay	Less than 1/256mm	none

There may be a variety of various sized sediments present in any given area. This size diversity demonstrates that over time a variety of transportation agents laid down the sedimentary material.

Geologists can measure the size of smaller materials by passing the material through screens with different sized openings. The point of determining size is to be able to recreate past environments. Size can provide clues to the original location of the material. Sedimentation is a continuous process.

Murky water: water carrying silt and clay sediments (suspended load) from upstream. Further upstream the materials are coarser.

The flowing water carries the material to the ocean where one of two things happen: the material is deposited on the offshore continental shelf, or the material is carried back inland to the inlets and bays.

Over time, the sediment thickly accumulates and may form typical coastal features such as sand bars and deltas. The continuous accumulation of sediment is why there is a continuing need to dredge harbors and rivers.

The lithification processes of cementation, compaction/dessification, and precipitation form sedimentary rocks.

Cementation: Sedimentary materials deposited in a pile are of different sizes. Consequently they have different sized spaces between grains. Some of these spaces are large enough to permit water to flow through them (sand sized or larger have large spaces between them).

Groundwater has lots of chemicals in it. As water moves through the spaces, the pH – measure of acidity – changes, and, drop by drop, chemicals are **precipitated** (deposited) along the edges of the grains. The spaces eventually become filled, and the precipitated chemicals hold the materials together.

The two most common cementing agents are Silica and Calcium Carbonate. **Silica (SiO_4)** is very hard (7 on the Mohs scale). Silica forms a rock that is very hard to break. **Calcium Carbonate ($CaCO_3$)** is less resistant to weathering (the calcium carbonate is easily dissolved).

Chemical impurities in flowing groundwater may collect within the spaces between sediment grains. These impurities cement the grains_together to form a rock.

Compaction and Dessification: the processes that affect fine grain sediments.

Silt, clay and extremely fine sand become compressed by the weight (pressure) of the dirt and other materials on top of them and eventually dry out.

Precipitation: Where chemicals in the groundwater precipitate as solutions in the underground cracks and crevices. Precipitation is the result of chemicals, originally deposited by groundwater, that have dried out on the surface of the material. Example: Water spots that harden on the shower walls. The two most common precipitatory agents are Silica and Calcium Carbonate. Calcium Carbonate formations are often found in caves, in the form of Stalactites and Stalagmites. **Stalactites** form from the roof. **Stalagmites** form on the floor. (Memory jogger: the "g" means ground up!)

The **Geode** is an example of silica precipitation. Quartz crystals form inside of a rock exterior. Precipitation doesn't occur between sediment grains, instead, whole cavities in existing rock material are filled.

Igneous Rocks

Igneous rocks form from the cooling and crystallization of a rock melt. **Melt:** the overall collective term used to describe molten and semi-molten rock material in the Earth. The melt is due to the heat present in the Earth and this heat is derived from two sources: the decay of radioactive elements and frictional forces and pressure within the Earth. As you go deeper into the Earth, the temperature increases. The various heat layers are collectively referred to as the **Geothermal Gradient**. Other forces can aid or hinder the melt.

Pressure: Rock stays solid for longer time periods if it is under pressure.

Presence of Water: Dependent on the pressure, the presence of water can delay or accelerate the melt process.

As rock materials move within the Earth, rocks in a liquid state move upward, seeking cracks in solid rock, and rocks in a solid state move downward.

Liquid rock slowly cools as it moves upwards. The upward movement can cause enough pressure and stress to move and/or fracture the solid rock.

Crystallization

Magma is rich in chemicals. As it cools, chemicals combine to form distinct mineral structures. As minerals form they either settle to the bottom of the magma well or continue to react and form a richer magma.

Bowen's Reaction Series is used to predict how and which minerals will solidify out of a melt. These predictions are primarily based on the heat of the magma.

Lavas on the surface have a temperature of around 2000 °F. By comparison, magma that cools underground can take millions of years because of the extremely high temperatures present below the Earth's surface.

Slow cooling: forms very large crystals of minerals in the rock. Very large grains are prominent. Example: Granite.

Quick Cooling: This allows less time for the crystal to cool and form. It results in smaller (sometimes microscopic) crystals. Example: Basalt.

Squelching (Instant Cooling): This cooling occurs almost instantaneously when lava flows into the ocean or is thrown into the air by an eruption. No crystals are formed and the rocks usually have a glassy appearance. Example: Obsidian.

The cooling rate of the igneous rock is very important because it produces a distinct texture that is a key factor in its identification.

Textural Results

Phaneritic: Igneous rock with mineral grains large enough to be seen with the naked eye. Grain size caused by slow cooling.

Aphanitic: Igneous rock with mineral crystals present, but the crystals are often too small to be seen without the aid of a microscope. Grain size caused by quick cooling.

Categories of Igneous Rocks

Extrusive: Igneous rocks that cool on or near the Earth's surface. Characterized by Aphanitic or Glassy textures.

Intrusive: Igneous rocks that cool deep within the Earth. Characterized by Phanaretic texture. Intrusive rocks never reach the surface during the cooling process. Instead, they are exposed after millions of years of weathering. Examples include Stone Mountain in Georgia or Half Dome in Yosemite National Park.

Glassy Texture: no detectable mineral crystals present. Caused by squelching (instant cooling).

Porphyritic: some large mineral crystals within an Aphanitic or Glassy ground mass (background). The background is also known as the **matrix** and presents a Checker-board texture. The magma cooled slowly, forming large grains, but before the magma was fully developed, it erupted upward through cracks, cooled quickly, and other minerals formed smaller crystals as the matrix. Example: Diamond Head in Hawaii is composed of volcanic basalt with large Olivine crystals.

Metamorphic Rocks

Metamorphism: changing a pre-existing rock into a new rock by heat and or pressure. Metamorphism is a process that is similar to that of putting a clay pot into a kiln. The clay doesn't melt, but a solid-state chemical reaction occurs that causes a change. The chemical bonds of adjoining atoms breakdown and allow the atoms to rearrange themselves, producing a substance with new properties.

Single Mineral Metamorphism: If the pre-existing rock is composed primarily of only one mineral, the metamorphic result is a rock with the same composition, but the crystal grains are larger and interlocked. For example, Sandstone is a cementation of silica. Under metamorphosis, the grains become larger and are fused together to form Quartzite. There are major differences in appearance and properties. Quartzite appears crystalline with very large crystals and is very hard. Another example: Metamorphism causes Limestone to become Marble. Limestone can be cut and used as building material, but it resists polishing, restricting its use as a decorative stone. Marble can be polished and utilized as very strong and decorative building material.

Multiple Mineral Metamorphism: If the pre-existing rock is composed of more than one mineral, then pre-existing minerals may align to give a new appearance, or recombination can occur within the rock, producing entirely new minerals. An example of this is the metamorphic change of Granite. It retains the same mineral composition but becomes Gneiss, ending up with the materials aligned, and giving it a striped appearance. Likewise, Garnet is a recombination of multiple minerals and is formed only by metamorphism.

Temperature and/or pressure cause metamorphism. The metamorphic effect may produce a change in the chemical and physical properties and/or appearance of the rock.

Types of Metamorphism

Contact Metamorphosis – Temperature: This requires the presence of a nearby magma chamber. The closer to the heat source, the more metamorphosis that takes place. This is a localized effect due to the presence of a magma chamber. The effect is measured in 10's to 100's of yards. Rocks formed during contact metamorphism tend not to be foliated (striped).

Regional Metamorphism – Deformation through pressure: This type of metamorphism is produced by the tectonic movement (drift) of continental plates. Continental drift exerts enormous pressure at the edges of the plates (where they abut). Rocks are forced into a semi-plastic state and the atoms break their bonds. The pressures involved cause the rocks to reform without breaking. An analogy for this type of metamorphism is that of chocolate chip cookies fresh and hot from the oven. Under pressure, they tend to bend rather than break. In the case of rock material, pressure compression causes the material to fold. Regional metamorphism has a widespread effect measured in 10's to 100's of miles. Example: The Appalachian Mountains have abundant metamorphic material because the mountains were the result of three collisions in the past between the North American and African plates. In regional metamorphism you end up with deformed rocks that are highly foliated.

Migrating Fluids – (Also called Metasomatism or Hydrothermal Alteration): Formed by groundwater heated by a magma chamber. Heated water (near steam) moves through cracks in the rocks. Over time, the water leeches minerals out of the rock. These minerals are concentrated in solution in the water and are transported to other locations to precipitate as a vein. The effect of migrating fluids tends to be localized and is measured in 10's to 100's of yards. This type of metamorphism is usually associated with the presence of large plutons.

Index Minerals: select minerals used to measure the metamorphic grade, which reflects the intensity of the metamorphic process. The presence of a particular index mineral provides information about the temperature and pressure involved in a metamorphic event. As a general rule of thumb: the closer to the heat source, the greater the metamorphic effect.

SKILL 19.3 Classify a given rock as sedimentary, igneous, or metamorphic

There are three major subdivisions of rock: sedimentary, metamorphic, and igneous.

Igneous rock is also known as basalt. Igneous rock is formed when either sedimentary or metamorphic rock buried deep underground succumbs to heat and pressure and is melted into magma. When the magma cools and hardens the resulting material is igneous rock.

Sedimentary rock is formed when exposed igneous or metamorphic rock erodes away and collects in water. Over time, the eroded particles are fused together by pressure, resulting in sedimentary rock. An example of sedimentary rock is sandstone.

Metamorphic rock is commonly called marble. Metamorphic rock is formed when either sedimentary or basalt rock buried deep in the Earth is surrounded by heat and pressure. These extreme conditions cause the rock to change; hence the new rock is called metamorphic rock.

COMPETENCY 20.0 UNDERSTAND THE STRUCTURE OF EARTH, THE DYNAMIC FORCES THAT SHAPE ITS SURFACE, THEORIES AND EVIDENCE OF CRUSTAL MOVEMENTS, AND THE EFFECTS OF CRUSTAL MOVEMENTS ON LANDSCAPES.

SKILL 20.1 Demonstrate an understanding of how Earth's internal structure can be inferred from the behavior of seismic waves

Seismology: The study of earthquakes.

Seismic waves are measured using a device called a Seismometer, a type of motion sensor. The seismometer is anchored to the Earth and a heavy weight is suspended on its frame. As the Earth's materials move, the weight also moves and electronically sends a signal to a recording device called a Seismograph. Movements are displayed as a series of lines on a recording chart called a Seismogram, reflecting the seismic energy detected at a particular location.

Types of Seismic Waves

P-Wave (Primary Wave): Also sometimes called a "Push-Pull Wave or Compression Wave," the P-Wave moves through both solids and liquids. The P-Wave has a pulsating, "push-pull" type of motion. It compresses material as it moves through it. The fastest moving of the seismic waves (4-7 Km/sec), the P-Wave is the first wave to reach the seismometers.

S-Wave (Secondary Wave) (Shake Wave): Moves only through solid material. Always shorter than a P-Wave, the S-Wave (2-5 Km/sec) is the second wave that reaches the seismometer. Motion is a sinuous "side to side" movement.

L-Wave (Surface Wave): The L-Wave is much slower than either the P or S-Waves, but creates a lot of ground movement. Because it is slower, the L-Wave takes longer to pass a location and consequently, the intense, undulating ground motion creates the greatest amount of damage in an earthquake. The L-Wave undulates with a rolling motion similar to ocean waves.

Measuring Magnitude and Intensity

Magnitude: the relative measure of how big an earthquake is (how much energy is released).

Intensity: the measure of observable effect in terms of damage and destruction caused by an earthquake.

Richter Scale: the primary scale used by seismologists to measure the magnitude of the energy released in an earthquake. It is a logarithmic scale.

A series of seismometers are used to locate the epicenter of an earthquake through a geometrical process called triangulation. A minimum of three seismometers is required to accurately triangulate the epicenter. Seismometers are also used to determine the magnitude and distance by plotting a travel-time curve, derived by measuring the time lag between the arrival of the P and S waves.

SKILL 20.2 Relate lithospheric plate movements to circulation in the mantle

The outermost part of Earth is known as the lithosphere. The lithosphere, which consists of the Earth's crust and upper most part of the mantle, is composed of cool rock, and responds to strain by deforming through brittle failure. For this reason, the lithosphere is fragmented into massive sections called tectonic plates. The asthenosphere is the region of the mantle directly below the lithosphere. Because of extreme pressure and temperature conditions, the asthenosphere is capable of liquid-like movement, and accommodates strain through plastic deformation of its heat-softened state.

The tectonic plates that compose the lithosphere are characterized by volcanic and seismic activity around each margin, and are capable of movement relative to other segments. Plate tectonics is a theory of geology that explains the large scale motion and seismic activity that occurs within the Earth's crust. This theory combines and supplements the two earlier plate tectonic theories of sea floor spreading and continental drift. Plate tectonics associates the forces that drive the motion of the plates with the Earth's internal flow of heat and material. Convections cells are believed to be the primary force driving plate motion.

In the geologic convection cell, material becomes heated in the asthenosphere by heat radiating from the Earth's core. When material is heated, particles begin to move more quickly, colliding more frequently, requiring more space and causing material to expand. Because particles of heated material are less tightly packed, the density of the heated material decreases. This heated, less dense material will rise toward the solid lithosphere. Less dense material will rise when surrounded by more dense material because of buoyant force. Fluid pressure increases with depth, and increased pressure is exerted in all directions. Buoyancy results from the unbalanced upward force that is exerted on the bottom of submerged, less dense material, as the fluid pressure is greater below the less dense material than above. When the heated material reaches the solid lithosphere, it can no longer rise and begins to move horizontally, dragging with it the lithosphere and causing movement of the tectonic plates. As the heated material moves, it pushes cooler, denser material in its path. Eventually, the cooler material sinks lower into the mantle where it is heated and rises again, continuing the cycle of the convection cell.

SKILL 20.3 Analyze evidence for seafloor spreading and plate tectonics (e.g., magnetic reversals)

Evidence for Plate Tectonics

Shape of the Continents: When graphically displayed, the continents look like they should largely fit together in a puzzle.

Paleomagnetism: As igneous rock cools, iron minerals within the rock will align much like a compass to the magnetic pole. Scientific research has shown that the magnetic pole periodically reverses in polarity. Normal Polarity is magnetic North and Reverse Polarity is magnetic South. Research also shows that the bands of rocks on either side of a seafloor spreading center are mirror images of each other with regards to magnetic polarity, and that the alignment of minerals indicate a periodic shift in polarity. The reversals in polarity can be visualized as alternating "stripes" of magnetic oceanic materials.

Age of the Rock: Besides being mirror images magnetically, dating research conducted on rocks on either side of a spreading center also indicate a mirroring of age. The age of the rock on either side of a spreading center are mirror images and become progressively older as you move away from the center. The youngest rock is always found directly at the spreading center. In comparison to continental rock materials, the youngest rock is found on the ocean floor, consistent with the tectonic theory of cyclic spreading and subduction. Overall, oceanic material is roughly 200 million years old, while most continental material is significantly older, with age measured in billions of years.

Climatology: This is one of the most compelling arguments supporting plate movement. Cold Areas show evidence of once having been hot and vice-versa. In example, coal needs a hot and humid climate to form. It does not form in the areas of extreme cold. Although Antarctica is extremely cold, it has huge coal deposits. This indicates that at one time in the past, Antarctica must have been much closer to the equator.

Evidence of Identical Rock Units: Rock units can be traced across ocean basins. Many rocks are distinctive in feature, composition, etc. Identical rock units have been found on multiple continents, usually along the edges of where the plates once appear to have joined.

Topographic Evidence: Topographic features can be traced across ocean basins. Some glacial deposits, stream channels, and mountain ranges terminate on one continent near the water's edge and resume on another continent in relatively the same position.

Fossil Evidence: Limited range fossils that could not swim or fly are found on either side of an ocean basin.

SKILL 20.4 Apply the theory of plate tectonics to explain ocean floor topography, landscape development, and geologic phenomena (e.g., volcanism, earthquakes) and to predict plate motions

Tectonic Plate Movement

Plate tectonic movement results from the motion induced in the lithosphere by the rise and fall of convection cell material in the asthenosphere.

Plate Boundaries: the points at which the edges of the tectonic plates abut.

Three motions characterize interactions at the plate boundaries: separation, collision, or lateral movement. Those motions directly correlate with the categories of plate boundaries, which are Divergent, Convergent, and Transform. The geologic and geographic effects that result from the motion depend on the location of the boundaries and the types of material involved.

Divergent Boundary: The plates are separating and moving away from each other.

Ocean/Ocean Boundaries: The materials involved are composed of heavy and dense, but very thin, dark colored oceanic lithospheric material, usually Basalt. As the magma rises, the ocean floor begins to dome upward. The upward pressure eventually forces an underwater rip in the center of the dome and the magma erupts. The erupted materials cool rapidly and build upward, forming Mid-Ocean Ridges, which are fairly common and found all over the globe. The ocean floor is constantly being pushed apart at these boundaries, causing Sea Floor Spreading. This results in the creation of huge oceanic plates.

Continental/Continental Boundaries: The materials involved are composed of less dense, but very thick, light colored continental lithospheric material, usually Granite. The same principles of force and motion present in divergent ocean/ocean boundaries apply to divergent continental/continental boundaries. However, as the erupted material eventually cools, a Rift Valley forms between the adjoining volcanic peaks. In many places around the world, these valleys play an important agricultural role because of the richness of volcanic soil.

Convergent Boundary: The plates are moving toward each other and collide.

Ocean/Ocean Boundaries: These plates are forced together by the spreading of the ocean floor. Tremendous frictional forces are created as the plates collide and some of the oceanic material builds upward, while other oceanic material bends downward. The leading edges of the boundaries meet and the forces involved push some material upward through the lithosphere to become a volcano. The built up materials may eventually break the ocean surface to become volcanic islands. This effect is so widespread that the islands form groupings of volcanic islands called Volcanic Arcs. This volcanism is of the explosive type and the quick release of fantastic strain and pressure causes devastating Deep Focus Earthquakes. Although some material is pushed upward, other oceanic material bends downward forming deep trenches and the leading edges of this plate subduct back into the asthenosphere.

Subduction Zone: A long, narrow belt where a lithospheric plate dives into the asthenosphere. The rate of subduction is relatively equal to the rate of formation of new oceanic lithospheric material at divergent boundary spreading centers. In effect, the ocean floor recycles itself.

Ocean/Continental Boundaries: The colliding plates produce effects relatively similar to ocean/ocean collisions, but the difference in density between the materials involved causes the oceanic plate to subduct under the continental plate. Subduction forces the continental materials upward, creating a line of on-shore volcanic mountains along the subduction zone.

Continental/Continental Boundaries: Both edges are too light to subduct. Instead, one will over ride over the other causing an uplift of material.

Transform Boundary: The plates move laterally with respect to each other. As the plates grind sideways, intense frictional forces are created as the lithospheric materials try to oppose the movement. A transform boundary may be found in any location where plates abut. They may be composed of any type of lithospheric material (oceanic or continental), and they produce extreme seismic effects when the pressure between moving boundaries is released. This sudden release of pressure creates widespread destruction along the fault lines.

COMPETENCY 21.0 UNDERSTAND WEATHERING, EROSIONAL, AND DEPOSITIONAL PROCESSES THAT CHANGE EARTH'S SURFACE AND THE RELATIONSHIP BETWEEN THESE PROCESSES AND LANDSCAPE DEVELOPMENT.

SKILL 21.1 Demonstrate an understanding of the processes of mechanical/physical, chemical, and biological weathering and factors that affect the rate at which rocks weather and soils are produced

Weathering: the physical and chemical breakdown and alteration of rocks and minerals at or near the Earth's surface. Weathering is typically caused by a combination of chemical and mechanical processes

- Mechanical (Also called Physical) Weathering: rock is broken into smaller pieces with no change in chemical or mineralogical composition. The resulting material still resembles the original material.
- Chemical Weathering: where a chemical or mineralogical change occurs in the rock and the resulting material no longer resembles the original material.

Factors Influencing Weathering

- Composition: Due to their composition, some rocks weather easier and will show more effects.
- Rock Structure: Does it contain cracks? Is it fractured? Water and other elements seep into cracks.
- Climate: The more water, the more the weathering effect. Additionally, the higher the temperature or the more the temperature varies, the greater the weathering effect.
- Topography: This factor determines the amount of surface area exposed to weathering. Smaller rocks are affected more because, collectively, they have less mass and more surface area than a boulder.
- Vegetation: Important weathering agent. Depending on the type of vegetation, it can either hinder or accelerate the weathering process. Although vegetation may leave less surface area exposed, the vegetation's root structures can produce a biological effect that accelerates the process.

Types of Mechanical Weathering

- Frost Wedging: This occurs when rock has a crack in which water collects and then freezes. Over time, as this cycle repeats itself, the expanding water gradually pushes the rock apart.
- Salt Crystal Growth: In a process similar to frost wedging, as water evaporates it leaves salt crystals behind. Eventually, these crystals build up and push the rock apart. This is a very small-scale effect and takes considerably longer than frost wedging to affect the rock material.
- Abrasion: This is a key factor in mechanical weathering. The motion of the landscape materials produces significant weathering effects, scouring, chipping, or wearing away of pieces of material. Abrasive agents include wind blown sand, water movement, and the materials in landslides.
- Biological Activity: This is a two-fold weathering agent.
    - Plants: Seeds will sometimes land in a crack in a rock and begin to grow inside the crack. The root structure eventually acts as a wedge, pushing the rock apart.
    - Animal: As animals burrow, the displaced material has an abrasive effect on the surrounding rock. Because of the limited number of burrowing animals, plant activity has a much greater weathering effect.
- Pressure Release (Exfoliation): Rock expands when compressive forces are removed, and bits of the rock break off during expansion. This can result in massive rock formations with rounded edges.
- Thermal Expansion and Contraction: Minerals within a rock will expand or contract due to changes in temperature. Dependent on the minerals in the rock, this expansion and contraction occurs at different rates and to different magnitudes. Essentially, the rock internally tears itself apart. The rock may look solid but when placed under pressure it easily crumbles.

Types of Chemical Weathering

- Oxidation (Rust): Oxygen atoms become incorporated into the formula of a mineral within a rock and the mineral becomes unstable and breaks off in flakes. Example: Iron oxide (FeO_2) changes to iron trioxide (FeO_3) due to the oxygen chemically imparted to the mineral.
- Solution: Due to their inherent composition, some minerals found in rocks easily dissolve into solution when exposed to a liquid. Example: Halite (Rock Salt) completely dissolves in water.
- Acids: Water and water vapor may combine with other elements and gases to form acids. Water (H_2O) and carbon dioxide (CO_2) can chemically combine to become Carbonic Acid (H_2CO_3). Sulfur Dioxide (SO_2) particles can chemically combine with water (H_2O) to form Sulfuric Acid (H_2SO_4).

- Biological Activity: Plant roots growing in the cracks of rocks not only cause mechanical wedging, but also secrete acids that cause chemical weathering.

Sediments and Soils

Sediment: fragments of broken rock produced by the weathering process. Soils form when sediments undergo the processes of leeching, accumulation, and addition of organic matter. Parent Material is the rock or sediment from which a soil is derived.

SKILL 21.2 Demonstrate an understanding of the processes of erosion by various agents (e.g., wind, water, glaciers) and factors that affect erosion rates and patterns

Stream Erosion

The action of streams causes various erosive effects.

- Hydraulic Action: It smoothes rocks and carves potholes. Potholes are holes bored into rock material by the swirling (hydraulic) action of a stream.
- Abrasion: Sand particles carried by water act like sandpaper, cutting and smoothing the landscape material.

Moving water in a stream has two major effects.

- It carves downwards and sideways. The downward carving is the first and most prominent action caused by a moving stream.
- It erodes the banks and beds of a stream, gradually changing the shape of the stream and its surrounding landscape.

Mass Wasting: the movement, by gravity, of Earth material down a slope.

Classifications of Mass Wasting

- **Landslide**: the rapid down-slope movement of dry material. The material moves as a unit.
- **Rock Slide**: A slab of rock slides off of a slope.
- **Debris Slide**: Piles of rocks slide down the slope.

Mass wasting is more commonly called a landslide. If snow is present it is called an avalanche. The material can move either slowly or quickly and be either consolidated or unconsolidated. Consolidated means a slab of rock and unconsolidated refers to sediment.

Landscape Alterations By Groundwater

Karst Topography: areas where large amounts of limestone are present. Groundwater is very effective in dissolving limestone, and forming caves and sinkholes. Chemical leeching combined with groundwater produces Carbonic acid ($CO_2 + H_20= H_2C0_3$), and this acid dissolves the limestone, riddling an area with underground holes.

Coastal Geomorphology

On a primary type of shoreline, very little reshaping has occurred.

- Drowned River Valleys: Cutting characterized by its V-shape. Example: Susquehanna River Valley or Delaware River Valley.
- Fjords: Cutting by Glaciers that is characterized by U-shaped cutting.
- Drumlins: Filling effect. Example: Cape Cod in Massachusetts and Long Island in New York.
- River Mouth Deltas: Filling effect. Example: The Mississippi and Columbia River deltas. The Mississippi River delta is a birdfoot delta. It has long channels that extend far out. The Columbia River doesn't have these because the longshore current keeps it clear.
- Volcanoes: Lava cones. Example: Hamauma Bay, Hawaii. It is the remains of a collapsed volcano that filled with ocean water.
- Faulting: Tensional breaking. Tectonic lifting or dropping to change the shape of the coast. Example: Montague Island in Alaska.

Marine processes and organisms have dramatically reconfigured a secondary type shoreline and the original shape of the coastline is unrecognizable.

- Barrier Islands: Barrier Islands make up 80% of the U.S. East Coast. They tend to be wave straightened.
- Wave Eroded (both straightened and irregular): The straightness is formed by ocean action. Retreating cliffs are typical of irregular shores.
- Cuspate Foreland: (Current sculpted). Characterized by huge, gentle curves in the shoreline. Example: The coastal area along the North Carolina/South Carolina borderline.
- Coral Reefs: Marine growth.
- Mangroves: Marine growth.

Transport

If the sediment particles are loose and dry, wind can be an important erosional factor in any climate. However, because of the nature of wind, it can only transport fine sediments such as sand, silt, and clay. Unlike streams, wind is not confined to a relatively narrow channel. It can transport sediment over long distances and vast areas.

Glacial Erosion

Glaciers are nature's bulldozers. As the glacier moves forward due to basal sliding, the underlying topography is severely abraded because of the immense pressure on the rock base due to the weight of the glacier. The key factor in the glacial erosion process is the meltwater. It causes frost wedging, which initiates the erosional sequence. As the glacier moves forward on the meltwater, some of the water seeps into cracks and freezes. This frost wedging causes a further widening and weakening of the rock material. The glacier plucks the fragments out of the cracks and pushes them along the base. These fragments act as a scouring pad. As they increase in size and amount, they abrade the topography. The grinding motion due to the glacial weight increases as the mass moves forward, picking up more fragments and causing striations in the underlying rock. Glaciers can move rock fragments varying in size from pebbles to entire boulders. Fine fragments are referred to as **rock flour**. Boulder sized rock units moved to other locations are called **eratics**.

SKILL 21.3 Relate depositional patterns to the properties of the transported particles

Wind velocity and size of the sediment determines the amount of material transported. Winds are generally stronger in desert areas than in humid climates. Although wind seldom moves particulates larger than sand grains, the wind-blown sand can act as a giant scouring agent, shaping isolated boulders, cobble, and pebbles into a Ventifact**:** a rock with a flat, wind-eroded surface. Desert Pavement (Regolith) is a thin, closely packed layer of gravel and is another feature of wind blown erosion. Essentially, the wind removes the fine sediments leaving behind the heavier rock material. This pebble size rock layer helps to protect the surface from further deflation.

Depositions

The loose sediment carried by the wind eventually falls back to the surface and can form a **loess**: unweathered, loosely consolidated angular grains of quartz, feldspar, and other minerals. Loess has high porosity and can form into layers exceeding 300 feet in depth. Soils that develop from the loess are usually very rich and extensively farmed, such as the grain fields of the American Midwest and Pacific Northwest.

In sharp contrast to the stratified loess are **sand dunes**: mounds of loose sand grains deposited by the wind. Dunes have the tendency to accumulate in regions that have strong winds blowing in the same direction. Although deserts are likely candidates to develop sand dunes, as evidenced by the Great Sahara Desert in Africa, which contains vast **sand seas**, patches of sand dunes are also found in other areas. Dunes are also common to beaches. Beach dunes are found along the shores of both coastlines and inland near the Great Lakes.

SKILL 21.4 Demonstrate an understanding of the processes by which given landscape features are formed

Differential Weathering

Differential weathering occurs when rocks on a landscape weather at different rates. The effect of these differences can create fantastic landscape features with some rocks upright, arched, or nested in deep depressions. Examples include Ship Rock, Devil's Tower, and the other mesa and butte formations in Monument Valley.

Desert Landforms

Spectacular landscape forms arise from the differentiated erosion of desert materials. Typical of this is the Colorado Plateau, where pockets of highly resistant materials may be surrounded by, or border, materials of lesser resistance. As these lesser resistant materials slowly erode away, they leave behind characteristic formations.

- Plateau: a broad, flat-topped area elevated above the land and partially bounded by cliffs.
- Mesa: a broad, flat-topped hill bounded by cliffs and capped with a resistant rock layer.
- Butte: a narrow, steep-sided, flat-topped pinnacle of resistant rock.
- Monocline: step-like folds of resistant rock layers protruding as ridges above the surface.
- Hogback: an eroded monocline that forms a steeply tilted ridge with equal sloped sides.
- Cuesta: an eroded monocline that forms a ridge with one steep side and one gently sloping side.

Another prominent geographic feature in the American Southwest is called the **Basin and Range**. This area is the result of faulting. The area is comprised of flat valley floors separating rugged mountains. These areas are bound by faults and tectonic movement along these faults have uplifted the mountains and dropped the valley floors as down-dropped blocks. As rain falls in the mountains, rapid erosion of the steep mountain faces cause deposition of materials on the valley floors. These can create Alluvial Fans at the base of the mountains. The fans widen as they flow out of the narrow canyons. Some of the sediment is carried out from the alluvial fan to form **Playa Lakes** further outward on the valley floor.

Playa lakes are very shallow and typically evaporate after a few days, leaving behind a thin layer of mud on the valley floor. When baked hard by the Sun, this forms a Playa, which is typically flat and cracked. If the runoff contained large amounts of dissolved salts, or salts are brought to the surface by groundwater, the playa surface will be covered by a bright layer of dried salt instead of the darker, sediment mud.

A **bajada** forms from the conjunction of the cone-shaped alluvial fans to form a broad, gently sloping depositional surface. A **pediment** forms uphill from a bajada as the cliff face erodes and retreats, leaving a gently sloping surface covered with a thin layer of gravel. The pediment's upper limit is marked by the point where the slope abruptly changes.

Glacial Erosional Features

After a glacier melts, it leaves behind its distinct mark on the landscape. One of the most common of these features is the **Alpine Glacier Valley**. These are usually easy to recognize. A characteristic of glacial landscaping is the U-shaped valley. These are usually situated in previously carved areas caused by streams. However, the glacier's movement straightens out the curves normally associated with streams and also carves the sides of valley, neatly removing or dramatically shortening any ridges that extend in its path. **Truncated Spurs** – the lowest part of the intruding ridges - are the result of this movement.

- Cirque: a steep-sided, rounded hollow at the head of a glacial valley. The cirque is one of the most prominent features associated with Alpine style glaciation.
- Horn: the sharp peak formed by the erosional action of cirques. The mountain is cut back on several sides, forming the prominence.
- Arete: sharp ridges that separate the valleys carved by glaciers.

Continental Erosional Features

- Till: the fragments that are abraded from the bedrock and deposi the path of the glacier. The till are usually angular shaped and uns
- Moraine: a body of till carried along or deposited by a glacier. This lo material falls from the side of the glacier and accumulates along the e of the ice path in the valleys.
- Lateral Moraine: piles of till along the sides of a glacier.
- Medial Moraine: a single long ridge of till carried down the central path of a glacier.
- End Moraine: a ridge of till that piles up at the edge of the ice sheet.
- Terminal Moraine: a type of end moraine that marks the furthest advance of the glacier.
- Recessional Moraine: a type of end moraine that marks the temporary terminus of receding glaciers.
- Ground Moraine: an extensive, thin layer of deposited till that creates the rolling topography of areas once affected by glaciation.
- Drumlin: a streamlined hill of till shaped like the bowl of an inverted spoon. The long axis of the drumlin is parallel to the direction of the ice movement.

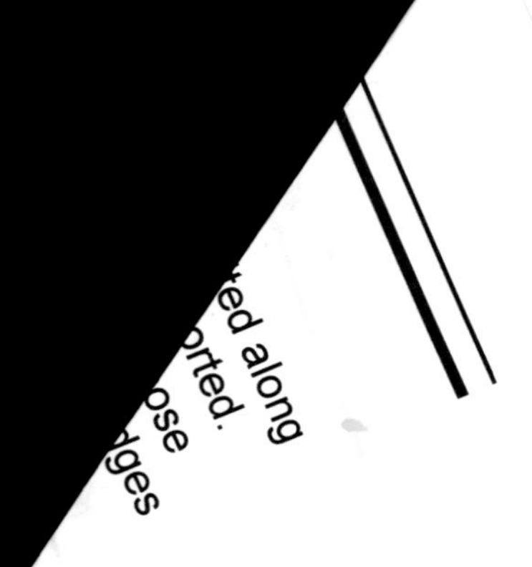

…NDERSTAND CHARACTERISTICS OF THE …JOR GEOLOGIC TIME DIVISIONS AND …ORIES AND SUPPORTING EVIDENCE …ARDING EARTH'S GEOLOGIC HISTORY AND …VOLUTION OF LIFE.

…les of stratigraphy (e.g., principle of … principle of superposition) to interpret …ta

…cks, soils, and sediments- are piled upon each other in …a. Understanding the relative orientation and arrangement of …ovides important information about the Earth's history and the …ng sequence of events and processes that helped to shape that history. …ertain assumptions come into play when determining the sequence of events and correlating stratigraphic layers. These assumptions are the basis for the Principles of Geology.

THE BASIC PRINCIPLES (LAWS) OF GEOLOGY

Principle of Uniformitarianism: Processes that are happening today also happened in the past.

Principle of Cross-Cutting Relations: A rock is younger than any rock it cuts across.

Principle of original Horizontality: Rock units are originally laid down flat. Something happened to cause them to change orientation.

Principle of Inclusion: Any rock enclosed within another rock must be older than the rock in which it is enclosed.

Principle of Original Lateral Continuity: A rock unit extends out in all directions.

Principle of Super Position: The rock on the bottom is older than the rock on top.

Principle of Biologic Succession: Fossils correspond to particular periods of time.

Stratigraphy: the study of regional landforms with the aim of detailing and understanding the sequence of events and relative timeframe in which those events occurred within the regions.

Sequence of Events: To understand the basic sequence of events for a particular landform, you must think in relative terms. In other words, something happened before or after to cause the event. At this point, don't be overly concerned about absolute dates, but concentrate instead on determining a sequence of events of a landform's strata in terms relative to each other.

SKILL 22.2 Demonstrate an understanding of the principles, applications, and limits of radioactive dating

(5)

Radiometric Dating: The **most accurate** method of absolute dating, this technique measures the decay of naturally occurring radioactive isotopes. These isotopes are great timekeepers because their rate of decay is constant. Elements decay because of the inherent structure of the nucleus of the atoms. Neutrons hold the positively charged protons together. However, the positive protons attempt to repel each other. In some heavy elements, the protons repel each other to such a degree that the proton tears itself apart (decays) and by losing protons, becomes another element. The decay starts the moment an isotope crystallizes in a rock unit, and chemicals, weathering, environment, or temperature does not affect the rate of decay.

The radioactive decay causes the mother element to change into a daughter element. The Mother-Daughter relationship of produced nuclides during the series of isotope decay is the basis for radiometric dating. Although many isotopes are used in radiometric dating, the most widely known method is referred to as **Carbon-14 dating**. Carbon-14 is unstable and decays, decomposes, and transmutes to Carbon-12. The dating process compares the ratio of Carbon-14 to Carbon-12 in an object. Since the decay occurs at a known rate, it is very predictable and can be used as a clock standard. However, Carbon-14 decays quickly and can only be used to date organic compounds less than 40,000 years old.

Knowing the **Half-Life** of the isotopes is the key factor in the radiometric dating process. If we know the half-life, we can compare the ratio of isotopes found in the object, and count backward to get an accurate date. The most common element checked is the ratio of Uranium to Lead. Example: 1 gram of 238Uranium. After 100 million years, you have 0.013g of 206Pb (lead) and 0.989 of 238U. After 4.5 billion years, you have 0.433g 206Pb and .500g of 238U. Therefore, the half-life of 238U is roughly 4.5 billion years.

Note: Only Carbon-14 can be used to date organic compounds. The other isotopes are not found in organic compounds.

Radiometric Isotopes Commonly Used in Absolute Dating

Mother Isotope	Daughter Isotope	Half-life (in years)	Dating Range (in years)
40K (Potassium)	10Ar (Aragon)	1.3 billion	>10 million
87 Rb (Rubidium)	87St (Strontium)	47 billion	>100 million
235U (Uranium)	407U (Uranium)	700 million	>1 million
14C (Carbon)	206 Pb (Lead)	5,730	>750<40,000

SKILL 22.3 Compare and contrast the environmental conditions and characteristic fossils of the various geologic periods

Principle of Biologic Succession: Fossils correspond to particular periods of time.

Guide fossils: These are fossils with a wide geographical distribution but narrow stratigraphic range. They are used to correlate the times of deposition of the layers above and below the disconformity. These guide fossils are excellent geologic tools because they existed only during a known geologic time range.

Type of Environment: By studying the fossil's records, we can reconstruct what type of environment was present. A combination of fossils and sediments can often show what type of environment was present.

Archean Eon

The oldest fossil found is approximately 3.4 - 3.5 billion years old. The Archean Eon is defined as 3.8 to 2.5 billion years ago. The early Earth was very hot, with a warm, toxic ocean. Totally devoid of Oxygen, it was composed of Hydrogen Sulfide, Methane, Ammonia, and Carbon Dioxide. Life began in the ocean. There wasn't an ozone (0_3) layer because there wasn't any oxygen (0_2) to be altered into ozone. Without ozone, Ultra-Violet *(UV)* radiation from the Sun scrambles the DNA inside a cell.

Early, Middle, and Late Proterozoic Eon

The Proterozoic Eon: 2.5 billion years ago (bya) to 570 million years ago (mya), is divided into 3 Periods.

Early Proterozoic: The Animike Group of banded iron formations formed. These Red Beds are important because they herald the appearance of significant amounts of oxygen on the Earth. The red color is produced by rust. The rust indicates the presence of oxygen acting upon the ferrous material present in the ocean, and eventually, on the land. The presence of significant amounts of oxygen allows ozone to form, which in turn, screens out the harmful ultra-violet (UV) rays. This makes life possible outside of the protective confines of the ocean. Around 1.9 billon years ago there is an abundance of primitive bacteria. We know of this diversity through the discovery of the Gunflint Chert, an assemblage of many different types of bacterial fossils.

Middle Proterozoic: Development of Eukayotic fossils (fossils other than bacteria).

Late Proterozoic: First evidence of multi-cellular organisms- **Edicaran Fauna**- at 1.0 billion years ago. Cells are organized into tissues and tissues are organized into organs.

The Phanerozoic Eon

The Phanerozoic Eon: 570 million years ago (mya) to present time, is divided into 3 Eras, the Paleozoic, the Mesozoic, and the Cenozoic.

Pealeozoic Era

The Paleozoic Era: 570 to 245 million years ago (mya), was a time of great evolutionary change and begins with the development of the organisms' ability to secrete hard parts. Both invertebrates and vertebrates were abundant.

Mesozoic Era

The Mesozoic Era: 245 to 66 million years ago (mya). The climate is changing throughout the Mesozoic. It starts as cool and dry because of the formation of Pangea. However, as Pangea breaks up, the climate warms throughout the Mesozoic, and it is very warm by the Cretaceous Period. Tropical conditions extend to 70 degrees north and south latitude. Dinosaurs appear.

Cenozoic Era: The Age of Mammals

The Cenozoic Era: 66 million years ago (mya) to present. Plants, marine invertebrates, and mammals are abundant, but dinosaurs are not. Primates first appear in the fossil record around 48 million years ago.

Primate Classification

Classified as Order Primata, with two suborders: Prosimian and Anthropoid.

1. **Prosimian**. (More primitive.) The Prosimians that remain today are small, nocturnal creatures.
2. **Anthropoid**. (Apes, monkeys, and man.) The split between Prosimian and Anthropoid occurred around 33-34 million years ago.

- Ramapithecus-the common ancestor to both man and ape-appeared around 10 million years ago.
- Australopithecus afarensis: appeared 3.5 million years ago. Bipedal, 3-4 ft. tall, with long arms and an ape-like jaw (jutting forward).
- Australopithecus africanus: Appeared *3-2* million years ago. Still unable to have articulated speech, primarily because of skull and neck construction.
- Australopithecus robustus: Appeared 2-1.5 million years ago. Flat face and forehead. Very heavily built.
- Australopithecus bosei: Appeared 2-1.5 million years ago. Contemporary to Australopithecus robustus. Very large build but slightly smaller than robustus.
- Homo habilis: Appeared around 2 million years ago. Face very ape-like. Walked upright. Used primitive tools.
- Homo erectus ("Peking Man and Java Man"): Appeared around 1.5 million years ago. Homo erectus is considered to be the first true species of humans.
- Homo sapiens (Archaic): Appeared between 500,000 and 250,000 years ago. Represents a transition between Homo erectus and Homo Sapiens.
- Homo sapiens neanderthalensis (Neanderthal): Appears 250,000 to 125,000 years ago. Neanderthals were short in height, but big boned and very heavyset.
- Homo sapiens sapiens (Cro-Magnon): First appeared 35,000 years ago. Had modern human type features. Homo sapiens sapiens eventually emerged as the sole surviving species of the Homo genus.

SKILL 22.4 Use stratigraphic and paleontological information to infer the geologic history of a given area

Theories on the origin of life

The origin of life and the environment from which life has formed is widely studied and theorized. Oparin developed the idea of a "primordial soup." He stated the coacervates, or organic material that resembles a lipid, can form out of an oxygen free environment through exposure to sunlight. These coacervates are not cells in and of themselves, but through "fusion" may develop into primitive cells. Generally it is accepted that amino acids can form from pre-biotic conditions. The amino acids can combine to form a lipid by-layer that is similar to the cell membrane. There is polymerization of nucleotides and RNA is developed. Ribosomes are formed and protein synthesis begins.

Fossils

Fossils are remains of organic material found in the bedrock. Fossils may be difficult to find as there are many Earth processes that destroy organic remains, such as metamorphism and igneous activity. Many of the fossils that are found are exoskeletons, shells, and bones. Soft tissue fossils are extremely rare. There are two major types of fossils: fossilized bodies (such as bones claws, teeth, and shells) and trace fossils or ichnofossils (footprints, nests, and dung).

Methods of fossilization

Carbonization: The process of compression and compaction of organic materials in anaerobic environment.

Mold: An impression of the organism in sediment. External mold is an impression of the outside of a shell; an internal mold is the impression of an inside of a shell. After the impression is made, the organism dissolves.

Cast: An organism dissolves leaving an empty void in the sediment. These cavities are filled forming a natural cast.

Permineralization: Minerals infiltrate into pores in the hard material of the organism (i.e. shell or bone). The mineral preserves the structure.

Replacement: The hard material from the structure is dissolved and replaced with other minerals. The size and structure are imperfectly preserved.

Use of the fossil record

Scientists use the fossil record in order to determine past environments at specific locations. Through the study of paleobotany, paleoclimatology, and paleoecology, scientists can create a succession for a specific area or can create a timeline for Earth's history. It is also helpful in determining how past climates have affected organisms so that we can determine how climate change might affect today's organisms.

SKILL 22.5 Apply the fossil record as evidence for evolutionary change

Fossils are the keys to understanding biological history. They are the preserved remnants left by an organism that lived in the past. Scientists have established the geological time scale to determine the age of a fossil. The geological time scale is broken down into four eras: the Precambrian, Paleozoic, Mesozoic, and Cenozoic. The eras are further broken down into periods that represent a distinct age in the history of Earth and its life. Scientists use rock layers called strata to date fossils. The older layers of rock are at the bottom. This allows scientists to correlate the rock layers with the era they date back to. Radiometric dating is a more precise method of dating fossils. Rocks and fossils contain isotopes of elements accumulated over time. The isotope's half-life is used to date older fossils by determining the amount of isotope remaining and comparing it to the half-life.

Dating fossils is helpful to construct an evolutionary tree. Scientists can arrange the succession of animals based on their fossil record. The fossils of an animal's ancestors can be dated and placed on its evolutionary tree. For example, the branched evolution of horses shows the progression of the modern horse's ancestors to be larger, to have a reduced number of toes, and have teeth modified for grazing.

COMPETENCY 23.0 UNDERSTAND THE PROCESSES BY WHICH WATER MOVES THROUGH THE HYDROLOGIC CYCLE, AND USE THIS KNOWLEDGE TO ANALYZE LOCAL WATER BUDGETS.

SKILL 23.1 Analyze the components of the hydrologic cycle (e.g., evaporation, runoff, transpiration, infiltration)

The hydrologic cycle of water movement is driven by solar radiation from the Sun. The cycle of evaporation from the oceans and precipitation over land is the methodology employed by nature to maintain the water balance at any given location. The Earth constantly cycles water. It evaporates from the sea, falls as rain, and flows over the land as it returns to the ocean. The constant circulation of water among sea, land, and the atmosphere is called the **hydrologic cycle**.

Evaporation

Water is constantly in motion on the Earth. As the water evaporates from the sea, it becomes water vapor in the atmosphere. Although a small amount of water evaporates from the land and inland waterways, the majority of evaporation occurs over the oceans. An additional small amount of evaporated water comes from plants as they breathe using the process of transpiration.

Precipitation

The water vapor in the atmosphere is returned to the Earth in the form of precipitation. Precipitation includes rain, hail, snow, and sleet. The amount of precipitation varies according to location, with some areas of Earth receiving plentiful moisture, and others receiving little. However, the overall proportional balance of evaporation and precipitation remains relatively constant.

Runoff

As the moisture returns to the Earth's surface in the form of precipitation, the liquid moves across the land according to the topology, with most of the water eventually flowing back into the oceans. Thus the cycle starts over.

SKILL 23.2 Evaluate the effects of various factors (e.g., vegetation, gradient, rock characteristics) on components of a local water budget

In sediments or soils, **porosity** refers to the amount of void or open space between grains. It is usually represented as a percentage or fraction from 0-1. In very loose sediments with large, round grains, porosity can be as high as 50%. In poorly sorted sediments with a variety of grain sizes, smaller particles fill the voids and porosity can range down to 20-30%. Rocks have much lower porosity, with sedimentary rocks being more porous than granitic rocks, which may have a porosity as low as 0.01 (1%). Fractures in the rock may also increase porosity and affect water flow in unpredictable ways. This is known as **secondary porosity**.

Permeability is the ability of sediments or soils to allow the flow of water or another liquid such as oil. Permeability is related to porosity, but also depends on the size and connectedness of the pore spaces. Permeability is expressed in units of cm^2. Generally, sandy or gravelly soils are much more permeable than clays or silts, even though clays and silts have a relatively high porosity. In clays and silts the pore spaces are so small that it is hard for water to pass through them. Water has a high **surface tension**, and therefore it cannot penetrate into very small spaces.

Permeability values of 10^{-3} to 10^{-6} cm^2 are considered to be high-medium permeability and make good groundwater aquifers (often sands and gravels or highly fractured rock), while permeability values of 10^{-11} cm^2 or smaller (often silts and clays or unfractured rock) are considered impermeable and are barriers to flow. Permeability is measured in the laboratory or the field using a pump test.

Water pressure is the height at which water will rise in a well, or **hydraulic head**. The height of water in an unconfined aquifer is known as the **water table**, which may fluctuate with rainfall, tides, or human extraction. Aquifers confined by a low-permeability layer may contain water under higher pressure. If a well is drilled into such an aquifer, the water may rise higher than the confining layer.

These various properties are combined into **Darcy's Law**, which predicts the rate of discharge of water through soils or sediment:

$$Q = \frac{-\kappa A}{\mu} \frac{(P_b - P_a)}{L}$$

where:
Q = discharge volume of water (cm^3/sec)
κ = intrinsic permeability of soil or sediment (cm^2)
A = cross-sectional area through which the water flows (cm^2)
$P_b - P_a$ = water pressure change over the distance L (Pa)
μ = viscosity of water (Pa-sec)
L = distance (cm)

This equation is also frequently written as:

$$q = -K(\Delta h/\Delta l)$$

where: q = Darcy flow velocity (cm/sec)
K = hydraulic conductivity (cm/sec)
Δh = change in water pressure or hydraulic head (m)
Δl = distance over which water travels (m)

The quantity ($\Delta h/\Delta l$), also notated as i, is known as the **hydraulic gradient**, or the change in hydraulic head over distance. Notice that water only flows from higher to lower hydraulic head, which is why the sign of the equation is negative. The greater the hydraulic gradient, the greater the flow will be.

The Darcy flow velocity q assumes that water takes a straight path through the aquifer. However, water actually has to navigate through the pore spaces and because of this, takes an indirect path through the sediments. The actual velocity of the water required to navigate through the pore spaces and create the Darcy flow velocity q is called the **mean porewater velocity**, and is higher than the Darcy velocity. This quantity is given by the following equation:

$$v = q/\phi$$

where: v = mean porewater velocity (cm/sec)
q = Darcy flow velocity
ϕ = porosity

Example: What is the mean porewater velocity in a sandy aquifer with a hydraulic conductivity of 1.5 cm/sec and a porosity of 0.43, if the hydraulic head decreases by 10 m over a distance of 1 km?

Solution: First, use the flow version of Darcy's law to calculate the Darcy flow velocity:

$$q = -1.5 \text{ cm/sec} \times -10 \text{ m} / 1000 \text{ m} = 0.015 \text{ cm/sec}$$

Next, use the equation for mean porewater velocity to find the solution:

$v = 0.015$ cm/sec / 0.43 = 0.035 cm/sec

SKILL 23.3 Analyze the energy transformations that occur as water moves through the hydrologic cycle

As water moves through each stage of the hydrologic cycle, it changes state (phase) and has an accompanying energy transfer. This transfer is based upon the basic laws of physics and chemistry and will involve either an exothermic or endothermic reaction. As the cycle begins over the oceans, the solar radiation heats the water sufficiently to cause the liquid to change phase.

Evaporation

In a closed system, a rise in temperature is accompanied by a rise in pressure. However, in the case of the hydrologic cycle where the system is relatively open, a rise in temperature is not necessarily accompanied by a rise in pressure. The increase in temperature in comparison to the surroundings causes high-speed molecules within the water to attempt to change phase (to become a gas). In a closed system phase equilibrium is reached where the flow of molecules caused by the rise in temperature and ambient pressure is roughly equal, and if the temperature rises further, more high-speed molecules escape into a gaseous state and the liquid boils away. However, in an open system such as the oceans, the release of molecules from liquid into a gaseous state continues without reaching equilibrium. As the molecules are continually removed, the liquid to gas process (evaporation) continues until no liquid is left. Given the volume of the oceans and the relatively cool temperatures involved, the oceans simply evaporate a thin layer of water, rather than the entire ocean. So why don't the oceans boil? Two factors keep this from happening. First, the temperature of the water is generally well below that required to boil water and the salinity of the water further raises the boiling point. Also, the remaining molecules (the slower ones) absorb heat from their surroundings (endothermic) and, in effect, help cause the ocean to remain relatively cool. Secondly, the atmospheric pressure remains constant, keeping the amount of high-speed molecules at a minimum.

Precipitation

Precipitation is generally the reverse of evaporation. As the heated, energetic water molecules in gaseous form rise in altitude, they encounter a different pressure and temperature environment and cool, giving off heat (exothermic). Eventually they cool enough to condense- return to a liquid phase- and fall back to the surface, usually in the form of rain.

Runoff

The energy transferred during the runoff part of the hydrologic cycle is largely the relationship of potential versus kinetic energy, and depends greatly on the topology of the area over which the water flows on its return path to the ocean.

COMPETENCY 24.0 UNDERSTAND THE PROCESSES BY WHICH WATER MOVES ON AND BENEATH EARTH'S SURFACE.

SKILL 24.1 Analyze the role of the hydrologic cycle in shaping Earth's surface

Groundwater

Groundwater is derived from precipitation during the hydrologic cycle. Groundwater is usually at a constant temperature and free of contaminants and suspended load. Only minimal treatment is required to remove man-induced toxins and lead. Groundwater is generally chemically uniform and classified as hardwater. **Hardwater**: water that has a high concentration of calcium, magnesium, and iron. Hardwater leaves red rings and a hard film because of its mineral deposits. Red deposits are from iron. Soap is not as sudsy in hardwater as it would be in soft water. Hardwater can be turned into **softwater** through the use of sodium in equipment designed to exchange sodium for the calcium, magnesium, and iron. Groundwater flows and the path taken by it somewhat mirrors the topography of the area.

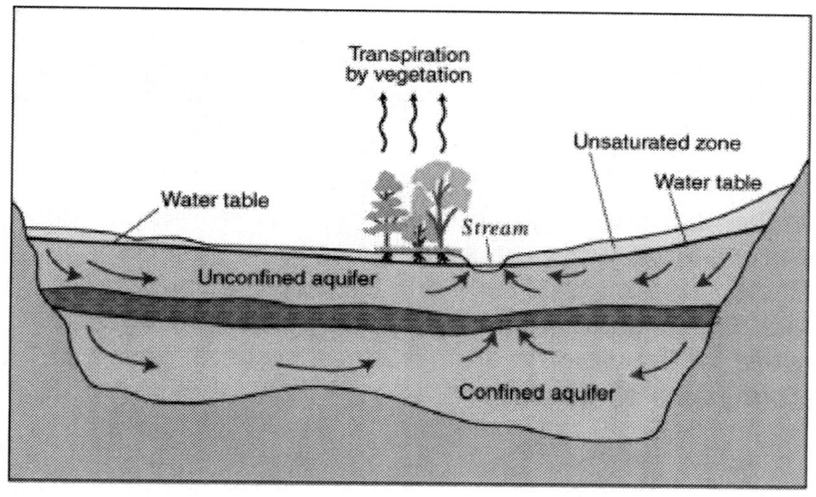

EXPLANATION

- High hydraulic-conductivity aquifer
- Low hydraulic-conductivity confining unit
- Very low hydraulic-conductivity bedrock
- ← Direction of ground-water flow

Landscape Alterations By Groundwater

Groundwater is very effective in dissolving limestone, forming caves and sinkholes. Chemical leeching combined with groundwater produces Carbonic acid ($CO_2 + H_20 = H_2C0_3$), and this acid dissolves the limestone, riddling an area with underground holes.

- Cave: an empty space underground. The majority of caves are formed by carbonate dissolution. 95% are made of limestone.
- Speleotherm: a general term for a deposit in a cave.
    - Stalactite: mineral formations from the ceiling.
    - Stalagmite: mineral formation built up from the floor.
    - Column: mineral formations at the top and bottom of the cave that have joined together.
- Sinkhole: a collapsed cave. Often a void in the limestone will fill with water and, during times of drought, the water recedes from the cave. The water supported the material in the cave and the newly unsupported weight of the cave ceiling collapses. Sinkholes are unpredictable in terms of when and where they will occur. They can be huge in scope and often become small lakes dotting the landscape.
- Thermal Spring (Hot Spring): These are common in volcanic regions where an active magma chamber is at depth. This heat source causes nearby groundwater to become warm where the water table is exposed to the surface (a spring).
- Geyser: a thermal spring that erupts. The processes behind the eruption are very similar to those involved in boiling water in a teakettle. A constriction forms in the connected chambers of a spring. The water heats under pressure, turns to steam, and erupts with great force past the constriction. The ejected steam condenses and returns to a liquid state. The water draws back into its chambers and the process begins again. Because it takes awhile for the water to drain back and reheat, geysers often erupt on a determinable schedule.

Desert Erosion

The majority of rainfall is sourced from evaporation of seawater. The greater the distance from the ocean, when taken in conjunction with the presence of mountains creating a rain shadow effect, the more likely the formation of deserts. Because deserts typically have sparse vegetation and the water cannot soak into the sun-baked ground, its runoff is rapid, and often creates a **Flash Flood**. These torrents erode the landscape and are laden with sediment that, as the floodwaters subside, coats the now dry streambed with a layer of sand and gravel. The rapid movement of the water also encourages a heavy downcutting effect, sculpting narrow canyons with vertical walls and graveled floors. The shortage of water slows the chemical weathering process to such a degree that minerals seldom break down into fine-grained clay products. Desert features usually look angular rather than rounded, due to the differentiated erosional effect on the materials present. In the desert, Limestone is much more resistant to erosion than in wet areas. Most igneous and metamorphic rocks are also resistant, and shale is the least resistant, forming a gentler slope.

SKILL 24.2 Analyze the factors affecting the flow of water in streams (e.g., discharge, sediment load, cross-sectional shape)

Streams: a body of water confined to a channel. Regardless of size, geologists call all moving bodies of water confined to a channel "streams".

Key Factors of a Stream

- Discharge: the volume of water flowing past a given point over a specific length of time.
- Gradient (Slope): the perpendicular angle of the stream channel. Gradient is extremely important in determining the effects of streams. It affects the way a stream changes the landscape. Gradient determines what is moved, the clarity of the stream, and the speed of water movement within a stream.
- Velocity: how fast a stream is moving. Velocity depends on the gradient or slope of a stream, and the steeper the slope, the higher the velocity. The slope is usually steepest at the Head of a stream.

Stream Transportation

- Load: general term used for material carried by a stream. This material is usually the unconsolidated debris that is the product of weathered rock material.
- Bed Load: material that sits on the bed. Usually sand and larger sized particles.
- Depending on its size, the bed load moves in different ways: Sand size: Moves through a process called Saltation (bouncing and hopping along the stream bed). Larger than sand size: Moves through rolling, sliding, and pushing motions. The larger sized the material, the higher the velocity required to move the material.
- Suspended Load: material that is light enough to stay suspended in the water column. Normally this includes silt and clay sized particles that make the water look muddy and cloudy.
- Dissolved Load: ions that dissolve into solution (chemicals leeched from the rocks). Example: The headwaters of the Rockies have a high concentration of calcium leeched from the limestone rocks.
- Competence: the largest particles that can be carried by the stream.
- Capacity Load or Capacity: the total amount of material that a stream can move by any means.

As the water volume and velocity changes, the stream load competence and capacity will also change. If the velocity of the stream is greater, it can hold a larger particle (competence) and move more material (capacity). Since the velocity depends on the gradient (slope), you usually find larger competence closer to the head of a stream, but more capacity near the mouth of a stream, where the mouth is wider.

Stream Deposition: Wherever the velocity slows deposition occurs.

Channel Deposition: Water moves in a curved path because of the rotation of the Earth. This rotational effect causes the water velocity to concentrate on the outside of the curves, where it erodes away the banks of the stream. Sediments are usually sorted by size due to the water's velocity. By the time you reach the mouth of a stream, only the fine-grained material remains.

Stream Patterns

- Dendritic: Most common pattern. Forms when a stream meets uniform resistance of underlying rock or sediment.
- Trellis: The stream flows along faults in rocks. Characterized by straight, parallel streams that turn at right angles.
- Radical: Centralized peak with drainage away.

SKILL 24.3 Analyze factors affecting the movement of groundwater (e.g., permeability, aquifers, gradient)

Groundwater Zones

- Zone of Aeration (Vadose Zone): the underground groundwater zone filled with both water and air.
- Zone of Saturation: the underground groundwater spaces totally filled with water.
- Water Table: the water table marks the top of the Zone of Saturation, and roughly follows the topography.

Aquifer: the porous and permeable layer of rock or sediment through which the groundwater moves freely. An aquifer can exist at any depth. The type of material the water is passing through determines the rate of flow in the aquifer. Depending on the composition of the soil, pockets of aquifers can form. Example: Limestone passes water easily, while sand passes water slowly but still is permeable and porous for forming an aquifer. However, silts and clays are porous, but non-permeable and become Aquitards.

Aquitards: non-pourous, non-permeable layers that trap water in an aquifer.

Porosity and Permeability

- **Porosity**: the amount of pore space in a rock or sediment.
- **Permeability**: the ability for a fluid to flow through a substance.

SKILL 24.4 Analyze a cross-sectional diagram of a water table and surrounding regolith and bedrock to predict the movement of groundwater and the behavior of wells

Regolith: The layer of loose rock resting on bedrock. Also called mantle rock, this constitutes the surface of most land.

Water Table: the water table marks the top of the Zone of Saturation, and roughly follows the topography.

Pumping Well: a screened well through which water is pumped out of the aquifer.

Artesian Well: a well that is sunk into an aquifer that is under pressure. Artesian wells are simply aquifers under pressure. The pressure is caused by the potential energy of the position of the water. Fully saturated zones have more water pushed into them. Artesian wells are often found in the mountains. The material at the top of the mountains is more porous because of the effects of weathering. The higher water table forces more pressure on the aquifer at the bottom of the slope. There is no difference in the water quality between regular wells and artesian wells.

Recharge: replenishing of the groundwater. Recharge is done naturally through the hydrological cycle.

Spring: a place where the water table intersects the land surface.

Cone of Depression: the lowering of the water table adjacent to a well. The deeper the well pipe and the amount of suction placed on it, the greater the cone of depression.

Porosity: the percent of pore space in the bedrock. The porosity indicates how much water the rock can "hold". Gravel sized rounded clasts of well sorted rock has the greatest porosity. Mud sized clasts (such as shale), or poorly sorted angular clasts have low porosity.

Permeability: The ability of a rock to let water pass through it. The greater the fracture in the bedrock, the higher the permeability.

Capillary fringe: The capillary fringe is the area in the zone of aeration where the water may move due to capillary action.

Zone of aeration: Area in the bedrock where the pore spaces are filled with air.

Zone of saturation or phreatic zone: Area in the bedrock where the pore spaces are filled with water.

Unconfined aquifer: Receives the majority of the water as recharge from the surface. Not bound by a confining layer.

Confined aquifer: usually found beneath an unconfined aquifer. Separated by an impermeable layer of rock.

Confining layer or aquitard: Layer of rock that restricts the flow of groundwater from one area to another.

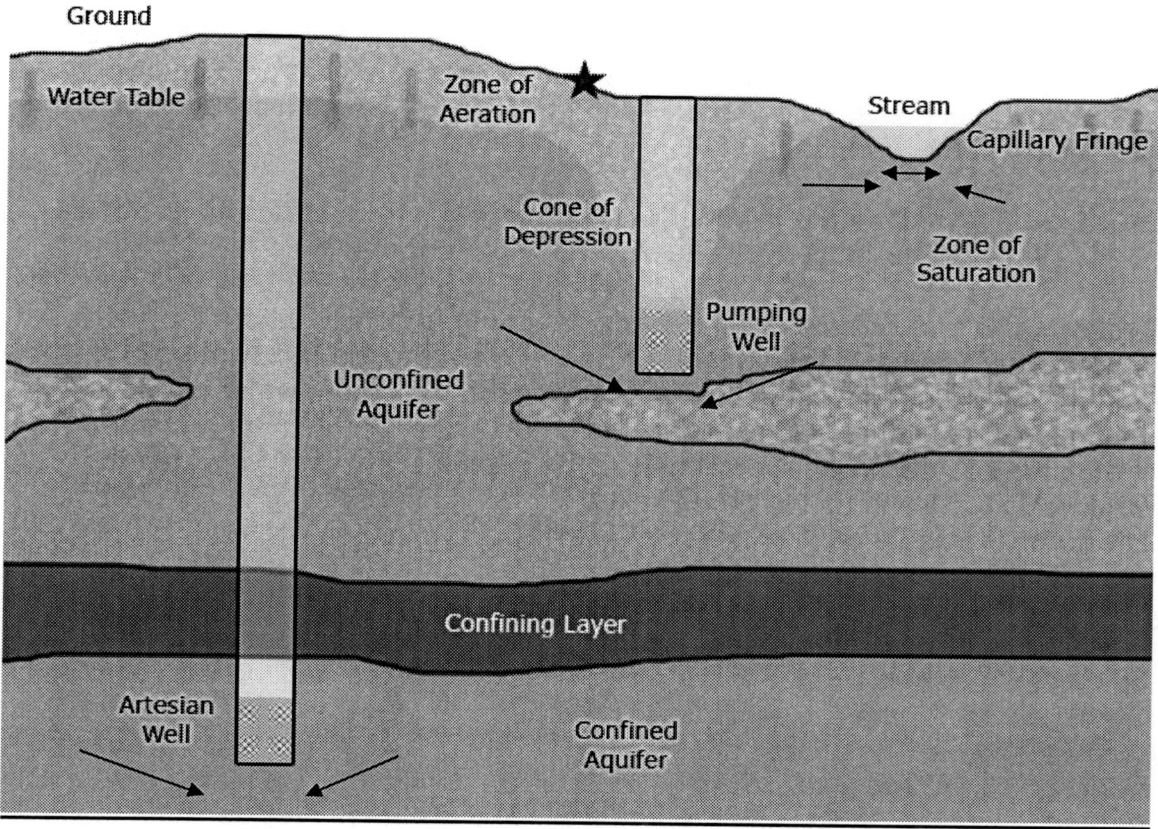

Figure 1: Cross-section of groundwater

Analysis of groundwater cross-section

The water table beneath the surface generally follows the topography of the surface. When the water table meets the surface, a stream, lake, pond, or wetland occurs. The relationship between a stream and the groundwater is one of equilibrium. Generally, the groundwater feeds the stream and the stream feeds water back into the ground.

Pumping wells act as a vacuum. As water is pumped out of the ground, the suction created causes a cone of depression. In times of drought, this zone of depression can get quite large. Other wells in the area, particularly if they are shallow, may run dry. If contamination occurred at the star on the diagram above, the pumping of the groundwater from the pumping well will pull the contamination down into the aquifer. The more pumping that takes place, the closer the contamination plume would get to the pumping well.

The confining layer, or aquitard, separates the confined aquifer from the unconfined aquifer. Wells that tap the confined aquifer are often artesian wells. Since the confining layer does not allow the transfer of water from the unconfined aquifer, pumping of water in the confined aquifer does not cause a cone of depression in the water table.

SKILL 24.5 Analyze the interactions between groundwater and surface water (e.g., springs, swamps, marshes)

Groundwater and surface water interact. A spring is located where the groundwater intersects the surface. A spring is usually the headwaters of a stream. As the stream is fed by the groundwater, the groundwater is also fed by the stream. Therefore, if pumping of the groundwater occurs near a stream, the stream may be depleted. Conversely, if the stream is pumped for water, the water table will lower as the groundwater will continue to recharge the stream. The same is true for contamination plumes. Contamination will freely move between the groundwater and the stream water.

Wetlands (swamps and marshes), serve a very important purpose in the interaction between surface water and groundwater. The wetland will serve as a recharge area for the groundwater. The vegetation filters out contaminates before they enter the ground or stream. The wetland also acts as an area to moderate runoff into a stream. Sediment is able to settle in the marsh before it enters the stream. In times of drought a wetland is able to provide water to the stream and replenish the groundwater supply.

COMPETENCY 25.0 UNDERSTAND THE STRUCTURE, COMPOSITION, AND PROPERTIES OF EARTH'S OCEANS AND THE CAUSES AND PROPERTIES OF CURRENTS AND WAVES.

SKILL 25.1 Analyze the composition of seawater (e.g., elements, dissolved gases, salinity)

Seventy percent of the Earth's surface is covered with saltwater which is termed the hydrosphere. The mass of this saltwater is about 1.4×10^{24} grams. The ocean waters continuously circulate among different parts of the hydrosphere. There are seven major oceans: the North Atlantic Ocean, South Atlantic Ocean, North Pacific Ocean, South Pacific Ocean, Indian Ocean, Arctic Ocean, and the Antarctic Ocean.

Pure water is a combination of the elements hydrogen and oxygen. These two elements make up about 96.5% of ocean water. The remaining portion is made up of dissolved solids. The concentration of these dissolved solids determines the water's salinity. Salinity is the number of grams of dissolved salts in 1,000 grams of seawater. The average salinity of ocean water is about 3.5%. In other words, one kilogram of seawater contains about 35 grams of salt. This is also sometimes measured in ppt (parts per thousand). Sodium Chloride, or salt (NaCl), is the most abundant of the dissolved salts. The dissolved salts also include smaller quantities of magnesium chloride, magnesium and calcium sulfates, and traces of several other salt elements. Salinity varies throughout the worlds oceans. The total salinity of the oceans varies from place to place and also varies with depth. Salinity is low near river mouths where the ocean mixes with fresh water, and salinity is high in areas with high evaporation rates.

SKILL 25.2 Analyze the relationship between the physical properties of ocean water (e.g., temperature, pressure, density, light) and depth

The temperature of the ocean water varies with different latitudes and with ocean depths. Ocean water temperature is constant up to depths of 90 meters (m). The temperature of surface water will drop rapidly from 28° C at the equator to -2° C at the Poles. The freezing point of seawater is lower than the freezing point of pure water. Pure water freezes at 0° C. The dissolved salts in seawater help to keep its freezing point at -2° C. The freezing point of seawater may vary depending on its salinity in a particular location.

The ocean can be divided into three temperature zones. The surface layer consists of a relatively warm water and exhibits most of the wave action present. The area where the wind and waves churn and mix the water is called the mixed layer. This is the layer where most living creatures are found due to abundant sunlight and warmth. The second layer is called the thermocline and it becomes increasingly cold as its depth increases. This change is due to the lack of energy from sunlight. The layer below the thermocline continues to the deep dark, very cold, and semi-barren ocean floor. Pressures on the ocean bottom are immense, and only invertebrates can survive there, however hydrothermal vent communities do exist at these depths.

SKILL 25.3 Analyze forces that affect ocean currents (e.g., Coriolis effect, wind, density)

World weather patterns are greatly influenced by ocean surface currents in the upper layer of the ocean. These currents continuously move along the ocean surface in specific directions. Ocean currents that flow deep below the surface are called sub-surface currents. These currents are influenced by such factors as the location of landmasses in the current's path and the Earth's rotation.

Surface currents are caused by winds and are classified by temperature. Cold currents originate in the Polar regions and flow through surrounding water that is measurably warmer. Those currents with a higher temperature than the surrounding water are called warm currents and can be found near the equator. These currents follow swirling routes around the ocean basins and the equator.

The Gulf Stream and the California Current are the two main surface currents that flow along the coastlines of the United States. The Gulf Stream is a warm current in the Atlantic Ocean that carries warm water from the equator to the northern parts of the Atlantic Ocean. Benjamin Franklin studied and named the Gulf Stream. The California Current is a cold current that originates in the Arctic regions and flows southward along the west coast of the United States.

Differences in water density also create ocean currents. Water found near the bottom of oceans is the coldest and the most dense. Water tends to flow from a denser area to a less dense area. Currents that flow because of a difference in the density of the ocean water are called density currents. Water with a higher salinity is more dense than water with a lower salinity. Water that has a salinity different from the surrounding water may form a density current.

The movement of ocean water is also caused in part by the wind, the Sun's heat energy, the Earth's rotation, the Moon's gravitational pull on Earth, and by underwater earthquakes. Most ocean waves are caused by the impact of winds. Wind blowing over the surface of the ocean transfers energy (friction) to the water and causes waves to form. Waves are also formed by any seismic activity on the ocean floor. A wave formed by an earthquake is called a seismic sea wave. These powerful waves can be very destructive with wave heights increasing to 30 meters or more near the shore.

Sample Test

Directions: The following are multiple choice questions.
Select from each grouping the best answer.

1. Which layer of the atmosphere would you expect most weather to occur?

A. troposphere
B. thermosphere
C. mesosphere

2. What percentage of earth's surface is covered by water?

A. 61%
B. 71%
C. 81%

3. Which layer of the earth's atmosphere contains the Ozone layer?

A. thermosphere
B. troposphere
C. stratosphere

4. Copernicus developed a theory that is known as

A. baycenter
B. heliocentric
C. geocentric

5. The boundary that separates the crust from the mantle is known as

A. Moho
B. shadow zone
C. catacastic

6. The product of intrusive activities would result in forming a

A. cinder cone
B. volcanic pipe
C. dike

7. A star's light and heat are produced by

A. magnetism
B. electricity
C. nuclear fusion

8. The center of an atom is called

A. micron
B. nucleus
C. electron

9. An important food source for animals in a water biome

A. shrimp
B. plankton
C. seaweed

10. The smallest piece of an element is called a/an

A. compound
B. nucleus
C. atom

11. An instrument that measures relative humidity is known as

A. psychrometer
B. anemometer
C. barometer

12. Removing salts from ocean water by heating is called

A. filtration
B. distillation
C. freezing

13. When molecules in the air cool and combine to form rain, _______ has occurred.

A. condensation
B. convection
C. radiation

14. Which instrument measures wind direction?

A. anemometer
B. barometer
C. wind vane

15. The most important cause of erosion is

A. water
B. wind
C. air

16. An anemometer measures

A. wind velocity
B. temperature
C. relative humidity

17. The boundary that develops when a cold air mass meets a warm air mass

A. cold front
B. warm front
C. stationary front

18. When the sun, moon and earth are aligned in a straight line what type of tides are produced?

A. neap tides
B. high tides
C. spring tides

19. North of the equator, currents move in which direction?

A. counter-clock wise
B. clockwise
C. northerly

20. Rocks that serve as aquifers are

A. impermeable
B. permeable
C. igneous

21. Volcanoes with violent eruptions are known as

A. shield volcanoes
B. dome volcanoes
C. cinder volcanoes

22. The Richter scale measures

A. compressions
B. focus
C. magnitude

23. The earth's outer core is probably

A. liquid
B. solid
C. rock-bed

24. What are the two most abundant elements found in the earth's crust?

A. oxygen and oxides
B. oxygen and cabonates
C. oxygen and silicon

25. The San Andreas Fault is classified as a

A. transform fault
B. oblique-slip fault
C. reverse fault

26. Batholiths are the largest structures of which type of rock activity?

A. intrusive rock
B. extrusive rock
C. magma

27. The main agents of chemical weathering are

A. water, oxygen, $C0_2$
B. water, oxygen, sulfur
C. water, oxygen, nitrogen

28. Soil classified as porous is called

A. clay soil
B. laterites soil
C. sandy soil

29. Intrusive igneous rock forms

A. glassy texture
B. small crystals
C. large crystals

30. Which types of rocks are rich sources of fossil remains'?

A. sedimentary rock
B. metamorphic rock
C. intrusive rock

31. The best preserved animal remains have been discovered in

A. resin
B. lava
C. tar-pits

32. The Mid-Atlantic is a major area of which type plate movement?

A. subduction plate movement
B. divergent plate
C. convergent plate

33. When lava cools quickly on the earth's surface the newly formed rock is called

A. clastic
B. intrusive
C. extrusive

34. When a dyke forms with magma flowing in a tub-like structure this is known to be a/an

A. extrusive activity
B. intrusive activity
C. metaphoric activity

35. A caldera is formed when a large depression collapses. This is the result of a

A. sinkhole
B. aquifer
C. volcanic eruption

36. Trenches observed on the sea floor are the results of

A. interaction
B. divergence
C. subduction

37. Alfred Wegener's hypothesis of continental drift was not supported until scientists began studying

A. sea floor
B. mountain ranges
C. volcanoes

38. These massive waves are caused by the displacement of ocean water, and are often the result of underwater earthquakes.

A. epicenters
B. tidal waves
C. tsunamis

39. Sea floor spreading occurs when the earth's crust is stretched and pulled apart in a process called

A. slippage
B. rifting
C. drifting

40. The layer of the atmosphere that is in a plasma state and aids in communication

A. Thermosphere
B. Ionosphere
C. Mesosphere

41. A stream erodes bedrock by grinding sand and rock fragments against each other. This process is defined as:

A. dissolving
B. transportation
C. abrasion

42. Rocks formed from magma are:

A. igneous
B. metamorphic
C. sedimentary

43. Rocks formed by the intense heating or compression of pre-existing rocks are classified as

A. igneous
B. metamorphic
C. sedimentary

44. Rocks made of loose materials that have been cemented together are:

A. igneous
B. metamorphic
C. sedimentary

45. River valley glaciers produce

A. U-shaped erosion
B. V-shaped erosion
C. S-shaped erosion

46. The life cycle of a river with the most cutting power and erosion is known as which stage?

A. youth stage
B. mature stage
C. old age

47. The result of radioactive decay

A. parent element
B. daughter element
C. half-life

48. The most abundant dry gas found in the atmosphere is

A. oxygen
B. nitrogen
C. CO_2

49. A natural groundwater outlet through which boiling water and steam explodes into the air is called a ______.

A. sinkhole
B. artesian system
C. geyser

50. Which of the following rocks make the best aquifer?

A. granite
B. basalt
C. sandstone

51. Sediments that settle out from rivers are called

A. deposits
B. boulders
C. sandstone

52. A hole that remains in the ground after a block of glacier ice melts is called a

A. pothole
B. sinkhole
C. kettle

53. The first sign that a tsunami is approaching a shore is

A. a sudden flatten of the waves
B. water moving from the shore
C. large wall of water on horizon

54. Mountains that have been squeezed into wavelike patterns are called

A. fold mountains
B. dome mountains
C. fault-block mountains

55. The largest ocean is the

A. Atlantic
B. Pacific
C. Indian

56. The major surface current that flows along the east coast of the United States is known as the

A. Bermuda Current
B. Mexican Current
C. Gulf Stream

57. The formation of ocean waves is caused by

A. earth's rotation
B. the moon
C. the wind

58. The most abundant compound found in sea water is

A. chloride
B. calcium carbonate
C. magnesium chloride

59. The distance between two meridians is measured in degrees of

A. longitude
B. latitude
C. magnitude

60. A contour line that has tiny comb-like lines along the inner edge indicates a

A. depression
B. mountain
C. valley

61. Fossils that are used to date strata are called

A. datum fossils
B. index fossils
C. true fossils

62. Which of the following causes the aurora borealis?

A. gases escaping from earth
B. particles from the sun
C. particles from the moon

63. The layer of the atmosphere that shields earth from harmful ultraviolet radiation is called

A. ionic layer
B. ozone layer
C. equatorial layer

64. The layer of the earth's atmosphere that is closest to the earth's surface is the

A. stratosphere layer
B. thermosphere layer
C. troposphere layer

65. The sun transfers its heat to other objects by

A. conduction
B. radiation
C. convection

66. As an air mass expands, it becomes

A. cooler
B. warmer
C. denser

67. Air moving northward from the horse latitudes produces a belt of winds called the

A. prevailing westerlies
B. north westerlies
C. trade winds

68. Which type of cloud always produces precipitation?

A. altostratus
B. cirrostratus
C. nimbostratus

69. An air mass that forms over the Gulf of Mexico is called

A. polar
B. maritime
C. continental

70. Spring tides will occur when the moon is in its

A. quarter phases
B. full and new phases
C. half phases

71. Air pressure is measured using a

A. barometer
B . hydrometer
C. physcrometer

72. The two most abundant elements found in stars are

A. hydrogen and calcium
B. hydrogen and helium
C. hydrogen and neon

73. A comet's tail always points _______ from the sun.

A. towards
B. perpendicular
C. away

74. The dark areas observed on the sun are known as

A. solar flares
B. prominences
C. sun spots

75. An example of distance in degrees of latitude is

A. 55° north
B. 93° east
C. 25° west

76. A scale use to measure the hardness of a mineral is known as the

A. Bowen's scale
B. Mohs' scale
C. Harding scale

77. When a gas changes to a liquid this process is known as

A. evaporation
B. condensation
C. dissolution

78. A fan-shaped river deposit is better known as a

A. levee
B. flood plain
C. delta

79. When heat energy is trapped by the gases in the Earth's atmosphere this process is called

A. greenhouse effect
B. coriolis effect
C. constant effect

80. Winds in the Northern Hemisphere are deflected to the

A. north
B. left
C. right

81. Water vapor and ________ trap heat in the atmosphere.

A. carbon dioxide
B. nitrogen
C. sodium nitrate

82. The frontal system that forms when a cold air mass meets a warm air mass and does not change position is defined as a

A. occluded front
B. stationary front
C. warm front

83. Surface ocean currents are caused by which of the following

A. temperature
B. density changes in water
C. wind

84. The length of time it takes for two waves to pass in a row is called

A. wave length
B. wave period
C. wave crest

85. Circulation of the deep ocean currents is the result of

A. equatorial currents
B. surface currents
C. density currents

86. Chains of undersea mountains associated with the spreading of the seafloor are known as _______.

A. ocean trenches
B. mid ocean ridges
C. seamounts

87. A shallow, calm area of water located between a barrier island and a beach area is defined as a/an _____.

A. atoll
B. coral reef
C. lagoon

88. Closed contour lines noticed on a topographical map indicate which type of information?

A. rivers and lakes
B. hills
C. mountains

89. The heliocentric model was developed by which famous scientist?

A. Kepler
B. Copernicus
C. Newton

90. The phases of the moon are the result of its _______ in relation to the sun.

A. revolution
B. rotation
C. position

91. A telescope that collects light by using a concave mirror and can produce small images is called a ___________.

A. radioactive telescope
B. reflecting telescope
C. refracting telescope

92. The measuring unit to measure the distance between stars is called

A. astronomical unit
B. light-year
C. parsec

93. The largest planet found in the solar system is

A. Pluto
B. Jupiter
C. Saturn

94. The famous scientist who discovered the elliptical orbits

A. Kepler
B. Copernicus
C. Galilee

95. The planet with retrograde rotation is

A. Pluto
B. Uranus
C. Venus

96. A star's brightness is referred to as

A. magnitude
B. mass
C. apparent magnitude

97. Clouds of gas and dust where new stars originate are called

A. black holes
B. super novas
C. nebulas

98. The transfer of heat from the earth's surface to the atmosphere is called ____.

A. conduction
B. radiation
C. convection

99. The ozone layer is found in the

A. stratosphere layer
B. mesosphere layer
C. exosphere layer

100. The coldest zone of the atmosphere is found in the

A. thermosphere
B. mesosphere
C. stratosphere

101. Winds in high pressure areas tend to blow

A. clockwise
B. counterclockwise
C. along the center

102. When warm air meets cold air this is defined as a

A. cold front
B. occluded front
C. warm front

103. The fastest velocity of a river is found where?

A. bottom
B. center
C. sides

104. As a glacier melts the sea level tends to:

A. rise
B. sink
C. evaporate

105. The largest groups of minerals found in the earth's crust are

A. silicates
B. carbonates
C. quartz

106. Used to measure the magnitude of an earthquake.

A. Richter scale
B. epicometer
C. seismograph

107. These are types of folds:

A. anticlines and synclines
B. faults and folds
C. fractures and shearings

108. Breaks in rocks which indicate movement are known as

A. fractures
B. folds
C. faults

109. The collision of two continental plates is called a

A. folded mountain range
B. volcanic mountain range
C. block mountain range

110. Plates that move in the same direction are termed

A. divergent faults
B. convergent faults
C. transform faults

111. Studying the positions of layered rock is referred to as

A. relative ages
B. index fossils
C. disconformity

112. The smallest division of geologic time is defined as

A. Periods
B. Eras
C. Epochs

113. The most common fossils of the Paleozoic Era are

A. angiosperms
B. trilobites
C. endotherms

114. Contamination may enter groundwater by

A. air pollution
B. leaking septic tanks
C. photochemical processes

115. Which is a form of precipitation?

A. snow
B. frost
C. fog

116. A dead star is called a _____.

A. White Dwarf
B. Super Giant
C. Black Dwarf

117. Roughly ninety percent of all geologic time is said to be __________.

A. Paleozoic
B. Pre-Cambrian
C. Mesozoic

118. The massive change in biological conditions that marked the beginning of life forms on earth is known as ________.

A. Oxygen Revolution
B. Carbon Revolution
C. Trilobite Revolution

119. Water is a truly unique material. It has the property of ________.

A. Adhesion
B. Cohesion
C. Both

120. The following is not a form of satellite used to track weather:

A. NEXRAD
B. Geostationary
C. Polar Orbitting

121. Over the course of our planet's history Earth has had _____ atmosphere(s).

A. one
B. two
C. three

122. Which is not a principle law of geology?

A. Cross Cutting
B. Faulting
C. Super position

123. The red beds are important because they indicate the presence of _______ in the geologic record.

A. Carbon
B. Ammonia
C. Oxygen

124. Tornadoes are most likely to occur in what season?

A. Spring
B. Summer
C. Autumn

125. Which scale is used to measure hurricanes?

A. Fujita Scale
B. Saffir-Simpson Scale
C. Richter Scale

Answer Key

1. A
2. B
3. C
4. B
5. A
6. C
7. C
8. B
9. B
10. C
11. A
12. B
13. A
14. C
15. A
16. A
17. A
18. C
19. B
20. B
21. C
22. C
23. A
24. C
25. A
26. A
27. A
28. C
29. C
30. A
31. C
32. B
33. C
34. B
35. C
36. C
37. A
38. C
39. B
40. B
41. C
42. A
43. B
44. C
45. A
46. A
47. B
48. B
49. C
50. C
51. A
52. C
53. B
54. A
55. B
56. C
57. C
58. A
59. A
60. A
61. B
62. B
63. B
64. C
65. B
66. B
67. A
68. C
69. B
70. B
71. A
72. B
73. C
74. C
75. A
76. B
77. B
78. C
79. A
80. C
81. A
82. B
83. C
84. B
85. C
86. B
87. C
88. B
89. B
90. C
91. B
92. C
93. B
94. A
95. C
96. A
97. C
98. A
99. A
100. B
101. A
102. C
103. B
104. A
105. A
106. C
107. A
108. C
109. A
110. C
111. A
112. C
113. B
114. B
115. A
116. C
117. B
118. A
119. C
120. A
121. C
122. B
123. C
124. A
125. B

Rationales for Sample Questions

1. Which layer of the atmosphere would you expect most weather to occur?
A. Troposphere
The troposphere is the lowest portion of the Earth's atmosphere. It contains the highest amount of water and aerosol. Because it touches the Earth's surface features, friction builds. For all of these reasons, weather is most likely to occur in the Troposphere.

2. What percentage of earth's surface is covered by water?
B. 71%
The earth's surface is nearly ¾ covered with water. The Pacific Ocean is the largest body of moving water. Of course there are other oceans, lakes, rivers, and glaciers as well.

3. Which layer of the earth's atmosphere contains the Ozone layer?
C. Stratosphere
The stratosphere is located above the troposphere and below the mesosphere. It has layers striated by temperature. The warmest portion, the ozone layer, is warm because it absorbs solar ultraviolet radiation.

4. Copernicus developed a theory that is known as
B. Heliocentric
Copernicus' theory stated that the planets revolved around the sun (helios), as opposed to prior belief that the planets revolved around the Earth (geocentric).

5. The boundary that separates the crust from the mantle is known as
A. Moho
The Mohorovicic Discontinuity separates oceanic and/or continental crust from the Earth's mantle.

6. The product of intrusive activities would result in forming a
C. dike
A dike is formed when upwelling magma cools and solidifies beneath the surface, an intrusive activity.

7. A star's light and heat are produced by
C. nuclear fusion
Nuclear fusion is the process in which hydrogen atoms fuse together to form helium atoms, releasing massive amounts of energy during the fusion. It's the fusion of atoms, not combustion, which causes the star to shine.

8. The center of an atom is called
B. nucleus
The center of the atom is the nucleus. The nucleus of the atom is composed of nucleons, which when electrically charged are protons and when electrically neutral are neutrons. However, the electrons swirl around the nucleus in a large region called the Electron Cloud.

9. An important food source for animals in a water biome
B. plankton
Drifting organisms that inhabit the water column are called plankton. They may be phytoplankton or zooplankton. Phytoplankton are autotrophs and form the base of the aquatic food chain.

10. The smallest piece of an element is called a/an
C. atom
An atom is the smallest particle of the element that has the properties of that element. All of the atoms of a particular element are the same. The atoms of each element are different from the atoms of the other elements.

11. An instrument that measures relative humidity is known as
A. psychrometer
A psychrometer measures relative humidity. The other choices, anemometer and barometer, measure wind speed and atmospheric pressure, respectfully.

12. Removing salts from ocean water by heating is called
B. distillation
In the process of distilling ocean water the saline water is heated, producing water vapor that is in turn condensed, forming fresh water. The salt is left behind as waste but the water is used in many areas for drinking supply.

13. When molecules in the air cool and combine to form rain, _____ has occurred.
A. condensation
Condensation is the change in matter from a denser phase, such as a gas (or vapor) to a liquid. Condensation commonly occurs when a vapor is cooled to a liquid.

14. Which instrument measures wind direction?
C. wind vane
Of the choices given, an anemometer measures wind speed (velocity), a barometer measures atmospheric pressure and a wind vane indicates wind direction.

15. The most important cause of erosion is
A. water
Erosion is most often caused by water. This can be acid rain eroding rocks, rivers eroding riverbeds, oceans eroding beaches and cliffs, etc. In addition, wind is another source of erosion.

16. An anemometer measures
A. wind velocity
Of the choices given, an anemometer measures wind speed (velocity), temperature would be measured by a thermometer, and relative humidity is measured with a psychrometer.

17. The boundary that develops when a cold air mass meets a warm air mass
A. cold front
Fronts are always labeled according to the approaching air mass. Therefore, a cold air mass meeting and displacing a warm air mass would be called a cold front.

18. When the sun, moon and earth are aligned in a straight line what type of tides are produced?
C. spring tides
Spring tides are produced when the Earth, Sun, and Moon are in a line. Therefore, spring tides occur during the full moon and the new moon. Neap tides occur during quarter moons. They occur when the gravitational forces of the Moon and the Sun are perpendicular to one another (with respect to the Earth).

19. North of the equator, currents move in which direction?
B. clockwise
North of the equator, currents move clockwise. South of the equator, currents move counter clockwise.

20. Rocks that serve as aquifers are
B. permeable
Aquifers are underground areas of water-bearing permeable rock from which groundwater can be collected.

21. Volcanoes with violent eruptions are known as
C. cinder volcanoes
Cinder volcanoes are some of the most violent volcanoes because of the immense pressure of gas built up within the neck of the volcanic tube. When it overcomes the resistance offered by the surrounding rock, it rips off the top of the cone. A huge mass of liquid magma and Pyroclastic Rock are flung outward in a violent explosion.

22. The Richter scale measures
C. magnitude
The richter scale is used to measure the magnitude of earthquakes. Focus and compressions refer to areas of activity, but are not examples of a scale for measuring.

23. The earth's outer core is probably
A. liquid
The Earth's inner core is mathematically hypothesized to be a solid iron and nickel core. The outer core, surrounding the inner core, is so hot that it is believed to be molten iron (liquid state). Combined, they are responsible for Earth's magnetism.

24. What are the two most abundant elements found in the Earth's crust?
C. oxygen and silicon
Earth's crust is composed of 47% oxygen and 28% silicon.

25. The San Andreas Fault is classified as a
A. transform fault
The San Andreas fault is considered a transform fault because sections of the Earth's crust (the Pacific and North American Plates) slide side-by-side past each other.

26. Batholiths are the largest structures of which type of rock activity?
A. intrusive rock
Batholiths are large portions of igneous intrusive rock deep within the Earth's crust that form from cooled magma.

27. The main agents of chemical weathering are
A. water, oxygen, CO_2
Water is the greatest factor in chemical weathering. Glaciers erode entire valleys. Rainfall pounds way at topographic surface features. Rivers erode riverbeds and river edges. Oceans erode shorelines and cliffs. Oxygen is also a factor in weathering. Air movement can have erosional factors. Most importantly, wind can transport material to other areas, having both erosional and depositional results. Carbon dioxide combines with water to produce carbonic acid, which erodes rock structures and some of our man made monuments.

28. Soil classified as porous is called
C. sandy soil
Sandy soil has a high sand content. The sand molecules have many spaces in-between, making the soil porous. This soil does not hold water well.

29. Intrusive igneous rock forms
C. large crystals
Intrusive igneous rock forms large crystals. This rock is formed from magma that cools and solidifies within the earth. Because it is surrounded by pre-existing rock, the magma cools slowly, and the rocks are coarse grained. The crystals are usually large enough to be seen by the unaided eye.

30. Which types of rocks are rich sources of fossil remains'?
A. sedimentary rock
Sedimentary rock has the most abundant fossil collection. This is because, over time the layers of sand and mud at the bottom of lakes & oceans turned into rocks due to compression. Plants and animals that died and fell to the bottom were part of the compressional process by which the many layers were eventually turned into stone, encapsulating a fossil.

31. The best preserved animal remains have been discovered in
C. tar pits
Tar pits provide a wealth of information when it comes to fossils. Tar pits are oozing areas of asphalt, which were so sticky as to trap animals. These animals, without a way out, would die of starvation or be preyed upon. Their bones would remain in the tar pits, and be covered by the continued oozing of asphalt. Because the asphalt deposits were continuously added, the bones were not exposed to much weathering, and we have found some of the most complete and unchanged fossils from these areas, including mammoths and saber toothed cats.

32. The Mid-Atlantic is a major area of which type plate movement?
B. divergent plate
The Mid- Atlantic is home to a submerged mountain range, which extends from the Arctic Ocean to beyond the southern tip of Africa. The divergent plate action results in sea floor spreading at a rate of about 2.5 centimeters per year (cm/yr), or 25 km in a million years, creating the vast ocean we recognize today.

33. When lava cools quickly on the earth's surface the newly formed rock is called
C. extrusive
Rock formed by the cooling of magma on the earth's surface is known as extrusive, as opposed to intrusive, which is formed by the cooling of magma below the Earth's surface.

34. When a dyke forms with magma flowing in a tub-like structure this is known to be a/an
B. intrusive activity
Dykes are thin, vertical veins of igneous rock. They form within fractures in the earth's crust. Intrusive activity forces magma into underground areas, which can seep into these existing fractures forming a dyke.

35. A caldera is formed when a large depression collapses. This is the result of a
C. volcanic eruption
A caldera is the collapse of land following a volcanic eruption. Once the underground store of magma and gas has been released in a volcanic explosion, there is not enough support, causing the ground to collapse. A caldera is sometimes confused with the area from which magma and gases are emitted (a crater).

36. Trenches observed on the sea floor are the results of
C. subduction
Trenches are created where two plates collide (converge). Plate collision causes denser oceanic crust to sink or slip beneath lighter continental crust. It is subducted and melted into the asthenosphere, producing a deep trench on the ocean floor parallel to the plate boundary.

37. Alfred Wegener's hypothesis of continental drift was not supported until scientists began studying
A. sea floor
Wegener's hypothesis of continental drift was supported by studies of the sea floor. In comparison to continental rock materials, the youngest rock is found on the ocean floor, consistent with the tectonic theory of cyclic spreading and subduction. Overall, oceanic material is roughly 200 million years old, while most continental material is significantly older, with age measured in billions of years.

38. These massive waves are caused by the displacement of ocean water, and are often the result of underwater earthquakes.
C. tsunamis
Earthquakes can trigger an underwater landslide or cause sea floor displacements that in turn, generate deep, omni-directional waves. Far out to sea these waves may be hardly noticeable. However, as they near the shoreline, the shallowing of the sea floor forces the waves upward in a "springing" type of motion.

39. Sea floor spreading occurs when the earth's crust is stretched and pulled apart in a process called
B. rifting
A rift is a place where the Earth's crust and lithosphere are being pulled apart. In rifts, no crust or lithosphere is produced. If rifting continues, eventually a mid-ocean ridge may form.

40. The layer of the atmosphere that is in a plasma state and aids in communication
B. Ionosphere
The Ionosphere is an area of free ions: positively charged ions, produced as a result of solar radiation striking the atmosphere. It is known for its production of aurora borealis and its benefits to radio transmission

41. A stream erodes bedrock by grinding sand and rock fragments against each other. This process is defined as
C. abrasion
Abrasion is the key form of mechanical weathering. It is a sandblasting effect caused by particles of sand or sediment. Abrasive agents include wind blown sand, water movement, and the materials in landslides bashing into each other.

42. Rocks formed from magma are
A. igneous
Igneous rocks are rocks that have formed from cooled magma. They are further classified as extrusive or intrusive according to location.

43. Rocks formed by the intense heating or compression of pre- existing rocks are classified as
B. metamorphic
Metamorphism is the process of changing a pre-existing rock into a new rock by heat and or pressure. Metamorphism is similar to that of putting a clay pot into a kiln. The clay doesn't melt, but a solid-state chemical reaction occurs that causes a change. The chemical bonds of adjoining atoms breakdown and allow the atoms to rearrange themselves, producing a substance with new properties.

44. Rocks made of loose materials that have been cemented together
C. sedimentary
Sediments are broken up rock material. Sand on a beach or pebbles in a mountain stream are typical examples. Sedimentary rocks are named for their source; they are rocks that form from sediments that lithify to become solid rock. Sedimentary rock is especially important for the finding of fossils.

45. River valley glaciers produce
A. U-shaped erosion
River valleys are typically V- shaped. The velocity and cutting power of a river is greatest at its center. However, glaciers broaden the area. Upon its retreat, a glacier typically leaves a U- shaped eroded valley.

46. The life cycle of a river with the most cutting power and erosion is known as which stage?
A. youth stage
Young streams have straight paths, no flood plain, a "V" shaped cutting profile, and high velocity with generally clear water and low suspended load. Old streams have lots of meanders, large flood plain, flat profile, low velocity, with murky, "muddy" waters because of a high-suspended load.

47. The result of radioactive decay
B. daughter element
The radioactive decay causes the (mother) element to change into an (daughter) element. The Mother-Daughter relationship of produced nuclides during the series of isotope decay is the basis for radiometric dating. Although many isotopes are used in radiometric dating, the most widely known method is referred to as Carbon-14 dating. Knowing the half-life (how long it takes for half of the material to decay) is the key factor in the radiometric dating process.

48. The most abundant dry gas found in the atmosphere is
B. Nitrogen
The atmosphere is composed of 78% Nitrogen, 21% Oxygen, and 1% other gasses.

49. A natural groundwater outlet through which boiling water and steam explodes into the air is called a
C. geyser
A geyser is a thermal spring that erupts. The processes behind the eruption are very similar to those involved in boiling water in a teakettle. A constriction forms in the connected chambers of a spring. The water heats under pressure, turns to steam, and erupts with great force past the constriction. The ejected steam condenses and returns to a liquid state. The water draws back into its chambers and the process begins again. Since it takes awhile for the water to drain back and reheat, geysers often erupt on a determinable schedule.

50. Which of the following rocks make the best aquifer?
C. sandstone
Sandstone makes the best aquifer because of its porosity. It has larger pores than granite or basalt, and is also likely to fracture in a way that is conducive to water movement and collection.

51. Sediments that settle out from rivers are called
A. deposits
Deposits are pieces of matter that settle out of the water and fall to the bottom, or are washed into a collection area, such as a delta. This can be terrestrial matter, biological matter, salts, or larger pebbles and rocks.

52. A hole that remains in the ground after a block of glacier ice melts is called a
C. kettle
As the outwash moves sediment alongside and in the path of a receding glacier, blocks of ice can be buried beneath the sediment. After years of erosion these blocks are uncovered and melt, leaving a shallow depression behind. When these depressions fill, they are known as Kettles, and become scenic lakes.

53. The first sign that a tsunami is approaching a shore is
B. water moving from the shore
The first sign that a tsunami is approaching is usually the retreat of water from the shoreline. When the water returns, it comes fast and washes well past its normal level in both distance and depth, destroying coastal areas and causing many losses.

54. Mountains that have been squeezed into wavelike patterns are called
A. fold mountains
During mountain building or compressional stress, rocks may deform to produce folds. Generally, a series is produced. The up-folds are called anticlines and the down-folds are known as synclines.

55. The largest ocean is the
B. Pacific
The four major oceans (listed in decreasing size) are the Pacific, Atlantic, Indian and Arctic.

56. The major surface current that flows along the east coast of the United States is known as the
C. Gulf Stream
The Gulf Stream begins in the Caribbean and ends in the northern North Atlantic. It is powerful enough to be seen from outer space and is one of the world's most studied current systems. It acts as the east coast boundary current plays an important role in the transfer of heat and salt to the poles.

57. The formation of ocean waves is caused by
C. the wind
Wind is the primary factor in the production of ocean waves. It is the energy and friction of wind action that transfers to the water to create waves.

58. The most abundant compound found in sea water is
A. chloride
Chloride is the compound found most often in sea water. Other compounds commonly found include sodium carbonate, magnesium and potassium compounds, sulfite, bromide, and silicate. NaCl is what we commonly refer to as sea salt. Of the two components, chloride is more readily available in the sea.

59. The distance between two meridians is measured in degrees of
A. longitude
Longitude describes the location of a place on Earth east or west of a line called the Prime Meridian. Longitude is given in degrees ranging from 0° at the Prime Meridian to 180° east or west

60. A contour line that has tiny comb-like lines along the inner edge indicates a
A. depression
Contour lines are shown as closed circles in elevated areas and as lines with miniature perpendicular lined edges where depressions exist. These little lines are called hachure marks.

61. Fossils that are used to date strata are called
B. index fossils
Index fossils are fossils of organisms that were known to be abundant at specific times in Earth's history. Presence of such fossils gives one an idea of what age the surrounding material came from.

62. Which of the following causes the aurora borealis?
A. particles from the sun
Aurora Borealis is a phenomenon caused by particles escaping from the sun. The particles escaping from the sun include a mixture of gases, electrons and protons, and are sent out at a force that scientists call solar wind. Together, we have the Earth's magnetosphere and the solar wind squeezing the magnetosphere and charged particles everywhere in the field. When conditions are right, the build-up of pressure from the solar wind creates an electric voltage that pushes electrons into the ionosphere. Here they collide with gas atoms, causing them to release both light and more electrons.

63. The layer of the atmosphere that shields earth from harmful ultraviolet radiation is called
B. ozone layer
The ozone layer is the part of the Earth's atmosphere that contains high concentrations of ozone (O_3). It is located in the stratosphere and absorbs UV radiation emitted from the sun, making life possible on Earth.

64. The layer of the earth's atmosphere that is closest to the earth's surface is the
C. troposphere layer
The troposphere is the layer of Earth's atmosphere that is the lowest (closest to the surface). It is the densest because it contains almost all the water vapor and aerosol found in the atmosphere. It is easy to conclude, then, that most weather phenomena occur here.

65. The sun transfers its heat to other objects by
B. radiation
Radiation is the process by which energy is transferred in the form of waves or particles. The Sun emits ultraviolet radiation in UVA, UVB, and UVC forms, but because of the ozone layer, most of the ultraviolet radiation that reaches the Earth's surface is UVA.

66. As an air mass expands it becomes
B. warmer
Air expends as heat is applied according to the laws of gasses.

67. Air moving northward from the horse latitudes produces a belt of winds called the
A. prevailing westerlies
The prevailing westerlies are the winds found in the middle latitudes between 30 and 60 degrees latitude. They blow from the high pressure area in the horse latitudes towards the poles.

68. Which type of cloud always produces precipitation?
C. nimbostratus
Nimbostratus clouds are seen as a thick, uniform, gray layer from which precipitation (significant rain or snow) is falling. Of the other choices offered, altostratus clouds appear as uniform white or bluish-gray layers that partially or totally obscure the sky, and cirrostratus are like a thin, nearly transparent, veil or sheet that partially or totally covers the sky. Only nimbostratus guarantees precipitation.

69. An air mass that forms over the Gulf of Mexico is called
B. maritime
Maritime air masses are moist, containing considerable amounts of water vapor, which is ultimately condensed and released as rain or snow. Maritime tropical air originates near the Gulf of Mexico and travels north-east across the warm Atlantic to affect western Europe, as well as north-west across the United States.

70. Spring tides will occur when the moon is in its
B. full and new phases
Spring tides are produced when the Earth, Sun, and Moon are in a line. Therefore, spring tides occur during the full moon and the new moon. Neap tides occur during quarter moons. They occur when the gravitational forces of the Moon and the Sun are perpendicular to one another (with respect to the Earth).

71. Air pressure is measured using a
A. barometer
A psychrometer measures relative humidity. A barometermeasures atmospheric pressure. A hydrometer is used to measure the specific gravity of a liquid.

72. The two most abundant elements found in stars are
B. hydrogen and helium
Hydrogen and helium are the only elements that occur naturally in our universe. It makes sense, then, that they are present in all areas, including stars.

73. A comet's tail always points ________ from the sun.
C. away
A comet's tail always points away from the sun. The sun's radiation is burning up the ice that makes the comet, and since it is projecting the material outward, the tail seems to be pointing away from the sun. Notice that this question does not use a specific direction (north, south, east, west) because comets move and are subject to the viewer's location and perception.

74. The dark areas observed on the sun are known as
C. sun spots
Larger dark spots called Sunspots appear regularly on the Sun's surface. These spots vary in size from small to 150,000 kilometers in diameter and may last from hours to months. The sunspots also cause solar flares that can accelerate to velocities of 900 km/hr, sending shock waves through the solar atmosphere.

75. An example of distance in degrees of latitude is
A. 55° north
Latitude is measured in degrees away from the equator. The equator marks 0°, and parallel lines moving around the globe are quantified in degrees north or south.

76. A scale use to measure the hardness of a mineral is known as the
B. Moh's scale
The Moh's scale of hardness measures the scratch resistance of minerals. The hardest material is diamond, and the frailest is talc. This means that diamond can scratch any surface, which is not true of less hard materials, such as talc.

77. When a gas changes to a liquid this process is known as
B. condensation
Condensation is the change in matter to a denser phase, such as a gas (or vapor) to a liquid. Condensation can occur when a vapor is cooled to a liquid or when a vapor is compressed.

78. A fan-shaped river deposit is better known as a
C. delta
Flowing water carries the material to the ocean where one of two things happen, the material is deposited on the offshore continental shelf or is carried back inland to the inlets and bays. Over time, the sediment thickly accumulates and may form typical coastal features such as sand bars and deltas.

79. When heat energy is trapped by the gases in the Earth's atmosphere this process is called
A. greenhouse effect
When greenhouse gases and heat build up, the Earth's surface and atmospheric temperature rises. The current and controversial hypothesis contends that if we cut the amount of rising $C0_2$ in the atmosphere, then things will cool down.

80. Winds in the Northern Hemisphere are deflected to the
C. right
The Earth is spinning on its rotational axis. Spin is greatest near the equator and least at the poles. The different velocities associated with the spin give rise to an effect on the air known as the Coriolis Force. The idea is that the result of the Coriolis effect is that winds in the north are deflected to the right, and winds in the south are deflected to the west.

81. Water vapor and ________ trap heat in the atmosphere.
A. carbon dioxide
Water vapor and carbon dioxide are both considered greenhouse gases because they can trap heat in the atmosphere. Other sources of greenhouse gasses include rice paddies and ruminant animals, which produce Methane.

82. The frontal system that forms when a cold air mass meets a warm air mass and does not change position is defined as a
B. stationary front
Fronts are the boundaries where one air mass meets another. A stationary front is a boundary between two air masses when neither is strong enough to displace the other.

83. Surface ocean currents are caused by which of the following
C. wind
A current is a large mass of continuously moving oceanic water. Surface ocean currents are mainly wind-driven and occur in all of the world's oceans (example: the Gulf Stream). This is in contrast to deep ocean currents which are driven by changes in density.

84. The length of time it takes for two waves to pass in a row is called
B. wave period
The wave period is the time required for two successive waves to pass. Wave crest is the tallest part of the wave. Wave length is measured from the crest of one wave to the crest of the next.

85. Circulation of the deep ocean currents is the result of
C. density currents
Unlike surface currents, deep ocean currents are driven by changes in density. These density differences may be caused by changes in salinity (halocline) or temperature (thermocline). Colder water sinks below warmer waters, causing a river (current) flowing below the warmer waters.

86. Chains of undersea mountains associated with the spreading of the seafloor are known as
B. mid ocean ridges
Mid ocean ranges are underwater mountains formed by plate tectonics. The underwater mountains are all connected, making a single mid-oceanic ridge system that is the longest mountain range in the world. The ridges are active sites with new magma constantly emerging onto the ocean floor and into the crust, resulting in sea floor spreading.

87. A shallow, calm area of water located between a barrier island and a beach area is defined as a/an
C. lagoon
A lagoon is known for its quiet movement of water. A lagoon is a body of shallow salt or brackish water separated from the sea by a shallow or exposed sandbank, coral reef, etc. Non-reef lagoon barriers are formed by wave-action or longshore currents depositing sediments. Because of their gentle atmosphere and brackish water, they are often nurseries for many baby fish and aquatic animals.

88. Closed contour lines noticed on a topographical map indicate which type of information?
B. hills
The rules of contouring dictate that contour lines are closed around hills, basins, or depressions. Because we know that depressions are shown using hachure marks, a closed contour line without such marks represents a hill.

89. The heliocentric model was developed by which famous scientist?
B. Copernicus
Copernicus is recognized for his heliocentric theory. The heliocentric theory postulates that the heavenly bodies rotate around the sun. Prior to his assertions, people believed in the geocentric model that held that all bodies rotated around the Earth. The geocentric model was supported by the church, so Copernicus' ideas were highly controversial.

90. The phases of the moon are the result of its _______ in relation to the sun.
C. position
The moon is visible in varying amounts during its orbit around the earth. One half of the moon's surface is always illuminated by the Sun (appears bright), but the amount observed can vary from full moon to none.

91. A telescope that collects light by using a concave mirror and can produce small images is called a
B. reflecting telescope
Reflecting telescopes are commonly used in laboratory settings. Images are produced via the reflection of waves off of a concave mirror. The larger the image produced the more likely it is to be imperfect.

92. The measuring unit to measure the distance between stars is called
C. parsec
Parsecs are the units used to describe the distance between stars. Astronomical units (AU) are used to describe the distances between celestial objects (example The Earth is 1.00 ± 0.02 AU from the Sun). Light years are a unit of length measuring the distance light travels in a vacuum in one year.

93. The largest planet found in the solar system is
B. Jupiter
The planets (in decreasing size) are Jupiter, Saturn (body- not inclusive of rings), Uranus, Neptune, Earth, Venus, Mars, Mercury (Pluto was thought to be the smallest planet, but is no longer classified as a planet).

94. The famous scientist who discovered the elliptical orbits
A. Kepler
The significance of Kepler's Laws is that it overthrew the ancient concept of uniform circular motion, which was a major support for the geocentric arguments. Although Kepler postulated three laws of planetary motion, he was never able to explain *why* the planets move along their elliptical orbits, only that they did.

95. The planet with retrograde rotation is
C. Venus
Venus has an axial tilt of only 3° and a very slow rotation. It spins in the direction opposite of its counterparts (who spin in the same direction as the Sun). Uranus is also tilted and orbits on its side. However, this is thought to be the consequence of an impact that left the previously prograde rotating planet tilted in such a manner.

96. A star's brightness is referred to as
A. magnitude
Magnitude is a measure of a star's brightness. The brighter the object appears, the lower the number value of its magnitude. The apparent magnitude is how bright an observer perceives the object to be. Mass has to do with how much matter can be measured, not brightness.

97. Clouds of gas and dust where new stars originate are called
C. nebulae
Nebulae are where new stars are born. They are large areas of gasses and dust. When the conditions are right, particles combine to form stars.

98. The transfer of heat from the earth's surface to the atmosphere is called
A. conduction
Radiation is the process of warming through rays or waves of energy, such as the Sun warms earth. The Earth returns heat to the atmosphere through conduction. This is the transfer of heat through matter, such that areas of greater heat move to areas of less heat in an attempt to balance temperature.

99. The ozone layer is found in the
A. stratosphere
The stratosphere is home to the ozone layer, which protects Earth from harmful UV radiation.

100. The coldest zone of the atmosphere is found in the
B. mesosphere
The mesosphere is the coldest layer of the atmosphere, with temperatures as low as -100°Celsius. Within this layer, temperature decreases with increasing altitude.

101. Winds in high pressure areas tend to blow
A. clockwise
High pressure systems are known for winds that flow clockwise and fair weather. Low pressure systems are accompanied by clouds and precipitation and winds flow counterclockwise.

102. When warm air meets cold air this is defined as a
C. warm front
When a warm air mass meets and displaces a cold air mass, the front is called a warm front.

103. The fastest velocity of a river is found where?
B. center
Mountain streams have little fining (sorting the material by size) due to their higher velocity, and low land streams are muddy because the velocity is less and erosion occurs on the bed and sides of the stream. Once a stream is at or close to base level, equilibrium is achieved between deposition and erosion. Erosion and deposition are controlled by the velocity of the stream. As the stream approaches base level, more of its energy is in a side-to-side cutting (meanders) than in down-cutting.

104. As a glacier melts the sea level tends to
A. rise
As a glacier melts, its water is distributed into nearby bodies of water, causing the sea level to rise.

105. The largest groups of minerals found in the earth's crust are
A. silicates
Silicates are the most abundant group of minerals found in the Earth' s crust. The two most abundant elements in the earth's crust are Oxygen (46.6%) and Silicon (27.7%). These combine together to form silicates, which some scientists believe make up as much as 90% of the Earth's crust.

106. Used to measure the magnitude of an earthquake.
C. seismograph
A seismograph is a machine used to measure the magnitude of an earthquake. As the Earth's materials move, the weight also moves and sends an electronic signal to a recording device called a seismograph. Movements are displayed as a series of lines on a recording chart called a Seismogram, reflecting the seismic energy detected at a particular location.

107. These are types of folds:
A. anticlines and synclines
Folded mountains are composed of up and down folds. The up-folds are called anticlines and the down-folds are known as synclines.

108. Breaks in rocks which indicate movement are known as
C. faults
Faults are rock fractures that indicate relative movement. Fractures are also breaks in the rock, but they show no evidence of movement. Folds are created from compression and are a forming of tectonic building.

109. The collision of two continental plates is called a
A. folded mountain range
The collision of two continental plates results in a folded mountain range. Two continental plates pushing against each other but not subducting, will cause the material to buckle, sometimes repeatedly, giving these mountains their characteristic ribbon appearance.

110. Plates that move in the same direction are termed
C. transform faults
Transform faults are areas where two plates move in the same direction. They are parallel, and do not collide, but may result in earthquakes if areas of the plates stick or have excessive pressure in sliding past each other.

111. Studying the positions of layered rock is referred to as
A. relative ages
The Earth's materials-rocks, soils, and sediments-are piled upon each other in layers called strata. Understanding the relative orientation and arrangement of the strata provides important information about the Earth's history and the ongoing sequence of events and processes that helped shape that history.

112. The smallest division of geologic time is defined as
C. epochs
Geologic time is divided into eons, eras, periods, and epochs (listed here in decreasing order of size).

113. The most common fossils of the Paleozoic Era are
B. trilobites
Trilobites flourished in the Paleozoic era. There were over 600 genera and 1000's of species. Trilobites were bottom dwellers and scavengers found in shallow to deep water. For an extremely long period of time, Trilobites were the dominant multi-cellular life form on the planet. Trilobites are very good guide fossils because they were extremely abundant and existed throughout the entire Paleozoic period. Their development underwent distinctive changes, and these differences are useful in subdividing the time period.

114. Contamination may enter groundwater by
B. leaking septic tanks
Leaking septic tanks allow contamination to slowly seep into the ground, where it is absorbed into the water table and infects the groundwater.

115. Which is a form of precipitation?
A. snow
Snow is a form of precipitation. Precipitation is the product of the condensation of atmospheric water vapor that falls to the Earth's surface. It occurs when the atmosphere becomes saturated with water vapor and the water condenses and falls out of solution. Frost and fog do not qualify as precipitates.

116. A dead star is called a _________.
C. Black Dwarf
The final phase of a lower main sequence star's life cycle can take two paths: most main sequence white dwarfs after a few billion years completely burn out to become what is called a black dwarf: a cold, dead star. Alternatively, if a White Dwarf is part of a Binary Star: two suns in the same solar system, instead of slowly cooling to become a Black Dwarf, it may capture hydrogen from its companion star.

117. Roughly ninety percent of all geologic time is said to be __________.
B. Pre-Cambrian
Pre-Cambrian Time: Comprised of the Hadean, Archean, and Proterozoic Eons, 87% of all geologic time is considered Pre-Cambrian.

118. The massive change in biological conditions that marked the beginning of life forms on earth is known as ________.
A. Oxygen Revolution
Between 4.6 and 3.6 billion years ago, we transition from an uninhabitable Earth, to the appearance of simple, single-celled bacteria. Around 2.5 billion years ago, the bacteria developed the ability of photosynthesis. This process released oxygen as a by-product and there was a massive release of oxygen as the bacteria multiplied. This massive release is called the Oxygen Revolution and it concurrently marks the beginning of the Proterozoic Eon.

119. Water is a truly unique material. It has the property of ________.
C. Both
A unique property of water is that water likes itself; it has a natural tendency to stick to itself. This property is based upon the polar nature of the water molecule. It attracts other water molecules. When the molecules stick together, they are attached through Hydrogen Bonds, giving the molecule a property called cohesion. Cohesion gives water an unusually strong surface tension, and its capillary action makes the water spread. When the water spreads, adhesion, the tendency of water to stick to other materials, allows water to adhere to solids, making them wet.

120. The following is not a form of satellite used to track weather:
A. NEXRAD
While all of these instruments are used to track weather, the NEXRAD Radar, Next Generation Doppler Radar, is not a satellite. It emits beams of energy that are reflected by the water droplets in the atmosphere. This type of radar is very useful for tracking and predicting rain and less useful for snow or sleet. Geostationary satellites move with the Earth's rotation. Since they always look at the same point, this allows for a view showing changes over periods of time. Polar Orbiting satellites follow an orbit from pole to pole. The Earth rotates underneath the satellite and gives a view of different areas. In effect, it produces slices of the Earth.

121. Over the course of our planet's history Earth has had _____ atmosphere(s).
C. three
Earth's initial atmosphere was composed of primarily hydrogen and smaller amounts of helium. However, most of the hydrogen and helium escaped into space very shortly after the earth was formed, approximately 4.6 billion years ago. A second atmosphere formed during the first 500 million years of Earth's history, as the gasses trapped within the planet were out- gassed during volcanic eruptions. This atmosphere was composed of carbon dioxide (CO_2), Nitrogen (N), and water vapor (H_2O), with smaller amounts of methane (CH_4), ammonia (NH_3), hydrogen (H), and carbon monoxide (CO). However, only trace quantities of oxygen were present. At around 3.5 billion years, Earth's third atmosphere began to form as the first life forms- simple, unicellular bacteria- appeared.

122. Which is not a principle law of geology?
B. faulting
The principle laws of geology are:

- Principle of Uniformitarianism: Processes that are happening today also happened in the past.
- Principle of Cross-Cutting Relations: A rock is younger than any rock it cuts across.
- Principle of Original Horizontality: Rock units are originally laid down flat. Something happened to cause them to change orientation.
- Principle of Super Position: The rock on the bottom is older than the rock on top.
- Principle of Biologic Succession: Fossils correspond to particular periods of time.

123. The red beds are important because they indicate the presence of _______ in the geologic record.
C. Oxygen
Formation of Red Beds: The Animike Group- banded iron formations- form. These Red Beds are important because they herald the appearance of significant amounts of oxygen on the Earth. The red color is produced by rust. The rust indicates the presence of oxygen acting upon the ferrous material present in the ocean, and eventually, on the land. The presence of significant amounts of oxygen allows ozone to form, which in turn, screens out the harmful ultra-violet (UV) rays. This makes life possible outside of the protective confines of the ocean.

124. Tornadoes are most likely to occur in what season?
A. Spring
Tornado: an area of extreme low pressure, with rapidly rotating winds beneath a cumulonimbus cloud. Tornadoes are normally spawned from a Super Cell Thunderstorm. They can occur when very cold air and very warm air meet, usually in the Spring. Tornadoes represent the lowest pressure points on the Earth and move across the landscape at an average speed of 30 mph.

125. Which scale is used to measure hurricanes?
B. Saffir-Simpson Scale
The Fujita Scale is used to measure the intensity and damage associated with tornadoes. The Saffir-Simpson Scale is used to classify hurricanes into five categories, with increasing numbers corresponding to lower central pressures, greater wind speeds, and large storm surges. Richter Scale: the primary scale used by seismologists to measure the magnitude of the energy released in an earthquake.

XAMonline, INC. 21 Orient Ave. Melrose, MA 02176

Toll Free number 800-509-4128

TO ORDER Fax 781-662-9268 OR www.XAMonline.com

NEW YORK STATE TEACHER CERTIFICATION EXAMINATION - NYSTCE - 2007

P0# Store/School:

Address 1:

Address 2 (Ship to other):

City, State Zip

Credit card number_______-________-_________-________ **expiration**_______

EMAIL ______________________________

PHONE **FAX**

13# ISBN 2007	TITLE	Qty	Retail	Total
978-1-58197-866-7	NYSTCE ATS-W ASSESSMENT OF TEACHING SKILLS- WRITTEN 91			
978-1-58197-867-4	NYSTCE ATAS ASSESSMENT OF TEACHING ASSISTANT SKILLS 095			
978-1-58197-854-4	CST BIOLOGY 006			
978-1-58197-855-1	CST CHEMISTRY 007			
978-1-58197-865-0	CQST COMMUNICATION AND QUANTITATIVE SKILLS TEST 080			
978-1-58197-632-8	CST EARTH SCIENCE 008			
978-1-58197-851-3	CST ENGLISH 003			
978-1-58197-862-9	CST FAMILY AND CONSUMER SCIENCES 072			
978-1-58197-858-2	CST FRENCH SAMPLE TEST 012			
978-1-58197-868-1	LAST LIBERAL ARTS AND SCIENCE TEST 001			
978-1-58197-863-6	CST LIBRARY MEDIA SPECIALIST 074			
978-1-58197-861-2	CST LITERACY 065			
978-1-58197-852-0	CST MATH 004			
978-1-58197-872-8	CST MULTIPLE SUBJECTS 002 SAMPLE QUESTIONS			
978-1-58197-850-6	CST MUTIPLE SUBJECTS 002			
978-1-58197-864-3	CST PHYSICAL EDUCATION 076			
978-1-58197-873-5	CST PHYSICS 009			
978-1-58197-853-7	CST SOCIAL STUDIES 005			
978-1-58197-859-9	CST SPANISH 020			
978-1-58197-860-5	CST STUDENTS WITH DISABILITIES 060			
			SUBTOTAL	
	FOR PRODUCT PRICES VISIT WWW.XAMONLINE.COM		**Ship**	$8.25
			TOTAL	

CPSIA information can be obtained at www.ICGtesting.com
Printed in the USA
LVOW031527250512

283343LV00001B/42/A

9 781581 976328